Constitutional Law: Laying Down the Law

ASPEN PUBLISHERS

Constitutional Law: Laying Down the Law

Robyn Scheina Brown

Kelly A. Koermer

 Wolters Kluwer

Law & Business

AUSTIN   BOSTON   CHICAGO   NEW YORK   THE NETHERLANDS

Aspen Publishers
Attn: Permissions Department
76 Ninth Avenue, 7th Floor
New York, NY 10011-5201

To contact Customer Care, e-mail customer.service@aspenpublishers.com,
call 1-800-234-1660, fax 1-800-901-9075, or mail correspondence to:

Aspen Publishers
Attn: Order Department
PO Box 990
Frederick, MD 21705

Printed in the United States of America.

1 2 3 4 5 6 7 8 9 0

ISBN 978-0-7355-8862-2

Library of Congress Cataloging-in-Publication Data

Brown, Robyn S.
  Constitutional law : laying down the law / Robyn Scheina Brown,
Kelly A. Koermer.
    p. cm.
  Includes bibliographical references and index.
  ISBN 978-0-7355-8862-2 (alk. paper)
  1. Constitutional law—United States. I. Koermer, Kelly A. II. Title.

  KF4550.B745 2011
  342.73—dc22

                                                    2010028982

About Wolters Kluwer Law & Business

Wolters Kluwer Law & Business is a leading provider of research information and workflow solutions in key specialty areas. The strengths of the individual brands of Aspen Publishers, CCH, Kluwer Law International and Loislaw are aligned within Wolters Kluwer Law & Business to provide comprehensive, in-depth solutions and expert-authored content for the legal, professional and education markets.

CCH was founded in 1913 and has served more than four generations of business professionals and their clients. The CCH products in the Wolters Kluwer Law & Business group are highly regarded electronic and print resources for legal, securities, antitrust and trade regulation, government contracting, banking, pension, payroll, employment and labor, and healthcare reimbursement and compliance professionals.

Aspen Publishers is a leading information provider for attorneys, business professionals and law students. Written by preeminent authorities, Aspen products offer analytical and practical information in a range of specialty practice areas from securities law and intellectual property to mergers and acquisitions and pension/benefits. Aspen's trusted legal education resources provide professors and students with high-quality, up-to-date and effective resources for successful instruction and study in all areas of the law.

Kluwer Law International supplies the global business community with comprehensive English-language international legal information. Legal practitioners, corporate counsel and business executives around the world rely on the Kluwer Law International journals, loose-leafs, books and electronic products for authoritative information in many areas of international legal practice.

Loislaw is a premier provider of digitized legal content to small law firm practitioners of various specializations. Loislaw provides attorneys with the ability to quickly and efficiently find the necessary legal information they need, when and where they need it, by facilitating access to primary law as well as state-specific law, records, forms and treatises.

Wolters Kluwer Law & Business, a unit of Wolters Kluwer, is headquartered in New York and Riverwoods, Illinois. Wolters Kluwer is a leading multinational publisher and information services company.

Summary of Contents

Contents   *ix*
Acknowledgments   *xiii*

Introduction   1

PART I: THE GOVERNMENT AND ITS POWERS

Chapter 1: Levels of Constitutional Scrutiny   7

Chapter 2: The Courts   11

Chapter 3: Congress   29

Chapter 4: The President   45

PART II: INDIVIDUAL RIGHTS AND LIBERTIES

Chapter 5: Due Process and Economic Freedoms   65

Chapter 6: The Right to Privacy   83

Chapter 7: Equal Protection   103

Chapter 8: Freedom of Expression   121

Chapter 9: Freedom of Religion   139

Chapter 10: The Right to Bear Arms   155

Chapter 11: The Constitution and the Criminal Justice System   173

Chapter 12: Voting Rights   193

Table of Cases   *207*

Contents

Acknowledgments   xiii

Introduction   1

PART I: THE GOVERNMENT AND ITS POWERS

Chapter 1: Levels of Constitutional Scrutiny   7

Chapter 2: The Courts   11

Introduction   11
Student Checklist   12
Supreme Court Cases   13
    Marbury v. Madison   13
    Elk Grove Unified School District v. Newdow   18
Case Questions   21
Hypothetical with Accompanying Analysis   22
Hypothetical for Student Analysis   24
Discussion Questions   24
Test Bank   27

Chapter 3: Congress   29

Introduction   29
Student Checklist   31

Supreme Court Cases   31
  Heart of Atlanta Motel v. United States   31
  Gonzales v. Raich   34
Case Questions   38
Hypothetical with Accompanying Analysis   38
Hypothetical for Student Analysis   40
Discussion Questions   40
Test Bank   42

Chapter 4: The President   45

Introduction   45
Student Checklist   46
Supreme Court Cases   47
  Youngstown Sheet & Tube Co. v. Sawyer   47
  Medellín v. Texas   51
Case Questions   56
Hypothetical with Accompanying Analysis   57
Hypothetical for Student Analysis   59
Discussion Questions   59
Test Bank   61

PART II: INDIVIDUAL RIGHTS AND LIBERTIES

Chapter 5: Due Process and Economic Freedoms   65

Introduction   65
Student Checklist   66
Supreme Court Cases   67
  West Coast Hotel Co. v. Parrish   67
  Kelo v. City of New London, Connecticut   72
Case Questions   75
Hypothetical with Accompanying Analysis   76
Hypothetical for Student Analysis   78
Discussion Questions   78
Test Bank   81

Chapter 6: The Right to Privacy   83

Introduction   83
Student Checklist   84
Supreme Court Cases   84

     Roe v. Wade   84
     Lawrence v. Texas   90
Case Questions   94
Hypothetical with Accompanying Analysis   95
Hypothetical for Student Analysis   97
Discussion Questions   97
Test Bank   100

Chapter 7: Equal Protection   103

Introduction   103
Student Checklist   104
Supreme Court Cases   105
     Brown v. Board of Education of Topeka, Kansas   105
     Grutter v. Bollinger   107
Case Questions   112
Hypothetical with Accompanying Analysis   113
Hypothetical for Student Analysis   115
Discussion Questions   115
Test Bank   118

Chapter 8: Freedom of Expression   121

Introduction   121
Student Checklist   122
Supreme Court Cases   123
     New York Times v. United States   123
     Ashcroft v. Free Speech Coalition   126
Case Questions   130
Hypothetical with Accompanying Analysis   131
Hypothetical for Student Analysis   133
Discussion Questions   133
Test Bank   136

Chapter 9: Freedom of Religion   139

Introduction   139
Student Checklist   140
Supreme Court Cases   141
     VanOrden v. Perry   141
     Gonzales v. O Centro Espirita Beneficente Uniao do Vegetal   143
Case Questions   148
Hypothetical with Accompanying Analysis   148
Hypothetical for Student Analysis   151
Discussion Questions   151
Test Bank   153

Chapter 10: The Right to Bear Arms   155

Introduction   155
Student Checklist   156
Supreme Court Cases   156
    United States v. Miller   *156*
    District of Columbia v. Heller   *159*
Case Questions   164
Hypothetical with Accompanying Analysis   164
Hypothetical for Student Analysis   167
Discussion Questions   168
Test Bank   170

Chapter 11: The Constitution and the Criminal Justice System   173

Introduction   173
Student Checklist   174
Supreme Court Cases   175
    Mapp v. Ohio   *175*
    Kennedy v. Louisiana   *180*
Case Questions   183
Hypothetical with Accompanying Analysis   183
Hypothetical for Student Analysis   187
Discussion Questions   187
Test Bank   190

Chapter 12: Voting Rights   193

Introduction   193
Student Checklist   194
Supreme Court Cases   195
    Harper v. Virginia Board Elections   *195*
    Crawford v. Marion County Election Board   *196*
Case Questions   201
Hypothetical with Accompanying Analysis   201
Hypothetical for Student Analysis   203
Discussion Questions   203
Test Bank   205

Table of Cases   *207*

Acknowledgments

We would like to extend our sincere gratitude to those individuals who provided invaluable input by reviewing this book: Mary M. Bachkosky, Anne Arundel Community College; Corey Ciocchetti, University of Denver; Timothy Dale, University of Wisconsin; Gordon P. Henderson, Widener University; Won Yon Jang, University of Wisconsin at Eau Claire; Richard Junger, Western Michigan; and Brian Steffen, Simpson College.

As always, we would like to thank our friends and families for providing their unconditional support and encouragement throughout this project.

Constitutional Law: Laying Down the Law

Introduction

This book is a workbook and not a textbook. It is not designed to instruct you on every nuance of the Constitution. As such, this book is not meant to be your *only* source on constitutional law. Instead, you should be using this *with* other sources on constitutional law, whether they are classroom discussions, a textbook, power points, or the like. Using this workbook, your textbook, and information provided by your instructor will enable you to master fully constitutional law and analysis.

Each chapter deals with a single constitutional provision or Amendment. With the exception of the introductory chapter on levels of constitutional scrutiny, each chapter is formatted in exactly the same way, containing eight separate sections: the Chapter Introduction; Student Checklist; Supreme Court Cases; Case Questions; Hypothetical with Accompanying Analysis; Hypothetical for Student Analysis; Discussion Questions; and Test Bank. It is designed to be user-friendly, to let you work through issues and scenarios dealing with constitutional powers and limitations to reinforce the concepts and to practice critical thinking skills that are necessary in analyzing every constitutional question.

HINTS TO FULLY UTILIZE THIS WORKBOOK

1. **Sometimes, there *is* no right answer . . .** Several of the issues you will tackle, whether in case questions, discussion questions, or hypothetical scenarios, do not have answers. The hypotheticals may be based upon cases that are currently pending in the courts or have not even been entertained by the courts. So, you may not find any binding precedent or persuasive authority on the issues. As such, you may be faced on occasion with what's called an "issue of first impression." When challenged by a case of first impression, your ultimate answer of whether the government's action is constitutional or not is not the most important part of your answer. What is critical is your thorough analysis of the problem and applying the known law to the facts. In some ways, it is like a math problem, in which it is important to show how you reached your answer. Many times when it comes to the law, the "winner" is not necessarily the person who has the stronger case. Rather, it may be the person who can make the stronger argument. Therefore, it is important to be thorough and explicit in reaching your conclusion.

2. **Sometimes there *is* a right answer, but you may personally disagree with it** . . . Students of the law are often confronted with laws and court decisions with which they do not personally agree. Your position may be very compelling. However, it is important when analyzing constitutional problem that you do not supplant the law with your personal beliefs. Recognizing that many of the issues in this book trigger very personal beliefs, some analysis questions will ask you to state your personal position. However, you will usually be asked to explain your legal rationale as to why you believe your personal position is correct.

3. **Appreciate the opposing argument** . . . Understanding and analyzing constitutional law requires a student to be able to understand the strengths and weaknesses of each side's positions. Anticipate counterarguments to your position, appreciate that argument, and formulate a well-reasoned refutation to the counterargument.

4. **Practice reading and analyzing constitutional law** . . . Being able to understand and analyze constitutional law is not always an innate skill. Many of the issues in this book are extremely complicated; so complicated, in fact, that at times the Supreme Court justices do not even agree on what the law should be. Consider the Supreme Court cases included in each chapter along with the cases you read in your main textbook in formulating your overall understanding of constitutional law. Use this body of knowledge and the steps used by the Court in its analysis in solving the hypotheticals in this book. There are a total of 24 hypotheticals in this book—12 that are analyzed for you, so you can practice, and another 12 without an analysis so you can test your skills. The more hypotheticals you work through, the easier they will become to analyze.

5. **Use plain English** . . . When analyzing the issues within this book, learn to express your thoughts in a clear, concise manner. Students frequently get more wrapped up in using "legalese" and not focusing on the substance of their answers.

6. **Cite to your legal authority** . . . It is critical to cite to the authority for any statements that you make about the law or that support your legal analysis. Citation illustrates that the concepts you are advancing are reliable. From an academic standpoint, citation will protect you from committing plagiarism. It is obvious that one must cite to the authority when quoting from that authority. It is also important to cite to the authority from which you extracted a legal concept.

7. **Employ the checklist** . . . The Student Checklist is designed as a roadmap to assist you in breaking down very complicated, multifaceted issues. Each checklist will take you through a step-by-step analysis of whichever constitutional provision about which you happen to be reading. You will find key vocabulary or "buzz words" in these checklists so you can analyze issues using the proper terms. Follow the checklist not only in your thought process but in your writing as well. Your analysis of an issue will not only be more thorough and comprehensive, but it will also be more accurate.

8. **Remember the ultimate constitutional question** . . . In almost every instance, the ultimate question in every constitutional case is "Does the government have the power to _____?" In fact, this phrase is often a very appropriate way to frame the overarching constitutional issue from which subissues may be derived. In conducting your analysis, be sure to explore if the body of the Constitution empowers the

government to act in a specific manner and that one or more of the Amendments do not restrict or take away such power.

9. **Professionalism is key ...** This book focuses on very *real* application to a very *real* world. Some of the topics may make you passionate, disturbed, or uncomfortable. It is appropriate to advance an argument with zeal and refute the opposition. It is never appropriate to make arguments personal or be disrespectful to classmates or colleagues.

10. **Enjoy your studies ...** The Constitution is an amazing document. Some scholars and Supreme Court justices believe that it is a living, breathing document that evolves with our society, while others believe it should be interpreted in the exact context in which it was written. Whichever way you consider the Constitution, it is impossible to ignore that it created the most stable and powerful democracy in history and is still relevant more than 200 years after its inception. It has guided us through more than two centuries of challenges, including civil strife, domestic unrest, and wars abroad. It has spurred great political debate and scholarly analysis. Even we authors grow more in awe of the Constitution as we continue to study the document. We hope that you enjoy the Constitution and constitutional law and debate as much as we do.

—R.S.B. & K.A.K.

Part I

The Government and Its Powers

Chapter 1

Levels of Constitutional Scrutiny

Studying constitutional law is essentially exploring governmental power and its limits. Government action is only lawful when the Constitution has given the government the authority to act. Before sinking our teeth into the complex and at times daunting subject of constitutional law, it might help our understanding to return very briefly to our basic American History class that we likely haven't given much thought to since high school. Following the American Revolution, in 1789 the Framers created the Constitution, which distributed responsibilities among the three branches of the federal government. In doing so, the Framers conferred a great deal of power to the legislative, executive, and judicial branches.

Having just escaped the tyranny of an English monarchy and a centralized government that had *too* much control over citizens' lives, some of the Framers (most notably, James Madison) became concerned that our newly formed government might also hold too much power over its citizens. Were we getting ourselves right back into the same predicament that we had just fought a war to escape? In order to allay those fears, constitutional amendments were proposed which would limit the government's powers. The Bill of Rights, as it is commonly known, comprises the first ten amendments to the Constitution. Ratified in 1791, the Bill of Rights' purpose is to prohibit the federal government from infringing on our basic human rights. Notably, it does not actually *give* citizens any rights that they don't already have. Instead, it prevents the federal government from infringing upon our pre-existing rights. Some of those rights discussed in more detail in this workbook include the freedom of speech, the freedom of religion, the right to privacy, and various protections against unfair prosecution for crimes.

Another important stage in our constitutional history occurred immediately after the Civil War. Following the Union's victory, several "reconstructionist" amendments were passed to help resolve some of the major controversies that had led to the war. Particularly relevant for our purposes was the Fourteenth Amendment, ratified in 1868, which has heavily influenced governmental powers through its Due Process and Equal Protection Clauses. This amendment

Level of Scrutiny	When Applied	Burden of Proof	Standard
HEIGHTENED SCRUTINY	**EQUAL PROTECTION** Government action motivated by **discriminatory intent** against a **suspect class** (*i.e.*, race or national origin) OR **Disparate treatment** of a member of a **suspect classification.** **SUBSTANTIVE DUE PROCESS** (Personal rights, such as the right to **privacy**) Government action infringes upon a **fundamental right** or freedom, enumerated or unenumerated. **FIRST AMENDMENT** Government action impairs the **content** of a message, the **freedom of assembly** or the **free exercise of religion.**	Burden is on the party seeking to have the government action upheld (*i.e.*, typically the government).	**STRICT SCRUTINY** There is a **compelling government interest**, and the government action is necessary and **narrowly tailored** to further the government interest. In determining if the action is narrowly tailored, the court must be convinced that there is **no less restrictive means** of achieving the compelling government interest.
MIDDLE LEVEL SCRUTINY	**EQUAL PROTECTION** Government action motivated by **intent to discriminate** on the basis of **gender** or **illegitimacy** OR **Disparate treatment** of one **sex** or of someone who is **illegitimate**, even when the government's language is neutral. **FIRST AMENDMENT** **(Time, place, and manner** regulation) Government action **impairs expression** but such impairment is not based upon the content of the message.	The burden is usually on the government, but there is no standard rule.	**INTERMEDIATE SCRUTINY** Government action serves an **important governmental objective** and discriminatory means employed are **substantially related** to achieving the important objective.

Level of Scrutiny	When Applied	Burden of Proof	Standard
MINIMAL (LOWER LEVEL) SCRUTINY	**EQUAL PROTECTION** Government action motivated by **intent** to treat a **non-suspect class** differently OR **Disparate treatment** of members of a **non-suspect class.** **SUBSTANTIVE DUE PROCESS** (Personal Rights) Government action infringes upon a **non-fundamental right** or freedom (*i.e.*, economic due process).	Burden is on the party seeking to have the government action declared unconstitutional.	**RATIONAL BASIS TEST** The government action has a **rational relationship** to a **legitimate government purpose.**

also allowed for the incorporation of the Bill of Rights against the states, meaning that state governmental powers could now be limited to the same extent that the federal government had already been limited for almost a century. So, essentially, the government did not have greater powers over one person or groups of people than over others.

In every constitutional challenge, one must consider both the powers that are conferred by the Constitution *and* the powers that are taken away or limited by the amendments. Additionally, it is extremely important to know what standard a court will apply when determining whether a governmental action is constitutional. The Supreme Court has helped in this regard by applying different levels of scrutiny depending upon the specific protection involved. Think of these levels as a spectrum. One end of the spectrum deals with circumstances in which fundamental rights or freedoms are limited or a suspect class of individuals is treated differently. Here, the government carries a heavy burden of establishing the constitutionality of its powers. On the opposite end of the spectrum we have circumstances involving non-fundamental rights or disparate treatment of non-protected classes, where the burden is not on the government but instead on the challenger to show that the government's power is limited. The Supreme Court has also established a test for the middle of the spectrum related to matters involving gender discrimination and illegitimacy. The chart above will help you see that spectrum more clearly as you determine the appropriate level of constitutional scrutiny to apply to the hypotheticals you will analyze throughout this book.

Ultimately, in every hypothetical you analyze, you will need to answer one fundamental question: **"Does the government have the power to undertake the challenged action?"** In answering that question, first determine if the branch of government has been granted the power to act under the Constitution. If the branch *does not* have the power, then the act is unconstitutional. If the branch *does* have the power, then you must determine if that power has been limited by an amendment. To make that determination, you will need to assess which level of scrutiny to apply based upon the nature of the governmental action. For example, if Congress enacts a law prohibiting the sale of child pornography, you would likely determine that Congress has the power to regulate the sale of an item based upon the Commerce Clause located in Article I of the Constitution. However, the regulation impacts a form of speech (*i.e.*, content) which is protected by the First Amendment. After consulting our chart, we know that heightened scrutiny is applied. Therefore, using a strict scrutiny analysis you must determine if (a) the government had a compelling interest in enacting the law, and (b) the government action was narrowly tailored to further that interest. In applying this test, it is likely that the government's interest of protecting children from sexual exploitation will be considered compelling. It is also likely that a prohibition on the sale of child pornography is narrowly tailored because there is no less restrictive means to protect children who would be the subject matter of the media and, therefore, victims of abuse and exploitation. In conclusion, because the Constitution has granted Congress the power to regulate interstate commerce and because the regulation is narrowly tailored toward furthering a compelling government interest, the Congressional prohibition of selling child pornography would be constitutional. This provides just one example of how to analyze properly the different levels of scrutiny in any given situation.

In the next few chapters, you'll review federalism and the origins of the federal government's powers enumerated in the Constitution. In the remaining chapters, you'll review civil liberties and civil rights as well as assess whether the government's powers are limited by one or more of the constitutional amendments. In those chapters, you'll see case excerpts, hypotheticals, and discussion questions. These tools will help you further explore governmental powers and limits, and they will shed light on how the levels of constitutional scrutiny are applied in "real life" situations. As we just explained, the levels of scrutiny are never discussed in a vacuum. Rather, they are analyzed in the context of the various constitutional provisions or the amendments. So, while you won't see any hypotheticals in this particular chapter, you *will* see them in every other chapter. Make sure, therefore, that before you turn the page to begin Chapter 2, you have a firm grasp on what the levels of constitutional scrutiny are all about and when they apply. It'll be worth the effort, we promise.

Chapter 2

The Courts

"The judicial Power of the United States, shall be vested in one supreme Court, and in such inferior Courts as the Congress may from time to time ordain and establish."

—Article III, Section 1.

INTRODUCTION

James Madison once wrote that "[t]he judiciary is beyond comparison the weakest of the three departments. . . . [I]t is in continual jeopardy of being overpowered, awed or influenced by its coordinate branches." Was he right? Is the judiciary the weakest branch of the U.S. government? Or, is it more like a silent partner—an integral part of our government's machinery yet one that, comparatively speaking, rarely takes center stage.

One thing that may shed light on whether any accuracy exists to Madison's comment is the fact that, although the judicial branch is not addressed in the Constitution until Article III, *after* both Congress and the President, textbooks teaching constitutional law almost without exception address the courts in one of the first chapters, *before* the other two branches. Why would that be? Why would a branch of government so unimportant or weak be the first priority in education? James Madison, of course, didn't have a crystal ball when he made those remarks. So perhaps he spoke too soon, before he could realize the silent power the judiciary would have on our system of government. Those powers, which will be discussed in detail throughout this chapter, can best be remembered as the four J's: Jurisdiction (*what* court has the power to hear a case); Justiciability (*why* a court will decline to consider the merits of a lawsuit); Judicial Restraint (*how* a court will deal with constitutional issues); and Judicial Review (*when* a court will overturn an unconstitutional law).

As you work your way through this chapter, keep Madison's prophecy in the back of your mind. Once you have completed learning about the judiciary, ask yourself whether you agree with his observations. Is it really the weakest link? You be the judge.

STUDENT *Checklist*

The Courts

1. Does the court have **jurisdiction** (*i.e.,* the **authority to hear the case**)?

■ Was it an **Article III** court created by the **Constitution**?
    Was a **federal question** raised?
    Was it a case affecting an **ambassador, public minister, or consul**?
    Was it a case of **admiralty and maritime** jurisdiction?
    Was the **United States a party**?
    Was it a controversy **between two or more states**?
    Was it a controversy **between a state and citizens of another state**?
    Was it a controversy **between citizens of different states**?
    Was it a controversy **between citizens of a state and a foreign nation or its citizens**?
    or

■ Was it an **Article I** court created by **Congress**? (Note: Because Article I courts are created by Congress, they are not guided by principals 2 through 4 below. Instead, they must observe the rules and regulations of the particular statute by which they were created.)

2. Is the case **justiciable** *(i.e.,* **appropriate** for the court's review)?

■ Is the issue **moot**?
    Was the issue **resolved** or did it **dissipate** during litigation, or
    ❑ Is the behavior capable of **repetition yet evading review**;
    ❑ Did the defendant **voluntarily cease** the illegal behavior; or
    ❑ Do **collateral consequences** warrant review by the court?

■ Is the issue not yet **ripe**?
    Was the lawsuit filed **before the harm occurred** or before the **threat of harm was imminent**?

■ Does the party bringing the action have **standing** (*i.e.,* does the plaintiff have a **stake** in the outcome of the case)?
    Did the plaintiff suffer an **injury in fact**;
    Is there a **causal connection** between the injury and conduct complained of; and
    Is it **likely** that the injury will be **redressed** by a favorable court decision?

■ Is the court being asked to issue an **advisory opinion**?
    Is the issue only an **abstract** or **hypothetical** question?

■ Does the issue present a **political question**?
    Has the political nature of the issue been **committed to another branch of government**; and
    Are there **no manageable standards** by which the court could resolve the issue?

3. Did the court exercise **judicial restraint** when interpreting a law?

■ Did the court observe **stare decisis**?

■ Did the court observe the **plain meaning rule**?

■ Did the court **avoid** deciding a case on constitutional grounds if it could be decided on non-constitutional grounds?

■ Did the court **presume** the law was constitutional, thus placing the **burden** on the challenger to show the law was unconstitutional?

■ Did the court **sever** any unconstitutional portions of the law to leave the remainder of the law intact?

4. Did the court properly exercise its powers of **judicial review**?

■ Did the Supreme Court review **legislative** or **executive acts** to determine their constitutionality?

■ Did the Supreme Court review **state court decisions** regarding **federal issues** if the decision did not rest on **independent state law grounds**?

SUPREME COURT CASES

MARBURY v. MADISON, 5 U.S. 137 (1803)

[In the 1800 presidential election, Democratic-Republican Thomas Jefferson defeated incumbent John Adams, a Federalist. The Federalists also lost their majority in Congress. In order to extend the Federalist influence into the new term, Congress created numerous judgeships, and Adams filled those positions with Federalists. Adams signed the commissions for the new judgeships and gave them to John Marhsall, his secretary of state, to deliver to the incoming judges. However, Marshall was unable to deliver all of the commissions before Jefferson took office. Once Jefferson was sworn in, he ordered his new secretary of state, James Madison, not to deliver the remaining commissions. William Marbury, upset that he had not received his commission as a justice of the peace for the District of Columbia, filed suit in the U.S. Supreme Court seeking a writ of mandamus (*i.e.*, demanding) that Madison deliver his commission. He filed the suit based on Section 13 of the Judiciary Act of 1789, which said that "the Supreme Court . . . shall have power to issue . . . writs of mandamus . . . to any courts appointed, or persons holding office, under the authority of the United States." Interestingly, by the time the case reached the Supreme Court, John Marshall had become the Chief Justice. He wrote the below opinion.]

At the last term on the affidavits then read and filed with the clerk, a rule was granted in this case, requiring the secretary of state to shew cause why a mandamus should not issue, directing him to deliver to William Marbury his commission as a justice of the peace for the county of Washington, in the district of Columbia.

No cause has been shewn, and the present motion is for a mandamus. The peculiar delicacy of this case, the novelty of some of its circumstances, and the real difficulty attending the points which occur in it, require a complete exposition of the principles, on which the opinion to be given by the court, is founded. . . .

The first object of inquiry is,

1st. Has the applicant a right to the commission he demands? . . .

It is . . . decidedly the opinion of the court, that when a commission has been signed by the President, the appointment is made; and that the commission is complete, when the seal of the United States has been affixed to it by the secretary of state. . . .

Mr. Marbury, then, since his commission was signed by the President, and sealed by the secretary of state, was appointed; and as the law creating the office, gave the officer a right to hold for five years, independent of the executive, the appointment was not revocable; but vested in the officer legal rights, which are protected by the laws of this country. To withhold his commission, therefore, is an act deemed by the court not warranted by law, but violative of a vested legal right.

This brings us to the second inquiry; which is,

2dly. If he has a right, and that right has been violated, do the laws of this country afford him a remedy? . . .

It is then the opinion of the court, . . . [t]hat, having this legal title to the office, he has a consequent right to the commission; a refusal to deliver which, is a plain violation of that right, for which the laws of his country afford him a remedy.

It remains to be inquired whether,

3dly. He is entitled to the remedy for which he applies. This depends on,

1st. The nature of the writ applied for, and, 2dly. The power of this court.

1st. The nature of the writ. . . .

This writ, if awarded, would be directed to an officer of government, and its mandate to him would be, to use the words of Blackstone, "to do a particular thing therein specified, which appertains to his office and duty and which the court has previously determined, or at least supposes, to be consonant to right and justice." Or, in the words of Lord Mansfield, the applicant, in this case, has a right to execute an office of public concern, and is kept out of possession of that right. These circumstances certainly concur in this case. . . .

It is true that the mandamus, now moved for, is not for the performance of an act expressly enjoined by statute.

It is to deliver a commission; on which subject the acts of Congress are silent. This difference is not considered as affecting the case. It has already been stated that the applicant has, to that commission, a vested legal right, of which the executive cannot deprive him. He has been appointed to an office, from which he is not removable, at the will of the executive; and being so appointed, he has a right to the commission which the secretary has received from the president for his use. The act of congress does not indeed order the secretary of state to send it to him, but it is placed in his hands for the person entitled to it; and cannot be more lawfully withheld by him, than by any other person. . . .

This, then, is a plain case for a mandamus, either to deliver the commission, or a copy of it from the record; and it only remains to be inquired,

Whether it can issue from this court.

The act to establish the judicial courts of the United States authorizes the supreme court "to issue writs of mandamus, in cases warranted by the principles and usages of law, to any courts appointed, or persons holding office, under the authority of the United States."

The secretary of state, being a person holding an office under the authority of the United States, is precisely within the letter of the description; and if this court is not authorized to issue a writ of mandamus to such an officer, it must be because the law is unconstitutional, and therefore absolutely incapable of conferring the authority, and assigning the duties which its words purport to confer and assign.

The constitution vests the whole judicial power of the United States in one supreme court, and such inferior courts as congress shall, from time to time, ordain and establish. This power is expressly extended to all cases arising under the laws of the United States; and consequently, in some form, may be exercised over the present case; because the right claimed is given by a law of the United States.

In the distribution of this power it is declared that "the supreme court shall have original jurisdiction in all cases affecting ambassadors, other public ministers and consuls, and those in which a state shall be a party. In all other cases, the supreme court shall have appellate jurisdiction."

It has been insisted, at the bar, that as the original grant of jurisdiction, to the supreme and inferior courts, is general, and the clause, assigning original jurisdiction to the supreme court, contains no negative or restrictive words; the power remains to the legislature, to assign original jurisdiction to that court in other cases than those specified in the article which has been recited; provided those cases belong to the judicial power of the United States.

If it had been intended to leave it in the discretion of the legislature to apportion the judicial power between the supreme and inferior courts according to the will of that body, it would certainly have been useless to have proceeded further than to have defined the judicial power, and the tribunals in which it should be vested. The subsequent part of the section is mere surplusage, is entirely without meaning, if such is to be the construction. If congress remains at liberty to give this court appellate jurisdiction, where the constitution has declared their jurisdiction shall be original; and original jurisdiction where the constitution has declared it shall be appellate; the distribution of jurisdiction, made in the constitution, is form without substance.

Affirmative words are often, in their operation, negative of other objects than those affirmed; and in this case, a negative or exclusive sense must be given to them or they have no operation at all.

It cannot be presumed that any clause in the constitution is intended to be without effect; and therefore such a construction is inadmissible, unless the words require it. . . .

When an instrument organizing fundamentally a judicial system, divides it into one supreme, and so many inferior courts as the legislature may ordain and establish; then enumerates its powers, and proceeds so far to distribute them, as to define the jurisdiction of the supreme court by declaring the cases in which it shall take original jurisdiction, and that in others it shall take appellate jurisdiction; the plain import of the words seems to be, that in one class of cases its jurisdiction is original, and not appellate; in the other it is appellate, and not original. If any other construction would render the clause inoperative, that is an additional reason for rejecting such other construction, and for adhering to their obvious meaning.

To enable this court then to issue a mandamus, it must be shewn to be an exercise of appellate jurisdiction, or to be necessary to enable them to exercise appellate jurisdiction.

It has been stated at the bar that the appellate jurisdiction may be exercised in a variety of forms, and that if it be the will of the legislature that a mandamus should be used for that purpose, that will must be obeyed. This is true, yet the jurisdiction must be appellate, not original.

It is the essential criterion of appellate jurisdiction, that it revises and corrects the proceedings in a cause already instituted, and does not create that cause. Although, therefore, a mandamus may be directed to courts, yet to issue such a writ to an officer for the delivery of a paper, is in effect the same as to sustain an original action for that paper, and therefore seems not to belong to appellate, but to original jurisdiction. Neither is it necessary in such a case as this, to enable the court to exercise its appellate jurisdiction.

The authority, therefore, given to the supreme court, by the act establishing the judicial courts of the United States, to issue writs of mandamus to public officers, appears not to be warranted by the constitution; and it becomes necessary to enquire whether a jurisdiction, so conferred, can be exercised.

The question, whether an act, repugnant to the constitution, can become the law of the land, is a question deeply interesting to the United States; but, happily, not of an intricacy proportioned to its interest. It seems only necessary to recognize certain principles, supposed to have been long and well established, to decide it. . . .

The powers of the legislature are defined, and limited; and that those limits may not be mistaken, or forgotten, the constitution is written. To what purpose are powers limited, and to what purpose is that limitation committed to writing, if these limits may, at any time, be passed by those intended to be restrained? The distinction, between a government with limited and unlimited powers, is abolished, if those limits do not confine the persons on whom they are imposed, and if acts prohibited and acts allowed, are of equal obligation. It is a proposition too plain to be contested, that the constitution controls any legislative act repugnant to it; or, that the legislature may alter the constitution by an ordinary act.

Between these alternatives there is no middle ground. The constitution is either a superior, paramount law, unchangeable by ordinary means, or it is on a level with ordinary legislative acts, and like other acts, is alterable when the legislature shall please to alter it.

If the former part of the alternative be true, then a legislative act contrary to the constitution is not law: if the latter part be true, then written constitutions are absurd attempts, on the part of the people, to limit a power, in its own nature illimitable.

Certainly all those who have framed written constitutions contemplate them as forming the fundamental and paramount law of the nation, and consequently the theory of every such government must be, that an act of the legislature, repugnant to the constitution, is void.

This theory is essentially attached to a written constitution, and is consequently to be considered, by this court, as one of the fundamental principles of our society. It is not therefore to be lost sight of in the further consideration of this subject.

If an act of the legislature, repugnant to the constitution, is void, does it, notwithstanding its invalidity, bind the courts, and oblige them to give it effect? Or, in other words, though it be not law, does it constitute a rule as operative as if it was a law? This would be to overthrow in fact what was established in theory; and would seem, at first view, an absurdity too gross to be insisted on. It shall, however, receive a more attentive consideration.

It is emphatically the province and duty of the judicial department to say what the law is. Those who apply the rule to particular cases, must of necessity expound and interpret that rule. If two laws conflict with each other, the courts must decide on the operation of each.

So if a law be in opposition to the constitution; if both the law and the constitution apply to a particular case, so that the court must either decide that case conformably to the law, disregarding the constitution; or conformably to the constitution, disregarding the law; the court must determine which of these conflicting rules governs the case. This is of the very essence of judicial duty.

If then the courts are to regard the constitution; and the constitution is superior to any ordinary act of the legislature; the constitution, and not such ordinary act, must govern the case to which they both apply.

Those then who controvert the principle that the constitution is to be considered, in court, as a paramount law, are reduced to the necessity of maintaining that courts must close their eyes on the constitution, and see only the law.

This doctrine would subvert the very foundation of all written constitutions. It would declare that an act, which, according to the principles and theory of our government, is entirely void; is yet, in practice, completely obligatory. It would declare, that if the legislature shall do what is expressly forbidden, such act, notwithstanding the express prohibition, is in reality effectual. It would be giving to the legislature a practical and real omnipotence, with the same breath which professes to restrict their powers within narrow limits. It is prescribing limits, and declaring that those limits may be passed as pleasure.

That it thus reduces to nothing what we have deemed the greatest improvement on political institutions—a written constitution—would of itself be sufficient, in America, where written constitutions have been viewed with so much reverence, for rejecting the construction. But the peculiar expressions of the constitution of the United States furnish additional arguments in favour of its rejection.

The judicial power of the United States is extended to all cases arising under the constitution.

Could it be the intention of those who gave this power, to say that, in using it, the constitution should not be looked into? That a case arising under the constitution should be decided without examining the instrument under which it arises? This is too extravagant to be maintained. . . .

. . . [I]t is apparent, that the framers of the constitution contemplated that instrument, as a rule for the government of *courts,* as well as of the legislature.

Why otherwise does it direct the judges to take an oath to support it? This oath certainly applies, in an especial manner, to their conduct in their official character. How immoral to impose it on them, if they were to be used as the instruments, and the knowing instruments, for violating what they swear to support?

The oath of office, too, imposed by the legislature, is completely demonstrative of the legislative opinion on this subject. It is in these words, "I do solemnly swear that I will administer justice without respect to persons, and do equal right to the poor and to the rich; and that I will faithfully and impartially discharge all the duties incumbent on me as according to the best of my abilities and understanding, agreeably to *the constitution,* and laws of the United States."

Why does a judge swear to discharge his duties agreeably to the constitution of the United States, if that constitution forms no rule for his government? If it is closed upon him, and cannot be inspected by him?

If such be the real state of things, this is worse than solemn mockery. To prescribe, or to take this oath, becomes equally a crime.

It is also not entirely unworthy of observation, that in declaring what shall be the *supreme* law of the land, the *constitution* itself is first mentioned; and not the laws of the United States generally, but those only which shall be made in *pursuance* of the constitution, have that rank.

Thus, the particular phraseology of the constitution of the United States confirms and strengthens the principle, supposed to be essential to all written constitutions, that a law repugnant to the constitution is void; and that *courts,* as well as other departments, are bound by that instrument. The rule must be discharged.

ELK GROVE UNIFIED SCHOOL DISTRICT v. NEWDOW, 542 U.S. 1 (2004)

[Michael Newdow challenged his daughter's recitation of the Pledge of Allegiance on First Amendment grounds. Sandra Banning, the girl's mother, sought to intervene or dismiss Newdow's lawsuit, claiming that she had legal custody of their daughter and it would not be in her daughter's best interest to be a part of the lawsuit.]

Each day elementary school teachers in the Elk Grove Unified School District (School District) lead their classes in a group recitation of the Pledge of Allegiance. Respondent, Michael A. Newdow, is an atheist whose daughter participates in that daily exercise. Because the Pledge contains the words "under God," he views the School District's policy as a religious indoctrination of his child that violates the First Amendment. A divided panel of the Court of Appeals for the Ninth Circuit agreed with Newdow. In light of the obvious importance of that decision, we granted certiorari to review the First Amendment issue and, preliminarily, the question whether Newdow has standing to invoke the jurisdiction of the federal courts. We conclude that Newdow lacks standing and therefore reverse the Court of Appeals' decision. . . .

In every federal case, the party bringing the suit must establish standing to prosecute the action. "In essence the question of standing is whether the litigant is entitled to have the court decide the merits of the dispute or of particular issues." *Warth v. Seldin,* 422 U.S. 490, 498, 95 S. Ct. 2197, 45 L. Ed. 2d 343 (1975). The standing requirement is born partly of " 'an idea, which is more than an intuition but less than a rigorous and explicit theory, about the constitutional and prudential limits to the powers of an unelected, unrepresentative judiciary in our kind of government.' " *Allen v. Wright,* 468 U.S. 737, 750, 104 S. Ct. 3315, 82 L. Ed. 2d 556 (1984) (quoting *Vander Jagt v. O'Neill,* 699 F.2d 1166, 1178-1179 (C.A.D.C. 1982) (Bork, J., concurring)).

The command to guard jealously and exercise rarely our power to make constitutional pronouncements requires strictest adherence when matters of great national significance are at stake. Even in cases concededly within our jurisdiction under Article III, we abide by "a series of rules under which [we have] avoided passing upon a large part of all the constitutional questions pressed upon [us] for decision." *Ashwander v. TVA,* 297 U.S. 288, 346, 56 S. Ct. 466, 80 L. Ed. 688 (1936) (Brandeis, J., concurring). Always we must balance "the heavy obligation to exercise jurisdiction," *Colorado River Water Conservation Dist. v. United States,* 424 U.S. 800, 820, 96 S. Ct. 1236, 47 L. Ed. 2d 483 (1976), against the "deeply rooted" commitment "not to pass on questions of constitutionality" unless adjudication of the constitutional issue is necessary, *Spector Motor Service, Inc. v. McLaughlin,* 323 U.S. 101, 105, 65 S. Ct. 152, 89 L. Ed. 101 (1944). See also *Rescue Army v. Municipal Court of Los Angeles,* 331 U.S. 549, 568-575, 67 S. Ct. 1409, 91 L. Ed. 1666 (1947).

Consistent with these principles, our standing jurisprudence contains two strands: Article III standing, which enforces the Constitution's case-or-controversy requirement, see *Lujan v. Defenders of Wildlife,* 504 U.S. 555, 559-562, 112 S. Ct. 2130, 119 L. Ed. 2d 351 (1992); and prudential standing, which embodies "judicially self-imposed limits on the exercise of federal jurisdiction," *Allen,* 468 U.S., at 751, 104 S. Ct. 3315. The Article III limitations are familiar: The plaintiff must show that the conduct of which he complains has caused him to suffer an "injury in fact" that a favorable judgment will redress. See *Lujan,* 504 U.S., at 560-561, 112 S. Ct. 2130. Although we have not exhaustively defined the prudential dimensions of the standing doctrine, we have explained that prudential standing encompasses "the general prohibition on a litigant's raising another person's legal rights, the rule barring adjudication of generalized grievances more appropriately addressed in the representative branches, and the requirement that a plaintiff's complaint fall within the zone of interests protected by the law invoked." *Allen,* 468 U.S., at 751, 104 S. Ct. 3315. See also *Secretary of State of Md. v. Joseph H. Munson Co.,* 467 U.S. 947, 955-956, 104 S. Ct. 2839, 81 L. Ed. 2d 786 (1984). "Without such limitations—closely related to Art. III concerns but essentially matters of judicial self-governance—the courts would be called upon to decide abstract questions of wide public significance even though other governmental institutions may be more competent to address the questions and even though judicial intervention may be unnecessary to protect individual rights." *Warth,* 422 U.S., at 500, 95 S. Ct. 2197.

One of the principal areas in which this Court has customarily declined to intervene is the realm of domestic relations. Long ago we observed that "[t]he whole subject of the domestic relations of husband and wife, parent and child, belongs to the laws of the States and not to the laws of the United States." *In re Burrus,* 136 U.S. 586, 593-594, 10 S. Ct. 850, 34 L. Ed. 500 (1890). . . . So strong is our deference to state law in this area that we have recognized a "domestic relations exception" that "divests the federal courts of power to issue divorce, alimony, and child custody decrees." *Ankenbrandt v. Richards,* 504 U.S. 689, 703, 112 S. Ct. 2206, 119 L. Ed. 2d 468 1992). We have also acknowledged that it might be appropriate for the federal courts to decline to hear a case involving "elements of the domestic relationship," *id.,* at 705, 112 S. Ct. 2206, even when divorce, alimony, or child custody is not strictly at issue. . . .

Thus, while rare instances arise in which it is necessary to answer a substantial federal question that transcends or exists apart from the family law issue, see, *e.g., Palmore v. Sidoti,* 466 U.S. 429, 432-434, 104 S. Ct. 1879, 80 L. Ed. 2d 421 (1984), in general it is appropriate for the federal courts to leave delicate issues of domestic relations to the state courts.

As explained briefly above, the extent of the standing problem raised by the domestic relations issues in this case was not apparent until August 5, 2002, when Banning filed her motion for leave to intervene or dismiss the complaint following the Court of Appeals' initial decision. At that time, the child's custody was governed by a February 6, 2002, order of the California Superior Court. That order provided that Banning had "'*sole* legal custody as to the rights and responsibilities to make decisions relating to the health, education and welfare of'" her daughter. *Newdow II,* 313 F.3d, at 502. The order stated that the two parents should "'consult with one another on substantial decisions relating to'" the child's "'psychological and educational needs,'" but it authorized Banning to "'exercise legal control'" if the parents could not reach "'mutual agreement.'" *Ibid.*

That family court order was the controlling document at the time of the Court of Appeals' standing decision. After the Court of Appeals ruled, however, the Superior Court held another conference regarding the child's custody. At a hearing on September 11, 2003, the Superior Court announced that the parents have "joint legal custody," but that Banning "makes the final decisions if the two . . . disagree." App. 127-128.

Newdow contends that despite Banning's final authority, he retains "an unrestricted right to inculcate in his daughter-free from governmental interference-the atheistic beliefs he finds persuasive." *Id.,* at 48, ¶78. The difficulty with that argument is that Newdow's rights, as in many cases touching upon family relations, cannot be viewed in isolation. This case concerns not merely Newdow's interest in inculcating his child with his views on religion, but also the rights of the child's mother as a parent generally and under the Superior Court orders specifically. And most important, it implicates the interests of a young child who finds herself at the center of a highly public debate over her custody, the propriety of a widespread national ritual, and the meaning of our Constitution.

The interests of the affected persons in this case are in many respects antagonistic. Of course, legal disharmony in family relations is not uncommon, and in many instances that disharmony poses no bar to federal-court adjudication of proper federal questions. What makes this case different is that Newdow's standing derives entirely from his relationship with his daughter, but he lacks the right to litigate as her next friend. . . .

Newdow's parental status is defined by California's domestic relations law. Our custom on questions of state law ordinarily is to defer to the interpretation of the Court of Appeals for the Circuit in which the State is located. See *Bishop v. Wood,* 426 U.S. 341, 346-347, 96 S. Ct. 2074, 48 L. Ed. 2d 684 (1976). In this case, the Court of Appeals, which possesses greater familiarity with California law, concluded that state law vests in Newdow a cognizable right to influence his daughter's religious upbringing. *Newdow II,* 313 F.3d, at 504-505. The court based its ruling on two intermediate state appellate cases holding that "while the custodial parent undoubtedly has the right to make ultimate decisions concerning the child's religious upbringing, a court will not enjoin the noncustodial parent from discussing religion with the child or involving the child in his or her religious activities in the absence of a showing that the child will be thereby harmed." *In re Marriage of Murga,* 103 Cal. App. 3d 498, 505, 163 Cal. Rptr. 79, 82 (1980). . . . Animated by a conception of "family privacy" that includes "not simply a policy of minimum state intervention but also a presumption of parental autonomy," 142 Cal. App. 3d, at 267-268, 190 Cal. Rptr., at 848, the state cases create a zone of private authority within which each parent, whether custodial or noncustodial, remains free to impart to the child his or her religious perspective.

Nothing that either Banning or the School Board has done, however, impairs Newdow's right to instruct his daughter in his religious views. Instead, Newdow requests relief that is more ambitious than that sought in *Mentry* and *Murga.* He wishes to forestall his daughter's exposure to religious ideas that her mother, who wields a form of veto power, endorses, and to use his parental status to challenge the influences to which his daughter may be exposed in school when he and Banning disagree. The California cases simply do not stand for the proposition that Newdow has a right to dictate to others what they may and may not say to his child respecting religion. *Mentry* and *Murga* are concerned with protecting "'the fragile, complex interpersonal bonds between child and parent,'" 142 Cal. App. 3d, at 267, 190 Cal. Rptr., at 848, and with permitting divorced parents to expose their children to the "'diversity of religious experiences [that] is itself a sound stimulant for a child,'" *id.,* at 265, 190 Cal. Rptr., at 847. The cases speak not at all to the problem of a parent seeking to reach outside the private parent-child sphere to restrain the acts of a third party. A next friend surely could exercise such a right, but the Superior Court's order has deprived Newdow of that status.

In our view, it is improper for the federal courts to entertain a claim by a plaintiff whose standing to sue is founded on family law rights that are in dispute when prosecution of the lawsuit may have an adverse effect on the person who is the source of the plaintiff's claimed standing. When hard questions of domestic relations are sure to affect the outcome, the prudent course is for the federal court to stay its hand rather than reach out to resolve a weighty question of federal constitutional law. There is a vast difference between Newdow's right to communicate with his child—which both California law and the First Amendment recognize—and his claimed right to shield his daughter from influences to which she is exposed in school despite the terms of the custody order. We conclude that, having been deprived under California law of the right to sue as next friend, Newdow lacks prudential standing to bring this suit in federal court.

The judgment of the Court of Appeals is reversed. *It is so ordered. . . .*

CASE QUESTIONS

MARBURY v. MADISON

1. How did the law at issue in this case directly conflict with the Constitution?

2. How did statutory construction play a role in the Court's decision? What did Chief Justice Marshall mean when he said, "[a]ffirmative words are often, in their operation, negative of other objects than those affirmed"?

3. What political influences do you think may have been behind the Court's decision in this case? Explain.

4. *Marbury v. Madison* has sometimes been criticized because the Court, by refusing to exercise one power (issuing the mandamus), in effect gave itself a much larger power nowhere explicitly mentioned in the Constitution (judicial review). Do you think this is a valid criticism? Explain.

ELK GOVE UNIFIED SCHOOL DISTRICT v. NEWDOW

1. What two types of standing did the Court recognize? Which type of standing was at issue in this case?

2. How did the following constitutional concepts play a role in the Court's opinion: separation of powers; judicial restraint; the right to privacy?

3. How did domestic relations play a large part in both the procedural history of the case as well as the Court's holding?

4. What if, subsequent to the Court's decision, the custody order between Newdow and Banning were modified, giving Newdow sole legal custody of his daughter; would that nullify the Court's opinion in this case? Would Newdow then be permitted to pursue his case? Explain.

HYPOTHETICAL WITH ACCOMPANYING ANALYSIS

Hypothetical

New Hampton is an ultra-conservative state that has enacted many controversial laws over the centuries. At the heart of the instant controversy is §3-1031 of the New Hampton Criminal Code. Enacted in 1798, it provides:

    (a) <u>Prohibited Conduct.</u> Any person, not being married, who voluntarily shall have sexual intercourse with any other person shall be guilty of fornication.

    (b) <u>Penalty.</u> A person who violates this section shall be guilty of a misdemeanor and on conviction shall be fined $10.

    Despite New Hampton's prohibition against fornication, the most recent conviction for the offense occurred in 1820. Additionally, only two other arrests have been made under §3-1031, both of which occurred over 50 years ago and dealt with acts of prostitution in a public place.

    Tara Henderson and Brandon Smith are unmarried adults who live in New Hampton and have recently become romantically involved with one another. They wish to move in together but have refrained from doing so out of fear that they will be prosecuted under §3-1031. They admit they aren't concerned about paying the $10 fine, but they maintain that the stigma associated with a criminal conviction would have a negative impact on both their personal and professional lives. Tara and Brandon filed suit in federal court seeking a declaratory judgment that §3-1031 violates their constitutional right to privacy. However, before their case came before the court for consideration, the New Hampton legislature repealed §3-1031 in its entirety. Discuss whether the court should reach the merits of Tara and Brandon's lawsuit.

Analysis

In order for a court to entertain the merits of any case, Article III requires that there be an actual "case or controversy" for judicial resolution. In other words, the issue must be "justiciable," or appropriate for the court's review. Justiciability encompasses the concepts of standing, ripeness, mootness, and political questions. They present a threshold question because they determine the power of a court to entertain a lawsuit. Warth v. Seldin, 422 U.S. 490 (1975). The issue in this hypothetical is whether the federal court has the power to hear the merits of Tara and Brandon's lawsuit. Three categories of justiciability are relevant when answering this question: first, whether the issue is ripe for the court's review; second, whether the parties have standing to challenge the law; and third, whether the lawsuit has become moot. Each will be addressed separately.

    First it must be determined whether the lawsuit filed by Tara and Brandon is ripe for review. Ripeness requires that "one challenging the validity of a criminal statue must show a threat of prosecution under the statute to present a case or controversy." Babbitt v. United Farm Workers National Union, 442 U.S. 289 (1979). "[P]ersons having no fears of state prosecution except those that are imaginary or speculative, are not to be accepted as appropriate plaintiffs." Younger v. Harris, 401 U.S. 37 (1971). The threat of prosecution must be "real" and "immediate." Golder v. Zwickler, 394 U.S. 103 (1969). In Poe v. Ullman, 367 U.S. 497 (1961), the plaintiffs challenged a Connecticut statute in existence since 1879 which criminally prohibited the use of contraceptive devices or giving medical advice about their use. The court declined to address the constitutionality of the statute because no live case or controversy existed. Individuals had only once been charged with violating the law in 1940, and those charges were dropped. The instant hypothetical presents a very similar scenario. The New Hampton statute, which was enacted in 1798, resulted in only one conviction that occurred almost 200 years ago. Additionally, the most recent arrests under the statute were over 50 years ago and were for prostitution, a situation entirely different from the one presented by Tara and Brandon. In short, neither plaintiff has offered any evidence that they were under a "real" and "immediate" threat of prosecution. To the contrary, all evidence points to the fact that New Hampton does not actively enforce §3-1031 and would not likely enforce it against Tara or Brandon.

A similar issue that must be addressed is whether Tara and Brandon had standing to challenge §3-1031. Standing is "a personal stake in the outcome of a controversy." Baker v. Carr, 369 U.S. 186 (1962). Standing requires (1) an injury in fact suffered by the plaintiff; (2) a causal connection between the injury and the conduct complained of; and (3) that a favorable court decision would likely redress the injury. Lujan v. Defenders of Wildlife, 504 U.S. 555 (1992). With regard to the first component, an "injury in fact" is "the invasion of a legally protected interest which is concrete and particularized and actual or imminent, not conjectural or hypothetical." *Id.* Once again, due to the complete lack of prosecution of §3-1031 and the unlikelihood that Tara or Brandon would face criminal charges for their actions, they will have a very difficult time meeting the first component of standing.

Even if Tara and Brandon could overcome issues of ripeness and standing, their lawsuit would still fail because it is now moot. Courts are prohibited from deciding cases "that cannot affect the rights of the litigants in the case before them." DeFunis v. Odegaard, 416 U.S. 312 (1974). In the instant hypothetical, §3-1031 was repealed by the New Hampton legislature. Fornication, therefore, is no longer a criminal act. The lawsuit filed by Tara and Brandon alleging the statute violates their constitutional rights no longer presents a live case or controversy. *See* Massachusetts v. Oakes, 491 U.S. 576 (1989).

In conclusion, the court cannot consider the merits of Tara and Brandon's challenge to §3-1031 for three alternative and independent reasons. First, the issue raised is not ripe for review; second, they do not have standing to bring the lawsuit; and third, any claims they may have had are now moot. Their lawsuit is, therefore, nonjusticiable.

Utopia is a nation half way around the world. Despite its name, it has been plagued for decades by violence and civil unrest. This past year, General Nemesis has become the new leader of Utopia. He has spoken freely about his plan to continue the violence and has also threatened to attack many other nations. In light of recent developments, the United States President, along with Congress's approval, has sent several thousand U.S. troops into Utopia in an attempt to restore peace. Congress has also appropriated several billion dollars to aid Utopian citizens in rebuilding their war-ravaged nation. The occupation of Utopia is a very divisive issue in the United States, and many groups are protesting our involvement in Utopian affairs.

One individual who is opposed to the military occupation of Utopia is Jerry Buttinski. Jerry, who is extremely outspoken in his political beliefs, has filed a federal lawsuit as a citizen of the United States against the President, the Vice President, and numerous congressional leaders. In his lawsuit, Jerry alleges that (1) the President and Congress are unconstitutionally ordering a war without proper justification; (2) the government's actions in occupying Utopia present a major threat to his life if General Nemesis should retaliate by attacking the United States; and (3) he is placed in constant fear of a full-scale nuclear war because of the government's actions.

Penny Pincher, another U.S. citizen, is also opposed to the U.S. occupation of Utopia but for a very different reason from Jerry. Penny firmly believes that as a taxpayer in this country, she has a voice in any governmental expenditures. She has filed suit in federal court seeking an injunction against the President and Congress from appropriating U.S. treasury funds to finance the ongoing military activity in Utopia. Penny maintains that she has a lesser quality of life because the money spent on Utopia has resulted in a reduction of public services in the United States and has caused a federal budget deficit.

Discuss whether the courts have the power to entertain the federal lawsuits initiated by Jerry and Penny, respectively.

DISCUSSION QUESTIONS

1. Research challenge: What did President Franklin D. Roosevelt do in the 1930s that almost permanently altered the composition of the Supreme Court? What was the ultimate result of his actions?

2. Wanda was driving drunk one afternoon in a small Connecticut town when she lost control of her vehicle and plowed into a crowd of people taking part in an Independence Day parade. Wanda, who is from Connecticut, seriously injured Courtney, a college student attending a Connecticut school but originally from Rhode Island. If Courtney decided to sue Wanda for the injuries she sustained in the accident, would a federal court have jurisdiction over her case? Explain. What other individuals might it be difficult to determine where they are domiciled for the purposes of diversity jurisdiction?

3. Research challenge: Only once in the history of our nation has the United States Supreme Court conducted a criminal trial. What were the circumstances of the case that is truly an anomaly in constitutional history? *See* Mark Curriden & Leroy Phillips, Jr., *Contempt of Court* (1999).

4. Of the three branches of government, the judiciary is the only one whose members are appointed rather than elected, and they (federal judges) hold office for life rather than for a fixed term. Why do you think the framers of the Constitution did this? What are the advantages and disadvantages of the judiciary's unique tenure in office?

5. Recently, Congress enacted a law that gave federal judges the power to authorize magistrates to preside over limited aspects of the trial process. Magistrates, although not judges, act in a similar capacity and help to alleviate the tremendous workload on federal court judges. Trudy Chapman was arrested and charged with federal child pornography offenses. If convicted, she could face over 20 years' imprisonment. When Trudy's case came for jury selection, a magistrate was appointed to oversee the process. Trudy objected, arguing that the seriousness of her case entitled her to an "Article III judge" rather than a magistrate. Her objection was noted, but the magistrate continued with the jury selection process in order to get her case to trial in a speedy manner. Were Trudy's constitutional rights violated? *Compare* Peretz v. United States, 501 U.S. 923 (1991), *with* Gomez v. United States, 490 U.S. 858 (1989).

6. Research challenge: Who was the only President later to serve as Chief Justice of the Supreme Court? Who was the only Justice to be impeached and why? How many times has the Constitution been amended to overturn a Supreme Court decision? When?

7. Do military tribunals operate the same way as Article III courts? When would a military tribunal have jurisdiction in a case?

8. Research challenge: Locate some cases in which the Supreme Court overturned its own precedent. Since our law is founded on the concept of *stare decisis*, why do you think the Court overruled itself in these particular cases?

9. Congress recently enacted a law which provides federal funds for the purchase of textbooks and other school supplies to parochial schools in several major cities. Bill and Cindy McCoy, residents of a small rural town in Arkansas, brought a federal lawsuit challenging the constitutionality of the law. Do they have standing? Why or why not? *Compare* Frothingham v. Mellon, 262 U.S. 447 (1923), *with* Flast v. Cohen, 392 U.S. 83 (1968).

10. Although Article III clearly establishes the Supreme Court as our nation's highest court, it states that inferior courts exist only "as the Congress may from time to time ordain and establish." Given that language, could Congress eliminate all lower federal courts? Article III also provides that the Supreme Court "shall have appellate Jurisdiction . . . under such Regulations as the Congress shall make." Could Congress also eliminate the Supreme Court's appellate jurisdiction entirely? What do you think might happen if Congress decided to do either or both of the above? Explain.

11. Revisit the section in the Student Checklist dealing with judicial restraint. Why do you think courts will only decide constitutional questions on the merits as a last resort? Why would a court want to avoid deciding a constitutional question?

12. Jeremy is convicted in state court of the misdemeanor of using profanity in a public place. He is sentenced to one month incarceration. Jeremy would like to challenge his conviction on the grounds that the statute at issue violates his First Amendment right to freedom of speech, but he knows that by the time his case gets through the appellate process he will long since have been released from jail. Is Jeremy's case justiciable? What additional facts might you want to know before you reach your conclusion? *See* Spencer v. Kemna, 523 U.S. 1 (1998).

13. How did ex-model and Playboy centerfold Anna Nicole Smith find herself before the United States Supreme Court in a case dealing with jurisdictional issues? What were the facts and holding in her case? *See* Marshall v. Marshall, 547 U.S. 293 (2006).

14. What is a class action lawsuit? What is its purpose and how does it potentially affect standing? What examples can you find of highly publicized class action lawsuits?

15. Research challenge: When did the President create what is known as an "Article II court"? What were the unique facts that led to its creation? Can you foresee the possibility of a similar court being created given current times? Explain.

16. What is a "Declaratory Judgment"? How is it not inconsistent with the principal of law that courts will only rule upon the merits of a case when an actual "case or controversy" exists? *See* Aetna Life Ins. Co. v. Haworth, 300 U.S. 227 (1937).

True/False

1. Judicial review encompasses the power of a court to invalidate unconstitutional acts of both the executive and legislative branches.

2. A federal court may not exercise judicial review of actions by state courts.

3. The Constitution gives Congress the power to regulate the Supreme Court's original and appellate jurisdiction.

4. Any time an issue involves another branch of government, it will not be decided by a court because the issue will be considered a political question.

5. Even though an issue has become moot, the court can still consider the merits of the issue under certain conditions.

Multiple Choice

6. Ben was recently fired from his job as a mechanic at Autoworks Unlimited. Ben maintains he was fired due to a physical handicap. He wants to sue Autoworks based on the Americans with Disabilities Act ("ADA") which was enacted by Congress in 1990. Can he properly file suit in a federal court?

   A. Yes, because he is raising a federal question.
   B. Yes, but only if he can first show a diversity of citizenship between himself and Autoworks.
   C. No, because his lawsuit would require the court to address a federal statute.
   D. No, because a citizen does not have standing to challenge a federal statute.

7. Revisit the above question. What if, after Ben filed suit in court, Autoworks rehired Ben and compensated him for lost earnings while he was unemployed. Should the court still consider the merits of Ben's lawsuit?

   A. No, because the issue is not yet ripe.
   B. No, because the issue has become moot.
   C. No, because Ben no longer has standing to bring the lawsuit.
   D. Yes.

8. Revisit the above question. Suppose that Ben was one of 75 plaintiffs who brought suit against Autoworks, all of whom alleged violations of the ADA.

If Ben alone were rehired and given back pay, should a court continue to hear the merits of the lawsuit?

A. No, because the plaintiffs as a whole no longer have standing.
B. Yes, but only if Ben gives express consent for the lawsuit to continue without him.
C. No, because the court would be issuing an advisory opinion.
D. Yes, as long as the other plaintiffs still maintain they suffered an injury from Autoworks' actions.

9. Carla wants to challenge the constitutionality of a recently enacted federal law which prohibits individuals of the same sex from marrying. In which of the following capacities would Carla most likely succeed as a plaintiff in getting a court to consider the merits of her complaint?

A. A citizen of the United States.
B. A taxpayer of the United States.
C. A homosexual woman who wishes to marry her partner but is unable to do so because of the federal law.
D. A heterosexual woman whose religious beliefs state that any individuals should be permitted to marry.

10. Revisit the above question. If a court were to consider the merits of Carla's challenge to the law, which of the following rules of judicial restraint should the court follow?

A. A court should presume the law is unconstitutional since it arguably infringes on an individual's right to privacy and equal protection.
B. A court should avoid deciding Carla's case on constitutional grounds if it can be decided on non-constitutional grounds.
C. Both A and B.
D. Neither A nor B.

Chapter 3

Congress

> "The Congress shall have Power to . . . provide for the
> general Welfare of the United States . . ."
> —**U.S. Constitution, Article 1, Section 8**

INTRODUCTION

The Framers of the Constitution created a bicameral legislature, with the House of Representatives and the Senate, to prevent the Congress from hastily or irrationally passing statutes. Under this bicameral system, elected representatives and senators vote on bills. A majority in both the House and the Senate is necessary to pass legislation.

While each house of Congress is left to determine its own internal operating procedures, Article I of the Constitution establishes the Congressional framework and qualifications for membership as detailed in the chart below.

	House	Senate
MEMBERSHIP	Each state is entitled to at least 1 Representative. Additional seats are apportioned to states based upon population as measured in the U.S. Census	2 Senators per state. Vice President casts vote in event of tie
TERM	2-year term (no term limits)	6-year term (no term limits)
LEADERSHIP	Speaker of the House	President of the Senate (Vice President of the United States)
CONSTITUTIONAL QUALIFICATIONS	U.S. Citizen for at least 7 years	U.S. citizen for at least 9 years

	House	Senate
	Resident of the state represented	Resident of the state represented
	Age 25 or over	Age 30 or over

Via specific constitutional provisions and constitutional amendments, Congress is expressly empowered to legislate statutes. Article I, Section 8 is the provision which enumerates most of Congress's powers, such as the powers to tax, spend, borrow, regulate commerce, coin money, and punish counterfeiters. In addition to these fiscal powers, Article I, Section 8 empowers Congress to establish the Post Office, federal courts, and a military, to protect intellectual property, to declare war, and to pass laws governing the District of Columbia. Notably, Article I, Section 8, Clause 18 contains the "Necessary and Proper Clause," which enables Congress to make any laws necessary for the federal government to execute its powers. Enumerated powers also exist in other areas of the Constitution. For example, Article II enables the Senate to participate in treaty making and to approve presidential appointments, and two voting rights amendments, the Nineteenth (removing sex as a voter qualification) and the Twenty-sixth (lowering the voting age to 18), explicitly state that "[t]he Congress shall have power to enforce this article by appropriate legislation."

The Supreme Court has also concluded that Congress possesses implied powers that are not enumerated in the Constitution or amendments. The seminal case on this topic was M'Culloch v. Maryland, 17 U.S. 316 (1819). At issue in *M'Culloch* was whether Congress had the power to establish a national bank. Maryland challenged the establishment of the bank, asserting that no such power was delineated in the Constitution. The Supreme Court disagreed with Maryland and considered the Necessary and Proper Clause along with the enumerated powers of taxing, spending, and borrowing. The Court concluded that the Constitution implies congressional powers essential to carrying out its enumerated powers. This decision was criticized as giving Congress too much power. Those supporting the Court's ruling believed that the executive and judiciary branches were sufficient checks on congressional powers.

Significant legislation emanated from the *M'Culloch* decision, ranging from the enactment of labor and antitrust laws, to the establishment of social security and passage of civil rights, criminal, agricultural, and environmental laws, among others. Congress has assumed such authority based upon implied powers arising mostly from the Commerce Clause (Art. I, Sec. 8, Cl. 3) and its taxing and spending powers. Without such implied powers, Congress could not have passed laws promoting social welfare. By virtue of a broad reading of these clauses and taxing authority, we have child labor laws (Hammer v. Dagenhart, 247 U.S. 251 (1918), and Bailey v. Drexel Furniture, 259 U.S. 20 (1922)); laws preventing child pornography (Miller v. California, 413 U.S. 15 (1973)); laws preventing discrimination in public accommodations such as hotels and restaurants (Heart of Atlanta and Katzenbach v. McClung, 379 U.S. 294 (1964)); laws preventing strip mining (Hodel v. Virginia Surface Mining and Reclamation Association, Inc., 452 U.S. 264 (1981)); and a law requiring employers to provide reasonable accommodations for people with disabilities (42 U.S.C.A. §12101).

Social welfare legislation abounded from the 1920s into the 1990s. During this time, the Supreme Court generally affirmed Congress's implied powers. However, in 1995, the Rehnquist Court heard a case involving gun-free school zones. United States v. Lopez, 514 U.S. 549 (1995). Under federal statute, it was a crime to possess a gun within 1,000 feet of a school. The federal government asserted that the Commerce Clause empowered Congress to pass such law. A sharply divided Court concluded that Congress did not have the power to create gun-free school zones by criminalizing the possession of a firearm near a school. The Court reasoned that possessing a gun near a school had nothing to do with commerce and that Congress had stretched its interpretation of the Commerce Clause too far in attempting to pass this law. The *Lopez* decision was the first to apply the brakes to Congress's interpretation of its implied powers. The *Lopez* case was not an anomaly, as it was followed five years later by *United States v. Morrison*, in which the Supreme Court struck down a provision of the Violence Against Women Act of 1994 providing for a civil remedy for the victim of gender-motivated violence. 529 U.S. 598 (2000). Although the pendulum has started to swing back slightly in the Court's interpretation of implied congressional powers, there is still a wealth of precedent and legislation supporting a broad interpretation of such powers.

STUDENT *Checklist*

Congressional Powers

Does Congress have the power to . . . ?

a. Is there an applicable enumerated power?

b. Is there an applicable implied power?

SUPREME COURT CASES

HEART OF ATLANTA MOTEL v. UNITED STATES,
379 U.S. 241 (1964)

[In this case, the parties agreed to the facts. The appellant operated the Heart of Atlanta Motel, which was accessible to several highways, two of which were interstate. The motel marketed to potential guests from outside of the State of Georgia, and approximately 75 percent of its guest were from outside the state. The motel refused to rent rooms to African-American patrons, even after the Civil Rights Act of 1964, which required equal access to public accommodations, was passed by Congress. The motel contended that the Act was unconstitutional, asserting that Congress had exceeded its powers, among other reasons. The United States challenged the motel's discriminatory practice and asserted that Congress had the power under the Commerce Clause (Article I, Section 8) to enact the Civil Rights Act of 1964.]

Mr. Justice CLARK delivered the opinion of the Court.

This is a declaratory judgment action, . . . attacking the constitutionality of Title II of the Civil Rights Act of 1964. . . . It is admitted that the operation of the motel brings it within the provisions of 201(a) of the Act and that appellant refused to provide lodging for transient Negroes because of their race or color and that it intends to continue that policy unless restrained.

The sole question posed is, therefore, the constitutionality of the Civil Rights Act of 1964 as applied to these facts. The legislative history of the Act indicates that Congress based the Act on 5 and the Equal Protection Clause of the Fourteenth Amendment as well as its power to regulate interstate commerce under Art. I, Sec. 8, cl. 3, of the Constitution.

The Senate Commerce Committee made it quite clear that the fundamental object of Title II was to vindicate "the deprivation of personal dignity that surely accompanies denials of equal access to public establishments." At the same time, however, it noted that such an objective has been and could be readily achieved "by congressional action based on the commerce power of the Constitution." S. Rep. No. 872, supra, at 16-17. Our study of the legislative record, made in the light of prior cases, has brought us to the conclusion that Congress possessed ample power in this regard, and we have therefore not considered the other grounds relied upon. . . .

In light of our ground for decision, it might be well at the outset to discuss the Civil Rights Cases, supra, which declared provisions of the Civil Rights Act of 1875 unconstitutional. We think that decision inapposite, and without precedential value in determining the constitutionality of the present Act. Unlike Title II of the present legislation, the 1875 Act broadly proscribed discrimination in "inns, public conveyances on land or water, theaters, and other places of public amusement," without limiting the categories of affected businesses to those impinging upon interstate commerce. In contrast, the applicability of Title II is carefully limited to enterprises having a direct and substantial relation to the interstate flow of goods and people, except where state action is involved. Further, the fact that certain kinds of businesses may not in 1875 have been sufficiently involved in interstate commerce to warrant bringing them within the ambit of the commerce power is not necessarily dispositive of the same question today. Our populace had not reached its present mobility, nor were facilities, goods and services circulating as readily in interstate commerce as they are today. Although the principles which we apply today are those first formulated by Chief Justice Marshall in Gibbons v. Ogden, 9 Wheat. 1 (1824), the conditions of transportation and commerce have changed dramatically, and we must apply those principles to the present state of commerce. The sheer increase in volume of interstate traffic alone would give discriminatory practices which inhibit travel a far larger impact upon the Nation's commerce than such practices had on the economy of another day. Finally, there is language in the Civil Rights Cases which indicates that the Court did not fully consider whether the 1875 Act could be sustained as an exercise of the commerce power. . . .

Since the commerce power was not relied on by the Government and was without support in the record it is understandable that the Court narrowed its inquiry and excluded the Commerce Clause as a possible source of power. In any event, it is clear that such a limitation renders the opinion devoid of authority for the proposition that the Commerce Clause gives no power to Congress to regulate discriminatory practices now found substantially to affect interstate commerce. . . .

While the Act as adopted carried no congressional findings the record of its passage through each house is replete with evidence of the burdens that discrimination by race or color places upon interstate commerce. . . . This testimony included the fact that our people have become increasingly mobile with millions of people of all races traveling from State to State; that Negroes in particular have been the subject of discrimination in transient accommodations, having to travel great distances to secure the same; that often they have been unable to obtain accommodations and have had to call upon friends to put them up overnight, and that these conditions had become so acute as to require the listing of available lodging for Negroes in a special guidebook which was itself "dramatic testimony to the difficulties" Negroes encounter in travel. These exclusionary practices were found to be nationwide, the Under Secretary of Commerce testifying that there is "no question that this discrimination in the North still exists to a large degree" and in the West and Midwest as well. This testimony indicated a qualitative as well as quantitative effect on interstate travel by Negroes. The former was the obvious impairment of the Negro traveler's pleasure and convenience that resulted when he continually was uncertain of finding lodging. As for the latter, there was evidence that this uncertainty stemming from racial discrimination had the effect of discouraging travel on the part of a substantial portion of the Negro community. This was the conclusion not only of the Under Secretary of Commerce but also of the Administrator of the Federal Aviation Agency who wrote the Chairman of the Senate Commerce Committee that it was his "belief that air commerce is adversely affected by the denial to a substantial segment of the traveling public of adequate and desegregated public accommodations." . . .

The power of Congress to deal with these obstructions depends on the meaning of the Commerce Clause. Its meaning was first enunciated 140 years ago by the great Chief Justice John Marshall in Gibbons v. Ogden, 9 Wheat. 1 (1824), in these words:

"The subject to be regulated is commerce; and . . . to ascertain the extent of the power, it becomes necessary to settle the meaning of the word. The counsel for the appellee would limit it to traffic, to buying and selling, or the interchange of commodities . . . but it is something more: it is intercourse . . . between nations, and parts of nations, in all its branches, and is regulated by prescribing rules for carrying on that intercourse. [At 189-190.] . . . .

"To what commerce does this power extend? The constitution informs us, to commerce 'with foreign nations, and among the several States, and with the Indian tribes.'

"It has, we believe, been universally admitted, that these words comprehend every species of commercial intercourse. . . . No sort of trade can be carried on . . . to which this power does not extend. [At 193-194.] . . . .

"The subject to which the power is next applied, is to commerce 'among the several States.' The word 'among' means intermingled. . . .

". . . [I]t may very properly be restricted to that commerce which concerns more States than one. . . . The genius and character of the whole government seem to be, that its action is to be applied to all the . . . internal concerns [of the Nation] which affect the States generally; but not to those which are completely within a particular State, which do not affect other States, and with which it is not necessary to interfere, for the purpose of executing some of the general powers of the government. . . .

"We are now arrived at the inquiry—What is this power?

"It is the power to regulate; that is, to prescribe the rule by which commerce is to be governed. This power, like all others vested in Congress, is complete in itself, may be exercised to its utmost extent, and acknowledges no limitations, other than are prescribed in the constitution. . . . If, as has always been understood, the sovereignty of Congress . . . is plenary as to those objects [specified in the Constitution], the power over commerce . . . is vested in Congress as absolutely as it would be in a single government, having in its constitution the same restrictions on the exercise of the power as are found in the constitution of the United States. The wisdom and the discretion of Congress, their identity with the people, and the influence which their constituents possess at elections, are, in this, as in many other instances, as that, for example, of declaring war, the sole restraints on which they have relied, to secure them from its abuse. They are the restraints on which the people must often rely solely, in all representative governments."

In short, the determinative test of the exercise of power by the Congress under the Commerce Clause is simply whether the activity sought to be regulated is "commerce which concerns more States than one" and has a real and substantial relation to the national interest. Let us now turn to this facet of the problem.

That the "intercourse" of which the Chief Justice spoke included the movement of persons through more States than one was settled as early as 1849, in the Passenger Cases, 7 How. 283, where Mr. Justice McLean stated: "That the transportation of passengers is a part of commerce is not now an open question." Again in 1913 Mr. Justice McKenna, speaking for the Court, said: "Commerce among the States, we have said, consists of intercourse and traffic between their citizens, and includes the transportation of persons and property." And only four years later in 1917 in Caminetti v. United States, 242 U.S. 470, Mr. Justice Day held for the Court:

> "The transportation of passengers in interstate commerce, it has long been settled, is within the regulatory power of Congress, under the commerce clause of the Constitution, and the authority of Congress to keep the channels of interstate commerce free from immoral and injurious uses has been frequently sustained, and is no longer open to question."

Nor does it make any difference whether the transportation is commercial in character. . . .

That Congress was legislating against moral wrongs in many . . . areas [such criminal enterprises, deceptive trade practices, fraudulent security transactions, and racial discrimination in professional football] rendered its enactments no less valid. In framing Title II of this Act Congress was also dealing with what it considered a moral problem. But that fact does not detract from the overwhelming evidence of the disruptive effect that racial discrimination has had on commercial intercourse. It was this burden which empowered Congress to enact appropriate legislation, and, given this basis for the exercise of its power, Congress was not restricted by the fact that the particular obstruction to interstate commerce with which it was dealing was also deemed a moral and social wrong.

It is said that the operation of the motel here is of a purely local character. But, assuming this to be true, "[i]f it is interstate commerce that feels the pinch, it does not matter how local the operation which applies the squeeze." . . .

Thus the power of Congress to promote interstate commerce also includes the power to regulate the local incidents thereof, including local activities in both the States of origin and destination, which might have a substantial and harmful effect upon that commerce. One need only examine the evidence which we have discussed above to see that Congress may—as it has—prohibit racial discrimination by motels serving travelers, however "local" their operations may appear. . . .

We, therefore, conclude that the action of the Congress in the adoption of the Act as applied here to a motel which concededly serves interstate travelers is within the power granted it by the Commerce Clause of the Constitution, as interpreted by this Court for 140 years. . . .

Affirmed.

GONZALES v. RAICH, 545 U.S. 1 (2005)

[The State of California passed the Compassionate Use Act of 1996, allowing seriously ill residents to use marijuana for medical purposes. Physicians, patients, and primary caregivers were exempt from prosecution for growing or possessing marijuana when its use was recommended by a physician. The federal Controlled Substances Act (CSA) criminalized even the medical use of marijuana. As such, those protected under California's Compassionate Use Act could still be prosecuted under federal law for growing, possessing, or distributing marijuana. The plaintiffs in this case, Mason and Raich, were seriously ill California residents whose doctors prescribed marijuana to treat serious medical conditions. Federal agents raided Mason's house and destroyed her marijuana plants. Both Mason and Raich sued the federal government, seeking an injunction preventing the enforcement of the federal CSA, arguing, among other things, that the CSA was unconstitutional because Congress did not have the power to pass the CSA. The plaintiffs specifically asserted that the Commerce Clause did not empower Congress to pass the CSA.]

Justice STEVENS delivered the opinion of the Court.

. . . In assessing the validity of congressional regulation, none of our Commerce Clause cases can be viewed in isolation. . . . The Commerce Clause emerged as the Framers' response to the central problem giving rise to the Constitution itself: the absence of any federal commerce power under the Articles of Confederation. For the first century of our history, the primary use of the Clause was to preclude the kind of discriminatory state legislation that had once been permissible. Then, in response to rapid industrial development and an increasingly interdependent national economy, Congress "ushered in a new era of federal regulation under the commerce power," beginning with the enactment of the Interstate Commerce Act in 1887, and the Sherman Antitrust Act in 1890, cases decided during that "new era," which now spans more than a century, have identified three general categories of regulation in which Congress is authorized to engage under its commerce power. First, Congress can regulate the channels of interstate commerce. Second, Congress has authority to regulate and protect the instrumentalities of interstate commerce, and persons or things in interstate commerce. Third, Congress has the power to regulate activities that substantially affect interstate commerce. Only the third category is implicated in the case at hand.

Our case law firmly establishes Congress' power to regulate purely local activities that are part of an economic "class of activities" that have a substantial effect on interstate commerce. . . .

Our decision in *Wickard* [v. Filburn, 317 U.S. 111 (1942)] is of particular relevance. In *Wickard*, we upheld the application of regulations promulgated under the Agricultural Adjustment Act of 1938, which were designed to control the volume of wheat moving in interstate and foreign commerce in order to avoid surpluses and consequent abnormally low prices. The regulations established an allotment of 11.1 acres for Filburn's 1941 wheat crop, but he sowed 23 acres, intending to use the excess by consuming it on his own farm. Filburn argued that even though we had sustained Congress' power to regulate the production of goods for commerce, that power did not authorize "federal regulation [of] production not intended in any part for commerce but wholly for consumption on the farm." Justice Jackson's opinion for a unanimous Court rejected this submission. He wrote:

> "The effect of the statute before us is to restrict the amount which may be produced for market and the extent as well to which one may forestall resort to the market by producing to meet his own needs. That appellee's own contribution to the demand for wheat may be trivial by itself is not enough to remove him from the scope of federal regulation where, as here, his contribution, taken together with that of many others similarly situated, is far from trivial."

Wickard thus establishes that Congress can regulate purely intrastate activity that is not itself "commercial," in that it is not produced for sale, if it concludes that failure to regulate that class of activity would undercut the regulation of the interstate market in that commodity.

The similarities between this case and *Wickard* are striking. Like the farmer in *Wickard*, respondents are cultivating, for home consumption, a fungible commodity for which there is an established, albeit illegal, interstate market. Just as the Agricultural Adjustment Act was designed "to control the volume [of wheat] moving in interstate and foreign commerce in order to avoid surpluses . . ." and consequently control the market price, a primary purpose of the CSA is to control the supply and demand of controlled substances in both lawful and unlawful drug markets. In *Wickard*, we had no difficulty concluding that Congress had a rational basis for believing that, when viewed in the aggregate, leaving home-consumed wheat outside the regulatory scheme would have a substantial influence on price and market conditions. Here too, Congress had a rational basis for concluding that leaving home-consumed marijuana outside federal control would similarly affect price and market conditions.

More concretely, one concern prompting inclusion of wheat grown for home consumption in the 1938 Act was that rising market prices could draw such wheat into the interstate market, resulting in lower market prices. The parallel concern making it appropriate to include marijuana grown for home consumption in the CSA is the likelihood that the high demand in the interstate market will draw such marijuana into that market. While the diversion of homegrown wheat tended to frustrate the federal interest in stabilizing prices by regulating the volume of commercial transactions in the interstate market, the diversion of homegrown marijuana tends to frustrate the federal interest in eliminating commercial transactions in the interstate market in their entirety. In both cases, the regulation is squarely within Congress' commerce power because production of the commodity meant for home consumption, be it wheat or marijuana, has a substantial effect on supply and demand in the national market for that commodity. . . .

In assessing the scope of Congress' authority under the Commerce Clause, . . . [w]e need not determine whether respondents' activities, taken in the aggregate, substantially affect interstate commerce in fact, but only whether a "rational basis" exists for so concluding. Given the enforcement difficulties that attend distinguishing between marijuana cultivated locally and marijuana grown elsewhere, and concerns about diversion into illicit channels, we have no difficulty concluding that Congress had a rational basis for believing that failure to regulate the intrastate manufacture and possession of marijuana would leave a gaping hole in the CSA. . . .

To support their contrary submission, respondents rely heavily on two of our more recent Commerce Clause cases. . . .

Those two cases, of course, are *Lopez*, and *Morrison*. As an initial matter, the statutory challenges at issue in those cases were markedly different from the challenge respondents pursue in the case at hand. . . .

At issue in *Lopez* was the validity of the Gun-Free School Zones Act of 1990, which was a brief, single-subject statute making it a crime for an individual to possess a gun in a school zone. The Act did not regulate any economic activity and did not contain any requirement that the possession of a gun have any connection to past interstate activity or a predictable impact on future commercial activity. Distinguishing our earlier cases holding that comprehensive regulatory statutes may be validly applied to local conduct that does not, when viewed in isolation, have a significant impact on interstate commerce, we held the statute invalid. We explained:

> "Section 922(q) is a criminal statute that by its terms has nothing to do with 'commerce' or any sort of economic enterprise, however broadly one might define those terms. . . . It cannot, therefore, be sustained under our cases upholding regulations of activities that arise out of or are connected with a commercial transaction, which viewed in the aggregate, substantially affects interstate commerce."

The statutory scheme that the Government is defending in this litigation is at the opposite end of the regulatory spectrum. As explained above, the CSA, enacted in 1970 as part of the Comprehensive Drug Abuse Prevention and Control Act, was a lengthy and detailed statute creating a comprehensive framework for regulating the production, distribution, and possession of five classes of "controlled substances." Most of those substances—those listed in Schedules II through V—"have a useful and legitimate medical purpose and are necessary to maintain the health and general welfare of the American people." The regulatory scheme is designed to foster the beneficial use of those medications, to prevent their misuse, and to prohibit entirely the possession or use of substances listed in Schedule I, except as a part of a strictly controlled research project.

While the statute provided for the periodic updating of the five schedules, Congress itself made the initial classifications. . . . That classification, unlike the discrete prohibition established by the Gun-Free School Zones Act of 1990, was merely one of many "essential part[s] of a larger regulation of economic activity, in which the regulatory scheme could be undercut unless the intrastate activity were regulated."

[*Morrison* focused upon The Violence Against Women Act of 1994, a statute which] created a federal civil remedy for the victims of gender-motivated crimes of violence. . . . Despite congressional findings that such crimes had an adverse impact on interstate commerce, we held the statute unconstitutional because, like the statute in *Lopez*, it did not regulate economic activity. We concluded that "the noneconomic, criminal nature of the conduct at issue was central to our decision" in *Lopez*, and that our prior cases had identified a clear pattern of analysis: " 'Where economic activity substantially affects interstate commerce, legislation regulating that activity will be sustained.' "

Unlike those at issue in *Lopez* and *Morrison*, the activities regulated by the CSA are quintessentially economic. "Economics" refers to "the production, distribution, and consumption of commodities." Webster's Third New International Dictionary 720 (1966). The CSA is a statute that regulates the production, distribution, and consumption of commodities for which there is an established, and lucrative, interstate market. Prohibiting the intrastate possession or manufacture of an article of commerce is a rational (and commonly utilized) means of regulating commerce in that product. Such prohibitions include specific decisions requiring that a drug be withdrawn from the market as a result of the failure to comply with regulatory requirements as well as decisions excluding Schedule I drugs entirely from the market. Because the CSA is a statute that directly regulates economic, commercial activity, our opinion in *Morrison* casts no doubt on its constitutionality.

CASE QUESTIONS

HEART OF ATLANTA MOTEL v. UNITED STATES

1. Define the term "inapposite." Why were the Civil Rights Cases inapposite?

2. Explain Congress's power to regulate interstate commerce.

3. What is the "determinative test of the exercise of power by the Congress under the Commerce Clause"?

4. What facts support the conclusion that the motel conducted interstate commerce?

GONZALES v. RAICH

1. In assessing Congress's authority, what level of constitutional scrutiny did the *Gonzales* Court apply? Applying such scrutiny, what did the Court conclude?

2. Explain how the Court applied *Wickard.*

3. Explain why the *Lopez* and *Morrison* decisions did not impact the Court's decision in *Gonzales.*

4. What was the federal interest in passing the CSA?

5. Explain why growing one's own marijuana for personal medical use impacts interstate commerce.

HYPOTHETICAL WITH ACCOMPANYING ANALYSIS

Hypothetical

Assume Congress passes a law requiring anyone who can afford health care insurance to purchase insurance if they are not covered. If a person who is required to purchase health care insurance fails to do so, they must pay a fine. Paul considers himself a relatively healthy person. He is 28, runs marathons, and has no known health problems. Paul can afford insurance and does not qualify for any publicly funded insurance. He does not want to "waste" his money on buying health care insurance. When Paul is fined for not buying health insurance, he asserts that the law is unconstitutional.

Analysis

In the matter at bar, it is likely that Congress does have the power to require a citizen to purchase health care insurance because there is a rational basis for concluding that not having health care insurance impacts interstate commerce. Studies have shown that there are serious financial consequences to being uninsured. When someone who is uninsured seeks health care, physicians and hospitals are not compensated for significant portions of the uninsured's care. As such, health care costs for the insured increases so as to cover the costs of the uninsured. This also means that health insurance premiums rise nationally. Health insurance providers cover medical procedures globally. Additionally, those who are uninsured tend to not seek preventative care. The uninsured may also not seek care until late stages of disease or illness when care is more costly. Also, because the uninsured tend not to seek preventative care as frequently as the insured and because the uninsured tend to seek care late, they may be left disabled or unable to work for longer periods of time, thus decreasing business productivity and impacting commerce. As health care for the uninsured raises health care costs and insurance premiums nationally and because many business which have uninsured workers and lose productivity undertake interstate commerce, there is a rational basis for concluding that being uninsured impacts interstate commerce. Therefore, Article 1, Section 8, Clause 3 empowers Congress to regulate health insurance and require the purchase of health care insurance.

HYPOTHETICAL FOR STUDENT ANALYSIS

Studies have shown that driving while texting, emailing, and/or using cell phone applications causes great distraction and leads to an increase in accidents. Congress wants drivers across the country to not be able to drive while texting, emailing, or using applications on their cell phones. As such, Congress requires any state receiving federal funding for highway improvements or maintenance to pass state laws banning texting, emailing, or using applications while driving. The State of Lasaka has a governor who likes to take risks and believes in personal autonomy. She refuses to sign legislation establishing the state ban. When the federal government revokes highway funding, the governor, on behalf of the State of Lasaka, challenges the law, asserting that Congress does not have the power to require the State of Lasaka to pass such a driving law. Assess the governor's chances of succeeding in her lawsuit.

DISCUSSION QUESTIONS

1. Why is an accurate U.S. Census important in the context of government?

2. Explain bicameralism. Why did the Framers believe bicameralism was so important? Do you think a bicameral legislature is still an effective form of government? Explain why or why not.

3. Read M'Culloch v. Maryland, 17 U.S. 316 (1819). Explain the holding in this case. *M'Culloch* is thought to be one of the most important cases in U.S. history. Explain why this case is so important.

4. Research challenge: Explain what a carpetbagger is and identify at least two members of Congress, past or present, which were thought to be carpetbaggers.

5. Research challenge: Identify the two senators from your state and list the Senate committees on which they serve.

6. Suppose that Congress decided to subpoena former President George W. Bush to testify regarding interrogation techniques authorized by the President for use against detainees at Guantanamo Bay. Also assume that Bush declined to testify, asserting that he did not have to testify because of executive privilege. Congress held Bush in contempt, and Bush appealed. See Chapter 4, Barenblatt v. United States, 360 U.S. 109 (1959), and United States v. Nixon, 418 U.S. 683 (1974).

7. What is the Dormant Commerce Clause?

8. What provision of the Constitution or its amendments vested power in Congress to pass the Voting Rights Act of 1965? *See* Katzenbach v. Morgan, 384 U.S. 641 (1966).

9. Congress passed the Defense of Marriage Act (DOMA). The act does two things. First, it defines marriage, for the purpose of applying federal laws, as being only between a man and a woman. Second, DOMA provides that one state need not recognize a legally valid, same-sex marriage from another state. Does Congress have the power to pass the second provision of the law relating to a state's recognition of same-sex marriages? Explain why or why not.

10. Has Congress declared war against Iraq or Afghanistan? Are these wars constitutional? Explain why or why not. Can you personally file a lawsuit to stop either of these wars? *See* Holtzman v. Schlesinger, 414 U.S. 1316 (1973), and 50 U.S.C §§ 1541-1548.

True/False

1. States have the power to draw House district lines after every census.

2. During a debate on the Senate floor, Senator Loudofthemouth stated that "the Senate Majority Leader is a rapist" and that that is why he does not want to pass a laws criminalizing violence against women. The statement that the Majority Leader is a rapist is factually untrue. Senator Loudofthemouth is immune from a slander lawsuit.

3. Senator Loudofthemouth published a campaign flier indicating that she was a supporter of legislation supporting women and criticized the Senate Majority Leader for not favoring such legislation, specifically stating that the "Majority Leader is a rapist." The statement that the Majority Leader is a rapist is factually untrue. Senator Loudofthemouth is immune from a slander lawsuit.

4. The Supreme Court determined that Congress has the power to enforce the Fifteenth Amendment.

5. Congress, and not the Supreme Court, actually extinguished the use of literacy tests as a means of racial discrimination in elections.

Multiple Choice

6. Assume Congress requires all private colleges receiving and/or distributing federal financial aid to allow military recruiters to attend any and all job fairs held by the colleges. Congress has the constitutional power to do so based upon:

   A. The Commerce Clause
   B. The War Powers Act
   C. The power to tax
   D. The power to spend

7. The _____ Amendment(s) give(s) Congress the authority to pass all appropriate statutes to enforce civil rights:

   A. Thirteenth Amendment
   B. Fourteenth Amendment
   C. Fifteenth Amendment
   D. All of the above

8. Congress's power to lay and collect taxes is vested by:

    A. Article 1, Section 8, Clause 1
    B. The Sixteenth Amendment
    C. Both A and B
    D. None of the above

9. Which Amendment limits congressional powers?

    A. Tenth
    B. Fourteenth
    C. Nineteenth
    D. Twenty-sixth

10. Which of the following congressional powers mirror powers of other branches

    A. Compulsory Process
    B. Holding hearings
    C. Contempt
    D. All of the above
    E. None of the above

Chapter 4
The President

> "The executive Power shall be vested in a President of the United States of America."
>
> **—Article II, Section 1**

INTRODUCTION

When examining the Constitution, we find that most issues involving Article II originate in Section 2, which enumerates the President's powers in both the domestic and foreign arenas. In addition to the powers of the President, issues have also arisen regarding what legal protections the President is entitled to in certain situations (*i.e.*, immunity and privilege) and what happens when a President has allegedly committed misconduct in office (*i.e.*, impeachment). These concepts may seem relatively straightforward, but things aren't always as they seem. Many issues related to the President aren't quite so simple, because an extraordinary amount of the President's power is implicit in nature. We call these "inherent powers." In other words, you won't find them explicitly mentioned *anywhere* in the Constitution or amendments. For example, nowhere does it talk about presidential privilege or immunity. That's why, when studying the presidency, it becomes crucial to look beyond the mere words of the Constitution. We must consider other sources that enlighten us about presidential power, including guidance from the Supreme Court, Congressional Acts, and even tradition. Once exploring these issues in detail, you should have a firm grasp of just who our Commander-in-Chief is and what he can or can't do under the cloak of the presidency.

STUDENT  *Checklist*

The President

1. Did the President engage in a constitutional **exercise** of his **power**?

■ Was it a **domestic** power?
  The power to **veto** legislation proposed by Congress?
  The power to **issue executive orders** or **proclamations**?
  The power to **appoint** or **remove** various officials?
  The power to issue **reprieves** or **pardons**?
  The power to **enforce the laws**?
  The power to exercise **emergency powers**?

■ Was it a **foreign** power?
  The power to **make treaties**?
  The power to **negotiate** with other **nations**?
  The power to enter into an **executive agreement** with another nation?
  The power to **initiate hostilities** against another nation and **commit troops** abroad?

■ If not an **explicit** power, did Congress **acquiesce** to the President's exercise of power?

2. Was the President constitutionally subjected to **impeachment** proceedings?

■ Was the President convicted of **treason, bribery**, or **other high crimes and misdemeanors**?

3. Was the President **immune** from liability for his actions?

■ Was the President engaged in an **official act (absolute civil immunity)**?

■ Was the President engaged in an action **unrelated** to the performance of duties (**no civil immunity**)?

■ Was the President subjected to a **criminal prosecution (no immunity)**?

4. Was the President protected from divulging **confidential information** by a **qualified** presidential **privilege**?

■ Did the President **assert** the privilege, thus establishing a **prima facie case of nondisclosure?**

■ Was the **presumption overcome** by a **need for the information** which was greater than the privilege?

SUPREME COURT CASES

YOUNGSTOWN SHEET & TUBE CO. v. SAWYER,
343 U.S. 579 (1952)

We are asked to decide whether the President was acting within his constitutional power when he issued an order directing the Secretary of Commerce to take possession of and operate most of the Nation's steel mills. The mill owners argue that the President's order amounts to lawmaking, a legislative function which the Constitution has expressly confided to the Congress and not to the President. The Government's position is that the order was made on findings of the President that his action was necessary to avert a national catastrophe which would inevitably result from a stoppage of steel production, and that in meeting this grave emergency the President was acting within the aggregate of his constitutional powers as the Nation's Chief Executive and the Commander in Chief of the Armed Forces of the United States. The issue emerges here from the following series of events:

In the latter part of 1951, a dispute arose between the steel companies and their employees over terms and conditions that should be included in new collective bargaining agreements. Long-continued conferences failed to resolve the dispute. On December 18, 1951, the employees' representative, United Steelworkers of America, C.I.O., gave notice of an intention to strike when the existing bargaining agreements expired on December 31. The Federal Mediation and Conciliation Service then intervened in an effort to get labor and management to agree. This failing, the President on December 22, 1951, referred the dispute to the Federal Wage Stabilization Board to investigate and make recommendations for fair and equitable terms of settlement. This Board's report resulted in no settlement. On April 4, 1952, the Union gave notice of a nationwide strike called to begin at 12:01 A.M. April 9. The indispensability of steel as a component of substantially all weapons and other war materials led the President to believe that the proposed work stoppage would immediately jeopardize our national defense and that governmental seizure of the steel mills was necessary in order to assure the continued availability of steel. Reciting these considerations for his action, the President, a few hours before the strike was to begin, issued Executive Order 10340, a copy of which is attached as an appendix, post, 72 S. Ct. 868. The order directed the Secretary of Commerce to take possession of most of the steel mills and keep them running. The Secretary immediately issued his own possessory orders, calling upon the presidents of the various seized companies to serve as operating managers for the United States. They were directed to carry on their activities in accordance with regulations and directions of the Secretary. The next morning the President sent a message to Congress reporting his action. Cong. Rec., April 9, 1952, p. 3962. Twelve days later he sent a second message. Cong. Rec., April 21, 1952, p. 4192. Congress has taken no action.

Obeying the Secretary's orders under protest, the companies brought proceedings against him in the District Court. Their complaints charged that the seizure was not authorized by an act of Congress or by any constitutional provisions. The District Court was asked to declare the orders of the President and the Secretary invalid and to issue preliminary and permanent injunctions restraining their enforcement. Opposing the motion for preliminary injunction, the United States asserted that a strike disrupting steel production for even a brief period would so endanger the well-being and safety of the Nation that the President had "inherent power" to do what he had done—power "supported by the Constitution, by historical precedent, and by court decisions." The Government also contended that in any event no preliminary injunction should be issued because the companies had made no showing that their available legal remedies were inadequate or that their injuries from seizure would be irreparable. Holding against the Government on all points, the District Court on April 30 issued a preliminary injunction restraining the Secretary from "continuing the seizure and possession of the plant ... and from acting under the purported authority of Executive Order No. 10340." 103 F. Supp. 569. On the same day the Court of Appeals stayed the District Court's injunction. 197 F.2d 582. Deeming it best that the issues raised be promptly decided by this Court, we granted certiorari on May 3 and set the cause for argument on May 12. 343 U.S. 937, 72 S. Ct. 775. . . .

The President's power, if any, to issue the order must stem either from an act of Congress or from the Constitution itself. There is no statute that expressly authorizes the President to take possession of property as he did here. Nor is there any act of Congress to which our attention has been directed from which such a power can fairly be implied. Indeed, we do not understand the Government to rely on statutory authorization for this seizure. There are two statutes which do authorize the President to take both personal and real property under certain conditions. However, the Government admits that these conditions were not met and that the President's order was not rooted in either of the statutes. The Government refers to the seizure provisions of one of these statutes (§201(b) of the Defense Production Act) as "much too cumbersome, involved, and time-consuming for the crisis which was at hand."

Moreover, the use of the seizure technique to solve labor disputes in order to prevent work stoppages was not only unauthorized by any congressional enactment; prior to this controversy, Congress had refused to adopt that method of settling labor disputes. When the Taft-Hartley Act was under consideration in 1947, Congress rejected an amendment which would have authorized such governmental seizures in cases of emergency. Apparently it was thought that the technique of seizure, like that of compulsory arbitration, would interfere with the process of collective bargaining. Consequently, the plan Congress adopted in that Act did not provide for seizure under any circumstances. Instead, the plan sought to bring about settlements by use of the customary devices of mediation, conciliation, investigation by boards of inquiry, and public reports. In some instances temporary injunctions were authorized to provide cooling-off periods. All this failing, unions were left free to strike after a secret vote by employees as to whether they wished to accept their employers' final settlement offer.

It is clear that if the President had authority to issue the order he did, it must be found in some provisions of the Constitution. And it is not claimed that express constitutional language grants this power to the President. The contention is that presidential power should be implied from the aggregate of his powers under the Constitution. Particular reliance is placed on provisions in Article II which say that "the executive Power shall be vested in a President . . . "; that "he shall take Care that the Laws be faithfully executed"; and that he "shall be Commander in Chief of the Army and Navy of the United States."

The order cannot properly be sustained as an exercise of the President's military power as Commander in Chief of the Armed Forces. The Government attempts to do so by citing a number of cases upholding broad powers in military commanders engaged in day-to-day fighting in a theater of war. Such cases need not concern us here. Even though "theater of war" be an expanding concept, we cannot with faithfulness to our constitutional system hold that the Commander in Chief of the Armed Forces has the ultimate power as such to take possession of private property in order to keep labor disputes from stopping production. This is a job for the Nation's lawmakers, not for its military authorities.

Nor can the seizure order be sustained because of the several constitutional provisions that grant executive power to the President. In the framework of our Constitution, the President's power to see that the laws are faithfully executed refutes the idea that he is to be a lawmaker. The Constitution limits his functions in the lawmaking process to the recommending of laws he thinks wise and the vetoing of laws he thinks bad. And the Constitution is neither silent nor equivocal about who shall make laws which the President is to execute. The first section of the first article says that "All legislative Powers herein granted shall be vested in a Congress of the United States . . . ." After granting many powers to the Congress, Article I goes on to provide that Congress may "make all Laws which shall be necessary and proper for carrying into Execution the foregoing Powers and all other Powers vested by this Constitution in the Government of the United States, or in any Department or Officer thereof."

The President's order does not direct that a congressional policy be executed in a manner prescribed by Congress—it directs that a presidential policy be executed in a manner prescribed by the President. The preamble of the order itself, like that of many statutes, sets out reasons why the President believes certain policies should be adopted, proclaims these policies as rules of conduct to be followed, and again, like a statute, authorizes a government official to promulgate additional rules and regulations consistent with the policy proclaimed and needed to carry that policy into execution. The power of Congress to adopt such public policies as those proclaimed by the order is beyond question. It can authorize the taking of private property for public use. It can make laws regulating the relationships between employers and employees, prescribing rules designed to settle labor disputes, and fixing wages and working conditions in certain fields of our economy. The Constitution did not subject this law-making power of Congress to presidential or military supervision or control.

It is said that other Presidents without congressional authority have taken possession of private business enterprises in order to settle labor disputes. But even if this be true, Congress has not thereby lost its exclusive constitutional authority to make laws necessary and proper to carry out the powers vested by the Constitution "in the Government of the United States, or in any Department or Officer thereof."

The Founders of this Nation entrusted the law making power to the Congress alone in both good and bad times. It would do no good to recall the historical events, the fears of power and the hopes for freedom that lay behind their choice. Such a review would but confirm our holding that this seizure order cannot stand.

The judgment of the District Court is affirmed.

Mr. Justice JACKSON, concurring in the judgment and opinion of the Court. . . .

The actual art of governing under our Constitution does not and cannot conform to judicial definitions of the power of any of its branches based on isolated clauses or even single Articles torn from context. While the Constitution diffuses power the better to secure liberty, it also contemplates that practice will integrate the dispersed powers into a workable government. It enjoins upon its branches separateness but interdependence, autonomy but reciprocity. Presidential powers are not fixed but fluctuate, depending upon their disjunction or conjunction with those of Congress. We may well begin by a somewhat oversimplified grouping of practical situations in which a President may doubt, or others may challenge, his powers, and by distinguishing roughly the legal consequences of this factor of relativity.

1. When the President acts pursuant to an express or implied authorization of Congress, his authority is at its maximum, for it includes all that he possesses in his own right plus all that Congress can delegate. In these circumstances, and in these only, may he be said (for what it may be worth), to personify the federal sovereignty. If his act is held unconstitutional under these circumstances, it usually means that the Federal Government as an undivided whole lacks power. A seizure executed by the President pursuant to an Act of Congress would be supported by the strongest of presumptions and the widest latitude of judicial interpretation, and the burden of persuasion would rest heavily upon any who might attack it.

2. When the President acts in absence of either a congressional grant or denial of authority, he can only rely upon his own independent powers, but there is a zone of twilight in which he and Congress may have concurrent authority, or in which its distribution is uncertain. Therefore, congressional inertia, indifference or quiescence may sometimes, at least as a practical matter, enable, if not invite, measures on independent presidential responsibility. In this area, any actual test of power is likely to depend on the imperatives of events and contemporary imponderables rather than on abstract theories of law.

3. When the President takes measures incompatible with the expressed or implied will of Congress, his power is at its lowest ebb, for then he can rely only upon his own constitutional powers minus any constitutional powers of Congress over the matter. Courts can sustain exclusive Presidential control in such a case only be disabling the Congress from acting upon the subject. Presidential claim to a power at once so conclusive and preclusive must be scrutinized with caution, for what is at stake is the equilibrium established by our constitutional system.

Into which of these classifications does this executive seizure of the steel industry fit? It is eliminated from the first by admission, for it is conceded that no congressional authorization exists for this seizure. That takes away also the support of the many precedents and declarations which were made in relation, and must be confined, to this category.

Can it then be defended under flexible tests available to the second category? It seems clearly eliminated from that class because Congress has not left seizure of private property an open field but has covered it by three statutory policies inconsistent with this seizure. In cases where the purpose is to supply needs of the Government itself, two courses are provided: one, seizure of a plant which fails to comply with obligatory orders placed by the Government, another, condemnation of facilities, including temporary use under the power of eminent domain. The third is applicable where it is the general economy of the country that is to be protected rather than exclusive governmental interests. None of these were invoked. In choosing a different and inconsistent way of his own, the President cannot claim that it is necessitated or invited by failure of Congress to legislate upon the occasions, grounds and methods for seizure of industrial properties.

This leaves the current seizure to be justified only by the severe tests under the third grouping, where it can be supported only by any remainder of executive power after subtraction of such powers as Congress may have over the subject. In short, we can sustain the President only by holding that seizure of such strike-bound industries is within his domain and beyond control by Congress. Thus, this Court's first review of such seizures occurs under circumstances which leave Presidential power most vulnerable to attack and in the least favorable of possible constitutional postures. . . .

MEDELLIN v. TEXAS, 552 U.S. 491 (2008)

The International Court of Justice (ICJ), located in the Hague, is a tribunal established pursuant to the United Nations Charter to adjudicate disputes between member states. In the *Case Concerning Avena and Other Mexican Nationals* (*Mex. v. U.S.*), 2004 I.C.J. 12 (Judgment of Mar. 31) (*Avena*), that tribunal considered a claim brought by Mexico against the United States. The ICJ held that, based on violations of the Vienna Convention, 51 named Mexican nationals were entitled to review and reconsideration of their state-court convictions and sentences in the United States. This was so regardless of any forfeiture of the right to raise Vienna Convention claims because of a failure to comply with generally applicable state rules governing challenges to criminal convictions.

In *Sanchez-Llamas v. Oregon*, 548 U.S. 331, 126 S. Ct. 2669, 165 L. Ed. 2d 557 (2006)—issued after *Avena* but involving individuals who were not named in the *Avena* judgment—we held that, contrary to the ICJ's determination, the Vienna Convention did not preclude the application of state default rules. After the *Avena* decision, President George W. Bush determined, through a Memorandum to the Attorney General (Feb. 28, 2005), App. to Pet. for Cert. 187a (Memorandum or President's Memorandum), that the United States would "discharge its international obligations" under *Avena* "by having State courts give effect to the decision."

Petitioner José Ernesto Medellín, who had been convicted and sentenced in Texas state court for murder, is one of the 51 Mexican nationals named in the *Avena* decision. Relying on the ICJ's decision and the President's Memorandum, Medellín filed an application for a writ of habeas corpus in state court. The Texas Court of Criminal Appeals dismissed Medellín's application as an abuse of the writ under state law, given Medellín's failure to raise his Vienna Convention claim in a timely manner under state law. We granted certiorari to decide: . . . does the President's Memorandum independently require the States to provide review and reconsideration of the claims of the 51 Mexican nationals named in *Avena* without regard to state procedural default rules? We conclude that neither *Avena* nor the President's Memorandum constitutes directly enforceable federal law that pre-empts state limitations on the filing of successive habeas petitions. We therefore affirm the decision below.

I

A

In 1969, the United States, upon the advice and consent of the Senate, ratified the Vienna Convention on Consular Relations (Vienna Convention or Convention), Apr. 24, 1963, [1970] 21 U.S.T. 77, T.I.A.S. No. 6820, and the Optional Protocol Concerning the Compulsory Settlement of Disputes to the Vienna Convention (Optional Protocol or Protocol), Apr. 24, 1963, [1970] 21 U.S.T. 325, T.I.A.S. No. 6820. The preamble to the Convention provides that its purpose is to "contribute to the development of friendly relations among nations." 21 U.S.T., at 79; *Sanchez-Llamas, supra*, at 337, 126 S. Ct. 2669. Toward that end, Article 36 of the Convention was drafted to "facilitat[e] the exercise of consular functions." Art. 36(1), 21 U.S.T., at 100. It provides that if a person detained by a foreign country "so requests, the competent authorities of the receiving State shall, without delay, inform the consular post of the sending State" of such detention, and "inform the [detainee] of his righ[t]" to request assistance from the consul of his own state. Art. 36(1)(b), *id.*, at 101.

The Optional Protocol provides a venue for the resolution of disputes arising out of the interpretation or application of the Vienna Convention. Art. I,

21 U.S.T., at 326. Under the Protocol, such disputes "shall lie within the compulsory jurisdiction of the International Court of Justice" and "may accordingly be brought before the [ICJ] . . . by any party to the dispute being a Party to the present Protocol." *Ibid.*

The ICJ is "the principal judicial organ of the United Nations." United Nations Charter, Art. 92, 59 Stat. 1051, T.S. No. 993 (1945). It was established in 1945 pursuant to the United Nations Charter. The ICJ Statute—annexed to the U.N. Charter—provides the organizational framework and governing procedures for cases brought before the ICJ. Statute of the International Court of Justice (ICJ Statute), 59 Stat. 1055, T.S. No. 993 (1945).

Under Article 94(1) of the U.N. Charter, "[e]ach Member of the United Nations undertakes to comply with the decision of the [ICJ] in any case to which it is a party." 59 Stat. 1051. The ICJ's jurisdiction in any particular case, however, is dependent upon the consent of the parties. See Art. 36, 59 Stat. 1060. The ICJ Statute delineates two ways in which a nation may consent to ICJ jurisdiction: It may consent generally to jurisdiction on any question arising under a treaty or general international law, Art. 36(2), *ibid.*, or it may consent specifically to jurisdiction over a particular category of cases or disputes pursuant to a separate treaty, Art. 36(1), *ibid.* The United States originally consented to the general jurisdiction of the ICJ when it filed a declaration recognizing compulsory jurisdiction under Art. 36(2) in 1946. The United States withdrew from general ICJ jurisdiction in 1985. See U.S. Dept. of State Letter and Statement Concerning Termination of Acceptance of ICJ Compulsory Jurisdiction (Oct. 7, 1985), reprinted in 24 I.L.M. 1742 (1985). By ratifying the Optional Protocol to the Vienna Convention, the United States consented to the specific jurisdiction of the ICJ with respect to claims arising out of the Vienna Convention. On March 7, 2005, subsequent to the ICJ's judgment in *Avena*, the United States gave notice of withdrawal from the Optional Protocol to the Vienna Convention. Letter from Condoleezza Rice, Secretary of State, to Kofi A. Annan, Secretary-General of the United Nations.

B

Petitioner José Ernesto Medellín, a Mexican national, has lived in the United States since preschool. A member of the "Black and Whites" gang, Medellín was convicted of capital murder and sentenced to death in Texas for the gang rape and brutal murders of two Houston teenagers. . . .

Medellín first raised his Vienna Convention claim in his first application for state postconviction relief. The state trial court held that the claim was procedurally defaulted because Medellín had failed to raise it at trial or on direct review. The trial court also rejected the Vienna Convention claim on the merits, finding that Medellín had "fail[ed] to show that any non-notification of the Mexican authorities impacted on the validity of his conviction or punishment." *Id.*, at 62. The Texas Court of Criminal Appeals affirmed. *Id.*, at 64-65.

Medellín then filed a habeas petition in Federal District Court. The District Court denied relief, holding that Medellín's Vienna Convention claim was procedurally defaulted and that Medellín had failed to show prejudice arising from the Vienna Convention violation. See *Medellín v. Cockrell*, Civ. Action No. H-01-4078 (SD Tex., June 26, 2003), App. to Brief for Respondent 86-92.

While Medellín's application for a certificate of appealability was pending in the Fifth Circuit, the ICJ issued its decision in *Avena*. The ICJ held that the United States had violated Article 36(1)(b) of the Vienna Convention by failing to inform the 51 named Mexican nationals, including Medellín, of their Vienna Convention rights. 2004 I.C.J., at 53-55. In the ICJ's determination, the United States was obligated "to provide, by means of its own choosing, review and reconsideration of the convictions and sentences of the [affected] Mexican nationals." *Id.*, at 72. The ICJ indicated that such review was required without regard to state procedural default rules. *Id.*, at 56-57.

The Fifth Circuit denied a certificate of appealability. *Medellín v. Dretke*, 371 F.3d 270, 281 (2004). The court concluded that the Vienna Convention did not confer individually enforceable rights. *Id.*, at 280. The court further ruled that it was in any event bound by this Court's decision in *Breard v. Greene*, 523 U.S. 371, 375, 118 S. Ct. 1352, 140 L. Ed. 2d 529 (1998) (*per curiam*), which held that Vienna Convention claims are subject to procedural default rules, rather than by the ICJ's contrary decision in *Avena*. 371 F.3d, at 280.

This Court granted certiorari. *Medellín v. Dretke*, 544 U.S. 660, 661, 125 S. Ct. 2088, 161 L. Ed. 2d 982 (2005) (*per curiam*) (*Medellín I*). Before we heard oral argument, however, President George W. Bush issued his Memorandum to the United States Attorney General, providing:

> I have determined, pursuant to the authority vested in me as President by the Constitution and the laws of the United States of America, that the United States will discharge its international obligations under the decision of the International Court of Justice in [*Avena*], by having State courts give effect to the decision in accordance with general principles of comity in cases filed by the 51 Mexican nationals addressed in that decision. App. to Pet. for Cert. 187a.

Medellín, relying on the President's Memorandum and the ICJ's decision in *Avena*, filed a second application for habeas relief in state court. *Ex parte Medellín*, 223 S.W.3d 315, 322-323 (Tex. Crim. App. 2006). Because the state-court proceedings might have provided Medellín with the review and reconsideration he requested, and because his claim for federal relief might otherwise have been barred, we dismissed his petition for certiorari as improvidently granted. *Medellín I, supra*, at 664, 125 S. Ct. 2088.

The Texas Court of Criminal Appeals subsequently dismissed Medellín's second state habeas application as an abuse of the writ. 223 S.W.3d, at 352. In the court's view, neither the *Avena* decision nor the President's Memorandum was "binding federal law" that could displace the State's limitations on the filing of successive habeas applications. *Ibid.* We again granted certiorari. 550 U.S. —, 127 S. Ct. 2129, 167 L. Ed. 2d 862 (2007). . . .

III

Medellín next argues that the ICJ's judgment in *Avena* is binding on state courts by virtue of the President's February 28, 2005 Memorandum. The United States contends that while the *Avena* judgment does not of its own force require domestic courts to set aside ordinary rules of procedural default, that judgment became the law of the land with precisely that effect pursuant to the President's Memorandum and his power "to establish binding rules of decision that preempt contrary state law." Brief for United States as *Amicus Curiae* 5. Accordingly, we must decide whether the President's declaration alters our conclusion that the *Avena* judgment is not a rule of domestic law binding in state and federal courts.

A

The United States maintains that the President's constitutional role "uniquely qualifies" him to resolve the sensitive foreign policy decisions that bear on compliance with an ICJ decision and "to do so expeditiously." Brief for United States as *Amicus Curiae* 11, 12. We do not question these propositions. . . . In this case, the President seeks to vindicate United States interests in ensuring the reciprocal observance of the Vienna Convention, protecting relations with foreign governments, and demonstrating commitment to the role of international law. These interests are plainly compelling.

Such considerations, however, do not allow us to set aside first principles. The President's authority to act, as with the exercise of any governmental power, "must stem either from an act of Congress or from the Constitution itself." *Youngstown, supra*, at 585, 72 S. Ct. 863; *Dames & Moore v. Regan*, 453 U.S. 654, 668, 101 S. Ct. 2972, 69 L. Ed. 2d 918 (1981).

Justice Jackson's familiar tripartite scheme provides the accepted framework for evaluating executive action in this area. First, "[w]hen the President acts pursuant to an express or implied authorization of Congress, his authority is at its maximum, for it includes all that he possesses in his own right plus all that Congress can delegate." *Youngstown*, 343 U.S., at 635, 72 S. Ct. 863 (Jackson, J., concurring). Second, "[w]hen the President acts in absence of either a congressional grant or denial of authority, he can only rely upon his own independent powers, but there is a zone of twilight in which he and Congress may have concurrent authority, or in which its distribution is uncertain." *Id.*, at 637, 72 S. Ct. 863. In this circumstance, Presidential authority can derive support from "congressional inertia, indifference or quiescence." *Ibid.* Finally, "[w]hen the President takes measures incompatible with the expressed or implied will of Congress, his power is at its lowest ebb," and the Court can sustain his actions "only by disabling the Congress from acting upon the subject." *Id.*, at 637-638, 72 S. Ct. 863.

B

The United States marshals two principal arguments in favor of the President's authority "to establish binding rules of decision that preempt contrary state law." Brief for United States as *Amicus Curiae* 5. The Solicitor General first argues that the relevant treaties give the President the authority to implement the *Avena* judgment and that Congress has acquiesced in the exercise of such authority. The United States also relies upon an "independent" international dispute-resolution power wholly apart from the asserted authority based on the pertinent treaties. Medellín adds the additional argument that the President's Memorandum is a valid exercise of his power to take care that the laws be faithfully executed.

1

The United States maintains that the President's Memorandum is authorized by the Optional Protocol and the U.N. Charter. Brief for United States as *Amicus Curiae* 9. That is, because the relevant treaties "create an obligation to comply with *Avena*," they "*implicitly* give the President authority to implement that treaty-based obligation." *Id.*, at 11 (emphasis added). As a result, the President's Memorandum is well grounded in the first category of the *Youngstown* framework.

We disagree. The President has an array of political and diplomatic means available to enforce international obligations, but unilaterally converting a non-self-executing treaty into a self-executing one is not among them. The responsibility for transforming an international obligation arising from a non-self-executing treaty into domestic law falls to Congress. *Foster*, 2 Pet., at 315; *Whitney*, 124 U.S., at 194, 8 S. Ct. 456; *Igartua-De La Rosa*, 417 F.3d, at 150. As this Court has explained, when treaty stipulations are "not self-executing they can only be enforced pursuant to legislation to carry them into effect."

Whitney, supra, at 194, 8 S. Ct. 456. Moreover, "[u]ntil such act shall be passed, the Court is not at liberty to disregard the existing laws on the subject." *Foster, supra*, at 315.

The requirement that Congress, rather than the President, implement a non-self-executing treaty derives from the text of the Constitution, which divides the treaty-making power between the President and the Senate. The Constitution vests the President with the authority to "make" a treaty. Art. II, §2. If the Executive determines that a treaty should have domestic effect of its own force, that determination may be implemented "in mak[ing]" the treaty, by ensuring that it contains language plainly providing for domestic enforceability. If the treaty is to be self-executing in this respect, the Senate must consent to the treaty by the requisite two-thirds vote, *ibid.*, consistent with all other constitutional restraints.

Once a treaty is ratified without provisions clearly according it domestic effect, however, whether the treaty will ever have such effect is governed by the fundamental constitutional principle that " '[t]he power to make the necessary laws is in Congress; the power to execute in the President.' " . . . As already noted, the terms of a non-self-executing treaty can become domestic law only in the same way as any other law-through passage of legislation by both Houses of Congress, combined with either the President's signature or a congressional override of a Presidential veto. See Art. I, §7. Indeed, "the President's power to see that the laws are faithfully executed refutes the idea that he is to be a law-maker." *Youngstown*, 343 U.S., at 587, 72 S. Ct. 863.

A non-self-executing treaty, by definition, is one that was ratified with the understanding that it is not to have domestic effect of its own force. That understanding precludes the assertion that Congress has implicitly authorized the President—acting on his own—to achieve precisely the same result. We therefore conclude, given the absence of congressional legislation, that the non-self-executing treaties at issue here did not "express[ly] or implied[ly]" vest the President with the unilateral authority to make them self-executing. See *id.*, at 635, 72 S. Ct. 863 (Jackson, J., concurring). Accordingly, the President's Memorandum does not fall within the first category of the *Youngstown* framework. . . .

2

We thus turn to the United States' claim that—independent of the United States' treaty obligations—the Memorandum is a valid exercise of the President's foreign affairs authority to resolve claims disputes with foreign nations. *Id.*, at 12-16. The United States relies on a series of cases in which this Court has upheld the authority of the President to settle foreign claims pursuant to an executive agreement. . . . In these cases this Court has explained that, if pervasive enough, a history of congressional acquiescence can be treated as a "gloss on 'Executive Power' vested in the President by §1 of Art. II." *Dames & Moore, supra*, at 686, 101 S. Ct. 2972 (some internal quotation marks omitted).

This argument is of a different nature than the one rejected above. Rather than relying on the United States' treaty obligations, the President relies on an independent source of authority in ordering Texas to put aside its procedural bar to successive habeas petitions. Nevertheless, we find that our claims-settlement cases do not support the authority that the President asserts in this case.

The claims-settlement cases involve a narrow set of circumstances: the making of executive agreements to settle civil claims between American citizens and foreign governments or foreign nationals. See, *e.g.*, *Belmont, supra*, at 327, 57 S. Ct. 758. They are based on the view that "a systematic, unbroken, executive practice, long pursued to the knowledge of the Congress and never before questioned," can "raise a presumption that the [action] had been [taken] in pursuance of its consent." *Dames & Moore, supra*, at 686, 101 S. Ct. 2972 (some internal quotation marks omitted). As this Court explained in *Garamendi*,

> Making executive agreements to settle claims of American nationals against foreign governments is a particularly longstanding practice. . . . Given the fact that the practice goes back over 200 years, and has received congressional acquiescence throughout its history, the conclusion that the President's control of foreign relations includes the settlement of claims is indisputable. 539 U.S., at 415, 123 S. Ct. 2374 (internal quotation marks and brackets omitted).

Even still, the limitations on this source of executive power are clearly set forth and the Court has been careful to note that "[p]ast practice does not, by itself, create power." *Dames & Moore, supra*, at 686, 101 S. Ct. 2972.

The President's Memorandum is not supported by a "particularly longstanding practice" of congressional acquiescence, see *Garamendi, supra*, at 415, 123 S. Ct. 2374, but rather is what the United States itself has described as "unprecedented action," Brief for United States as *Amicus Curiae* in *Sanchez-Llamas*, O.T. 2005, Nos. 05-51 and 04-10566, pp. 29-30. Indeed, the Government has not identified a single instance in which the President has attempted (or Congress has acquiesced in) a Presidential directive issued to state courts, much less one that reaches deep into the heart of the State's police powers and compels state courts to reopen final criminal judgments and set aside neutrally applicable state laws. *Cf. Brecht v. Abrahamson*, 507 U.S. 619, 635, 113 S. Ct. 1710, 123 L. Ed. 2d 353 (1993) ("States possess primary authority for defining and enforcing the criminal law" (quoting *Engle v. Isaac*, 456 U.S. 107, 128, 102 S. Ct. 1558, 71 L. Ed. 2d 783 (1982); internal quotation marks omitted). The Executive's narrow and strictly limited authority to settle international claims disputes pursuant to an executive agreement cannot stretch so far as to support the current Presidential Memorandum. . . . *It is so ordered.*

CASE QUESTIONS

YOUNGSTOWN SHEET & TUBE CO. v. SAWYER

1. Prior to the Court's decision in *Youngstown*, what was Congress's position on the government's seizure of private companies in order to settle labor disputes? Did *Youngstown* change this procedure?

2. What specific constitutional provisions did the Court consider when determining whether the President had the authority to seize the steel mills? Did the Court hold that the Constitution gave the President such authority under those provisions? Explain.

3. What three scenarios did Justice Jackson articulate with regard to presidential authority to act in any given situation? Which of those scenarios did the majority find applied in *Youngstown* and why?

4. Why do you think Justice Jackson's concurrence is quoted by subsequent Supreme Court decisions more frequently than the majority opinion?

MEDELLIN v. TEXAS

1. Outline the unique procedural history of this case.

2. Did the President's Memorandum work in favor of or against Medellín? Explain.

3. How did the Court revisit its previous decision in *Youngstown*? In which of the three scenarios described by Justice Jackson in *Youngstown* did the Court determine the President's actions in *Medellín* fell? Why?

4. What is the difference between a self-executing treaty and a non-self-executing treaty? How does that difference have a bearing on the outcome of the case?

5. Research challenge: What happened to Medellín subsequent to the Court's decision?

HYPOTHETICAL WITH ACCOMPANYING ANALYSIS

Hypothetical

President McIntosh has had a tumultuous presidency to say the least. During the past three years of his term, the United States has been engaged in a bloody war against Polaristan, a small country located just north of Antarctica. Since U.S. troops are not accustomed to fighting in such frigid conditions, many soldiers have become ill. Sam Bartlett, a corporal in the Marine Corps, was on a mission in Polaristan when he was wounded in battle. He died of exposure because he could not make it back to base quickly enough. Shirley Bartlett, Sam's mother, has filed a civil suit against the President for wrongful death. She maintains that had President McIntosh not committed troops to Polaristan, her son would still be alive today.

McIntosh, under tremendous pressure from the war, decided to get away from it all for the weekend and take a hunting expedition in his home state. However, what was supposed to be a relaxing couple of days turned into tragedy. While sitting in his tree stand, President McIntosh mistook another hunter for a deer. McIntosh, who never missed a shot, killed James Mandarin instantly with a single shot to the chest. Mary Mandarin, James's surviving widow, has filed a civil suit against the President for wrongful death based on the hunting incident gone awry.

Discuss the likelihood that the President can be successfully sued in the above scenarios.

Analysis

When confronted with situations related to the President, several constitutional issues could potentially arise. Those issues include whether the President exercised his domestic and/or foreign powers in a constitutional manner, whether an attempt was made to impeach the President, whether the President could successfully claim immunity for certain actions, and whether the President was protected by privilege from divulging allegedly confidential information. In the instant scenario, we must analyze the issue of immunity, including when it will apply and how much, if any, protection it will offer the President for his actions.

The law regarding presidential immunity is well established. In Nixon v. Fitzgerald, 457 U.S. 731 (1982), the Court gave credence to the concept of presidential immunity, despite the fact that it is nowhere explicitly mentioned in the Constitution. Immunity, explained the Court, is "a functionally mandated incident of the President's unique office, rooted in the constitutional tradition of the separation of powers and supported by our history." However, the existence of immunity is dependent upon the action being challenged as improper. In *Fitzgerald*, the Court determined that the President was protected by absolute immunity for all actions within the direct or "outer perimeter" of his authority. *Id.* In contrast to *Fitzgerald*, the Court in Jones v. Clinton, 520 U.S. 681 (1997), declared that the President was not immune from civil suit for actions the President undertook that were unrelated to the performance of his official duties. Thus, in the *Jones* case, the complainant was permitted to sue the President for alleged sexual harassment that had occurred before the President took office because the alleged conduct had nothing to do with his duties or responsibilities as the President.

Our next task is to analyze the two impending lawsuits against President McIntosh to determine whether he is protected by any degree of immunity. As to the first lawsuit, Shirley Bartlett is suing the President for the wrongful death of her son while serving in Polaristan. The presidential action that Shirley directly challenges is the committing of troops abroad. Clearly, that action by President McIntosh falls under his official duties as President. According to *Nixon v. Fitzgerald*, therefore, President McIntosh is protected by absolute immunity for his actions, and Shirley will not be permitted to bring suit against him. As to the second lawsuit, Mary Mandarin's wrongful death lawsuit stems from the President's accidental shooting of her husband during a hunting trip. In contrast to the first lawsuit, the second lawsuit has nothing to do with the President's official actions. To the contrary, the President took the trip to "relax" and "get away from it all for the weekend," thus supporting the fact that the shooting had nothing to do with his official duties. Therefore, according to *Jones v. Clinton*, the President is not protected by immunity, and Mary will be permitted to entertain her suit against President McIntosh.

Edenia is a tiny island nation located deep in the South Pacific. The United States has historically had very good diplomatic relations with Edenia. Recently, however, relations have become strained due to a raging civil war in Edenia and the fact that high-ranking government officials have ordered thousands of Edenian citizens to be murdered. In light of recent developments overseas, the President of the United States has unilaterally cut all ties with Edenia and officially denounced the Edenian government.

In direct response to the President's actions, Edenian officials have halted all trade with the United States. The primary Edenian export to our nation was the extract from the alleviata flower, which just happens to contain one of the primary ingredients used in virtually all pain relievers dispensed in the United States. The United States can only obtain alleviata extract from a small collection of South Pacific nations, so the lack of Edenia's exports have resulted in the skyrocketing prices of all pain relievers in the United States. As the prices continue to rise, many U.S. citizens can no longer afford to purchase simple pain relievers. As a result of the inflated prices and the disastrous effect it is having on our nation's health care industry, the President has issued an executive order stating that all U.S. pharmaceutical companies must freeze their prices for pain relievers until further notice. There is no federal law that either explicitly authorizes or prohibits the President from undertaking such action.

Discuss and analyze in depth the constitutionality of all presidential actions described above.

DISCUSSION QUESTIONS

1. Research challenge: When in our nation's history has the Electoral College chosen one individual as President and the popular vote chosen another? What were the ultimate results of those cases? *See, e.g.*, Bush v. Gore, 531 U.S. 98 (2000).

2. President Williams issued a pardon to Brett Chester, a high-raking executive official who had been convicted of extorting hundreds of thousands of dollars from the federal government. Williams placed upon that pardon a condition requiring Chester to make restitution for the money stolen. If Chester fails to fulfill the condition of the pardon, can the President revoke the pardon? What if the President had imposed the condition on Chester's pardon that he no longer be permitted to work in any government job; would that be constitutional?

3. Research challenge: Which constitutional amendments pertain to the presidency and what do those amendments say? What was going on in our nation that led to their passage?

4. What is "impeachment"? For what reasons may a President be impeached? When in our nation's history has the President been impeached, and what were the results of those proceedings?

5. Revisit the Hypothetical with Accompanying Analysis from this chapter. Assume further investigation revealed that President McIntosh had intentionally shot James Mandarin. Could the state bring criminal charges against the President for murder, or would immunity protect him from any prosecution? Could he be impeached for his actions? Explain.

6. If the President exercises a power not explicitly granted by the Constitution, does Congress have to consent to the President's exercise of that power in order for his actions to be constitutional? *See* Dames & Moore v. Regan, 453 U.S. 654 (1981).

7. Compare and contrast the pocket veto with the line item veto. Does the President have the authority to exercise these vetoes? Explain. *Compare* Okanogan Indians v. United States, 279 U.S. 655 (1929), *with* Clinton v. City of New York, 524 U.S. 417 (1998).

8. Why do you think the President has traditionally been granted far more power with regard to foreign affairs than with regard to domestic affairs? *See, e.g.,* United States v. Curtiss-Wright Export Corp., 299 U.S. 304 (1936).

9. Congress recently appropriated several billion dollars for the construction of a new space craft. President Bernaise, concerned at the growing rate of inflation in our country, has refused to allow the expenditure of funds needed in order to build the craft. Are the President's actions in withholding the money constitutional?

10. Research Challenge: What is known as "The Saturday Night Massacre," and what does it have to do with the powers of the President?

11. Does the President have the power to pardon himself? What language in the Constitution supports your answer? Explain.

12. What is the War Powers Resolution, and how does it affect the President?

13. President Henderson is definitely a woman of current times. Her most prized possession is her state-of-the-art Blackberry. She uses it on a daily basis to communicate with her cabinet, her friends, and even international heads of state. Of course, her Blackberry has the most recent, cutting-edge security system that has been deemed "impenetrable" by anyone other than the President. Unfortunately, President Henderson lost her Blackberry during a recent trip abroad, and it ultimately fell into the hands of Shirley Hack, a notorious computer hacker. Hack was able to penetrate the President's impenetrable security system within minutes. Is the information contained within President Henderson's Blackberry confidential? Why or why not?

14. Can the President lawfully permit the CIA to torture terrorists in order to get information from them? Why or why not?

True/False

1. Impeachment is the removal of President from office due to specific misconduct while in office.

2. Clemency refers to a presidential pardon of a group of people.

3. A presidential exercise of power may gain validity even though not expressly authorized by the Constitution if Congress explicitly consents or implicitly acquiesces to the President's actions.

4. Impoundment refers to the process by which the President refuses to spend congressionally appropriated funds.

5. In *Youngstown*, the Supreme Court upheld the President's seizure of the nation's steel mills on the basis that the nation was faced with an emergency and the seizure was authorized by the President's power as Commander-in-Chief of the armed forces.

Multiple Choice

6. The President has the power to:

   A. Commit U.S. troops abroad.
   B. Commit U.S. troops abroad and declare war.
   C. Commit U.S. troops abroad, declare war, and ratify treaties made by Congress.
   D. The President does not have any of the above powers.

7. The President has just vetoed proposed legislation whereby Congress sought to give millions of dollars to small businesses in order to help a troubled economy. Brett Michaels, a small business owner, was forced to close his shop after going bankrupt. He is now suing the President for civil damages, arguing that his bankruptcy and financial hardships are a direct result of the President's failure to sign the proposed legislation. Will Brett's lawsuit prevail?

   A. Yes, because the President is not above the law and is directly accountable to the citizens of this country for all of his actions.
   B. Yes, because the suit is directly traceable to one of the enumerated presidential powers mentioned in the Constitution, the veto power.
   C. No, because the President enjoys absolute immunity from civil suit for any official actions taken.
   D. No, because the President enjoys qualified immunity from civil suit for any official actions taken, and the action related to his veto power.

8. Which statement best represents the Supreme Court's holding in *Medellín v. Texas*?

   A. An international treaty is not binding law upon the United States unless it is either self-executing or Congress has enacted statutes implementing it; the President, therefore, lacked the power to enforce the international treaty.

   B. An international treaty is binding law upon the United States only if the President explicitly declares it to be such; the President, therefore, had the power to issue the Memorandum at issue in this case.

   C. Because the President's Memorandum was issued with Congress's implicit approval, the President had the power to make the international treaty binding upon the United States.

   D. Because the President is vested with significant authority when it comes to foreign affairs, the power to enforce the international treaty rested solely with the President and could not be challenged by the other branches of government.

9. Congress presents the President with a bill to fund stem cell research. The President takes no action on the bill, and five days later Congress adjourns. Which of the following has just occurred?

   A. The President has made a pocket veto of the bill.

   B. The President has made a line item veto of the bill.

   C. The President has made an executive veto of the bill.

   D. The bill will automatically become law because the President implicitly approved of it by taking no action.

10. Which of the following statements about presidential privilege is accurate?

    A. Article II of the Constitution expressly provides for presidential privilege, and it is absolute in nature.

    B. Article II of the Constitution expressly provides for presidential privilege, but it is qualified in nature.

    C. Article II of the Constitution does not expressly provide for presidential privilege, but the President nonetheless enjoys an absolute privilege.

    D. Article II of the Constitution does not expressly provide for presidential privilege, but the President nonetheless enjoys a qualified privilege.

II

Individual Rights and Liberties

Chapter 5

Due Process and Economic Freedoms

"No person shall . . . be deprived of life, liberty, or property without due process of law[.]"
—**The Fifth Amendment**

". . . [N]or shall any State deprive any person of life, liberty, or property, without due process of law[.]"
—**The Fourteenth Amendment**

INTRODUCTION

Think of a very long, winding road with several forks along the way. Once you have that picture in your mind, you've basically plotted the road map to this particular chapter. Due process covers a massive amount of ground. Its first fork comes when we determine *which* Due Process Clause applies—the one in the Fifth Amendment or the Fourteenth Amendment. Next, we must distinguish between substantive due process and procedural due process. And if our travels lead us down the fork dealing with substantive due process, we must further determine what type of individual rights are implicated.

The first fork is by far the easiest to navigate. When we come to that juncture, we'll find an arrow pointing us in the direction of the Fifth Amendment if we're dealing with actions of the federal government. The opposite arrow will point us to the Fourteenth Amendment if state governmental action is involved.

The second fork forces us to choose between substantive and procedural due process. This, too, is typically not a difficult task. Substantive due process means that laws cannot infringe upon an individual's inherent liberty interest. Procedural due process refers to the fact that the government must follow certain protocols before depriving you of a right. Think of the distinction in terms of a ball game. The game itself has to be fair (substantive due process), and it has to be played by rules that are also fair (procedural due process).

Of the two due process roads, the one leading us through an analysis of substantive due process is by far the more complex of the two. It's kind of like having an invisible "Keep Out" or "No Trespassing" sign in order to protect individuals from the government becoming *too* involved in certain areas of their lives. The law related to substantive due process seeks to protect an individual's liberty interest. The term "liberty" has been interpreted in two fashions (hence, our road has a fork within a fork). The first and more traditional definition deals with economic liberty, including the right to possess private property, engage in a certain livelihood or live in a certain place, or the right to freely enter into contracts. The second and more recent interpretation of liberty deals with fundamental rights, such as what individuals may do with their bodies or with other intimate details of their personal lives. Because the notion of "fundamental rights" has become such a popular and controversial topic in recent times, a niche of its own has been carved out of a more general due process discussion. This chapter, therefore, deals only with economic due process and leaves for the following chapter a detailed discussion of the right to privacy and how due process is implicated in that context. Keep in mind, the issues in this chapter might not be as "sexy" as those in the next chapter, but they are just as important to our daily lives.

Finally, when learning about the various economic freedoms to which individuals are entitled, don't look solely to due process. Two other sources play a role in our economic freedom. The first, referred to as the Takings Clause, is found in the Fifth Amendment. More commonly referred to as "eminent domain," it provides, "nor shall private property be taken for public use, without just compensation." The second source, although not relied upon with regularity in recent times, is the Contracts Clause found in Article I, §10 of the Constitution. It provides that "[n]o state shall . . . pass any . . . Law impairing the Obligation of Contracts." The combination of all three constitutional sources provide us with a solid framework for determining the appropriate balance between the power of the government to regulate property interests (*i.e.*, police powers) versus an individual's right to economic freedom. In a nutshell, these sources will tell us when, exactly, the government must Keep Out!

STUDENT *Checklist*

Due Process & Economic Freedoms

1. Which Due Process Clause is implicated?

▪ **Fifth Amendment:** Federal government

▪ **Fourteenth Amendment:** State governments

2. Is **substantive** or **procedural** due process implicated?

▪ **Substantive:** Is the individual challenging the **fundamental fairness** of the law as an unjust **interference** with a **protected liberty interest**? or

▪ **Procedural:** Is the individual challenging the **method** by which the government deprived him of a right?

3. If a violation of **substantive due process** is alleged:

■ Did the government action implicate a **fundamental right** (If so, continue analysis in Chapter 6, The Right to Privacy) or

■ Did the government action implicate an **economic liberty interest**? If so . . .

Based on the **Due Process Clause**,
❏ Did the challenging party meet its burden of proving that the law was **not rationally related** to a **permissible government interest**?
❏ Did the legislature act in an **arbitrary and irrational** manner?

Based on the **Takings Clause**,
❏ Did the government effectuate a **taking** of property (either a **direct** taking or **indirect** taking that **substantially impaired the value** of the property);
❏ For **public use**;
❏ Providing the individual with **just compensation (fair market value** of the property)?

Based on the **Contracts Clause**,
❏ Did a **state law** operate as a **substantial impairment** of a **contractual relationship**;
❏ Did the state show a **significant** and **legitimate public purpose** to justify the impairment?

4. If a violation of **procedural due process** is alleged:

■ Did the individual have a legitimate **entitlement** to a **protected liberty** or **property interest**?

■ Was the individual **deprived** of that liberty or property interest without due process of law, when considering:

The **private interest** that will be affected by the official action (*i.e.*, the greater the individual's stake in the outcome, the more procedural protections that will be requested);

The risk of **erroneous deprivation** of such interest through the procedures used;

The probable **value**, if any, of additional or substitute procedural safeguards; and

The **government's interest**, including any burden, that procedural requirements would entail?

SUPREME COURT CASES

WEST COAST HOTEL CO. v. PARRISH, 300 U.S. 379 (1937)

This case presents the question of the constitutional validity of the minimum wage law of the state of Washington.

The act, entitled "Minimum Wages for Women," authorizes the fixing of minimum wages for women and minors. . . .

The appellant conducts a hotel. The appellee Elsie Parrish was employed as a chambermaid and (with her husband) brought this suit to recover the difference between the wages paid her and the minimum wage fixed pursuant to the state law. The minimum wage was $14.50 per week of 48 hours. The appellant challenged the act as repugnant to the due process clause of the Fourteenth Amendment of the Constitution of the United States. The Supreme Court of the state, reversing the trial court, sustained the statute and directed judgment for the plaintiffs. Parrish v. West Coast Hotel Co., 185 Wash. 581, 55 P. (2d) 1083. The case is here on appeal.

The appellant relies upon the decision of this Court in Adkins v. Children's Hospital, 261 U.S. 525, 43 S. Ct. 394, 67 L. Ed. 785, 24 A.L.R. 1238, which held invalid the District of Columbia Minimum Wage Act (40 Stat. 960) which was attacked under the due process clause of the Fifth Amendment. On the argument at bar, counsel for the appellees attempted to distinguish the *Adkins* Case upon the ground that the appellee was employed in a hotel and that the business of an inn-keeper was affected with a public interest. That effort at distinction is obviously futile, as it appears that in one of the cases ruled by the *Adkins* opinion the employee was a woman employed as an elevator operator in a hotel. Adkins v. Lyons, 261 U.S. 525, at page 542, 43 S. Ct. 394, 395, 67 L. Ed. 785, 24 A.L.R. 1238. . . .

The Supreme Court of Washington has upheld the minimum wage statute of that state. It has decided that the statute is a reasonable exercise of the police power of the state. In reaching that conclusion, the state court has invoked principles long established by this Court in the application of the Fourteenth Amendment. The state court has refused to regard the decision in the *Adkins* Case as determinative and has pointed to our decisions both before and since that case as justifying its position. We are of the opinion that this ruling of the state court demands on our part a re-examination of the *Adkins* Case. The importance of the question, in which many states having similar laws are concerned, the close division by which the decision in the *Adkins* Case was reached, and the economic conditions which have supervened, and in the light of which the reasonableness of the exercise of the protective power of the state must be considered, make it not only appropriate, but we think imperative, that in deciding the present case the subject should receive fresh consideration. . . .

The principle which must control our decision is not in doubt. The constitutional provision invoked is the due process clause of the Fourteenth Amendment governing the states, as the due process clause invoked in the *Adkins* Case governed Congress. In each case the violation alleged by those attacking minimum wage regulation for women is deprivation of freedom of contract. What is this freedom? The Constitution does not speak of freedom of contract. It speaks of liberty and prohibits the deprivation of liberty without due process of law. In prohibiting that deprivation, the Constitution does not recognize an absolute and uncontrollable liberty. Liberty in each of its phases has its history and connotation. But the liberty safeguarded is liberty in a social organization which requires the protection of law against the evils which menace the health, safety, morals, and welfare of the people. Liberty under the Constitution is thus necessarily subject to the restraints of due process, and regulation which is reasonable in relation to its subject and is adopted in the interests of the community is due process.

This essential limitation of liberty in general governs freedom of contract in particular. More than twenty-five years ago we set forth the applicable principle in these words, after referring to the cases where the liberty guaranteed by the Fourteenth Amendment had been broadly described.

"But it was recognized in the cases cited, as in many others, that freedom of contract is a qualified, and not an absolute, right. There is no absolute freedom to do as one wills or to contract as one chooses. The guaranty of liberty does not withdraw from legislative supervision that wide department of activity which consists of the making of contracts, or deny to government the power to provide restrictive safeguards. Liberty implies the absence of arbitrary restraint, not immunity from reasonable regulations and prohibitions imposed in the interests of the community." Chicago, Burlington & Quincy R. Co. v. McGuire, 219 U.S. 549, 565, 31 S. Ct. 259, 262, 55 L. Ed. 328.

This power under the Constitution to restrict freedom of contract has had many illustrations. That it may be exercised in the public interest with respect to contracts between employer and employee is undeniable. Thus statutes have been sustained limiting employment in underground mines and smelters to eight hours a day (Holden v. Hardy, 169 U.S. 366, 18 S. Ct. 383, 42 L. Ed. 780); in requiring redemption in cash of store orders or other evidences of indebtedness issued in the payment of wages (Knoxville Iron Co. v. Harbison, 183 U.S. 13, 22 S. Ct. 1, 46 L. Ed. 55); in forbidding the payment of seamen's wages in advance (Patterson v. The Bark Eudora, 190 U.S. 169, 23 S. Ct. 821, 47 L. Ed. 1002); in making it unlawful to contract to pay miners employed at quantity rates upon the basis of screened coal instead of the weight of the coal as originally produced in the mine (McLean v. Arkansas, 211 U.S. 539, 29 S. Ct. 206, 53 L. Ed. 315); in prohibiting contracts limiting liability for injuries to employees (Chicago, Burlington & Quincy R. Co. v. McGuire, supra); in limiting hours of work of employees in manufacturing establishments (Bunting v. Oregon, 243 U.S. 426, 37 S. Ct. 435, 61 L. Ed. 830, Ann. Cas. 1918A, 1043); and in maintaining workmen's compensation laws (New York Central R. Co. v. White, 243 U.S. 188, 37 S. Ct. 247, 61 L. Ed. 667, L.R.A. 1917D, 1, Ann. Cas. 1917D, 629; Mountain Timber Co. v. Washington, 243 U.S. 219, 37 S. Ct. 260, 61 L. Ed. 685, Ann. Cas. 1917D, 642). In dealing with the relation of employer and employed, the Legislature has necessarily a wide field of discretion in order that there may be suitable protection of health and safety, and that peace and good order may be promoted through regulations designed to insure wholesome conditions of work and freedom from oppression. Chicago, Burlington & Quincy R. Co. v. McGuire, supra, 219 U.S. 549, at page 570, 31 S. Ct. 259, 55 L. Ed. 328.

The point that has been strongly stressed that adult employees should be deemed competent to make their own contracts was decisively met nearly forty years ago in *Holden v. Hardy*, supra, where we pointed out the inequality in the footing of the parties. We said (Id., 169 U.S. 366, 397, 18 S. Ct. 383, 390, 42 L. Ed. 780):

> "The legislature has also recognized the fact, which the experience of legislators in many states has corroborated, that the proprietors of these establishments and their operatives do not stand upon an equality, and that their interests are, to a certain extent, conflicting. The former naturally desire to obtain as much labor as possible from their employees, while the latter are often induced by the fear of discharge to conform to regulations which their judgment, fairly exercised, would pronounce to be detrimental to their health or strength. In other words, the proprietors lay down the rules, and the laborers are practically constrained to obey them. In such cases self-interest is often an unsafe guide, and the legislature may properly interpose its authority."

And we added that the fact "that both parties are of full age, and competent to contract, does not necessarily deprive the state of the power to interfere, where the parties do not stand upon an equality, or where the public heath demands that one party to the contract shall be protected against himself." "The state still retains an interest in his welfare, however reckless he may be. The whole is no greater than the sum of all the parts, and when the individual health, safety, and welfare are sacrificed or neglected, the state must suffer."

It is manifest that this established principle is peculiarly applicable in relation to the employment of women in whose protection the state has a special interest. That phase of the subject received elaborate consideration in Muller v. Oregon (1908), 208 U.S. 412, 28 S. Ct. 324, 326, 52 L. Ed. 551, 13 Ann. Cas. 957, where the constitutional authority of the state to limit the working hours of women was sustained. We emphasized the consideration that "woman's physical structure and the performance of maternal functions place her at a disadvantage in the struggle for subsistence" and that her physical well being "becomes an object of public interest and care in order to preserve the strength and vigor of the race." We emphasized the need of protecting women against oppression despite her possession of contractual rights. We said that "though limitations upon personal and contractual rights may be removed by legislation, there is that in her disposition and habits of life which will operate against a full assertion of those rights. She will still be where some legislation to protect her seems necessary to secure a real equality of right." Hence she was "properly placed in a class by herself, and legislation designed for her protection may be sustained, even when like legislation is not necessary for men, and could not be sustained." We concluded that the limitations which the statute there in question "places upon her contractual powers, upon her right to agree with her employer, as to the time she shall labor" were "not imposed solely for her benefit, but also largely for the benefit of all." . . .

The minimum wage to be paid under the Washington statute is fixed after full consideration by representatives of employers, employees, and the public. It may be assumed that the minimum wage is fixed in consideration of the services that are performed in the particular occupations under normal conditions. Provision is made for special licenses at less wages in the case of women who are incapable of full service. The statement of Mr. Justice Holmes in the *Adkins* Case is pertinent: "This statute does not compel anybody to pay anything. It simply forbids employment at rates below those fixed as the minimum requirement of health and right living. It is safe to assume that women will not be employed at even the lowest wages allowed unless they earn them, or unless the employer's business can sustain the burden. In short the law in its character and operation is like hundreds of so-called police laws that have been up-held." 261 U.S. 525, at page 570, 43 S. Ct. 394, 406, 67 L. Ed. 785, 24 A.L.R. 1238. And Chief Justice Taft forcibly pointed out the consideration which is basic in a statute of this character: "Legislatures which adopt a requirement of maximum hours or minimum wages may be presumed to believe that when sweating employers are prevented from paying unduly low wages by positive law they will continue their business, abating that part of their profits, which were wrung from the necessities of their employees, and will concede the better terms required by the law, and that while in individual cases, hardship may result, the restriction will ensure to the benefit of the general class of employees in whose interest the law is passed, and so to that of the community at large." Id., 261 U.S. 525, at page 563, 43 S. Ct. 394, 403, 67 L. Ed. 785, 24 A.L.R. 1238.

We think that the views thus expressed are sound and that the decision in the *Adkins* Case was a departure from the true application of the principles governing the regulation by the state of the relation of employer and employed. . . .

With full recognition of the earnestness and vigor which characterize the prevailing opinion in the *Adkins* Case, we find it impossible to reconcile that ruling with these well-considered declarations. What can be closer to the public interest than the health of women and their protection from unscrupulous and overreaching employers? And if the protection of women is a legitimate end of the exercise of state power, how can it be said that the requirement of the payment of a minimum wage fairly fixed in order to meet the very necessities of existence is not an admissible means to that end? The Legislature of the state was clearly entitled to consider the situation of women in employment, the fact that they are in the class receiving the least pay, that their bargaining power is relatively weak, and that they are the ready victims of those who would take advantage of their necessitous circumstances. The Legislature was entitled to adopt measures to reduce the evils of the "sweating system," the exploiting of workers at wages so low as to be insufficient to meet the bare cost of living, thus making their very helplessness the occasion of a most injurious competition. The Legislature had the right to consider that its minimum wage requirements would be an important aid in carrying out its policy of protection. The adoption of similar requirements by many states evidences a deepseated conviction both as to the presence of the evil and as to the means adapted to check it. Legislative response to that conviction cannot be regarded as arbitrary or capricious and that is all we have to decide. Even if the wisdom of the policy be regarded as debatable and its effects uncertain, still the Legislature is entitled to its judgment.

There is an additional and compelling consideration which recent economic experience has brought into a strong light. The exploitation of a class of workers who are in an unequal position with respect to bargaining power and are thus relatively defenseless against the denial of a living wage is not only detrimental to their health and well being, but casts a direct burden for their support upon the community. What these workers lose in wages the taxpayers are called upon to pay. The bare cost of living must be met. We may take judicial notice of the unparalleled demands for relief which arose during the recent period of depression and still continue to an alarming extent despite the degree of economic recovery which has been achieved. It is unnecessary to cite official statistics to establish what is of common knowledge through the length and breadth of the land. While in the instant case no factual brief has been presented, there is no reason to doubt that the state of Washington has encountered the same social problem that is present elsewhere. The community is not bound to provide what is in effect a subsidy for unconscionable employers. The community may direct its law-making power to correct the abuse which springs from their selfish disregard of the public interest. The argument that the legislation in question constitutes an arbitrary discrimination, because it does not extend to men, is unavailing. This Court has frequently held that the legislative authority, acting within its proper field, is not bound to extend its regulation to all cases which it might possibly reach. The Legislature "is free to recognize degrees of harm and it may confine its restrictions to those classes of cases where the need is deemed to be clearest." If "the law presumably hits the evil where it is most felt, it is not to be overthrown because there are other instances to which it might have been applied." There is no "doctrinaire requirement" that the legislation should be couched in all embracing terms. . . . This familiar principle has repeatedly been applied to legislation which singles out women, and particular classes of women, in the exercise of the state's protective power. . . . Their relative need in the presence of the evil, no less than the existence of the evil itself, is a matter for the legislative judgment.

Our conclusion is that the case of *Adkins v. Children's Hospital*, supra, should be, and it is, overruled. The judgment of the Supreme Court of the state of Washington is affirmed. Affirmed.

KELO v. CITY OF NEW LONDON, CONNECTICUT,
545 U.S. 469 (2005)

In 2000, the city of New London approved a development plan that, in the words of the Supreme Court of Connecticut, was "projected to create in excess of 1,000 jobs, to increase tax and other revenues, and to revitalize an economically distressed city, including its downtown and waterfront areas." 268 Conn. 1, 5, 843 A.2d 500, 507 (2004). In assembling the land needed for this project, the city's development agent has purchased property from willing sellers and proposes to use the power of eminent domain to acquire the remainder of the property from unwilling owners in exchange for just compensation. The question presented is whether the city's proposed disposition of this property qualifies as a "public use" within the meaning of the Takings Clause of the Fifth Amendment to the Constitution.

I

The city of New London (hereinafter City) sits at the junction of the Thames River and the Long Island Sound in southeastern Connecticut. Decades of economic decline led a state agency in 1990 to designate the City a "distressed municipality." In 1996, the Federal Government closed the Naval Undersea Warfare Center, which had been located in the Fort Trumbull area of the City and had employed over 1,500 people. In 1998, the City's unemployment rate was nearly double that of the State, and its population of just under 24,000 residents was at its lowest since 1920.

These conditions prompted state and local officials to target New London, and particularly its Fort Trumbull area, for economic revitalization. To this end, respondent New London Development Corporation (NLDC), a private nonprofit entity established some years earlier to assist the City in planning economic development, was reactivated. In January 1998, the State authorized a $5.35 million bond issue to support the NLDC's planning activities and a $10 million bond issue toward the creation of a Fort Trumbull State Park. In February, the pharmaceutical company Pfizer Inc. announced that it would build a $300 million research facility on a site immediately adjacent to Fort Trumbull; local planners hoped that Pfizer would draw new business to the area, thereby serving as a catalyst to the area's rejuvenation. After receiving initial approval from the city council, the NLDC continued its planning activities and held a series of neighborhood meetings to educate the public about the process. In May, the city council authorized the NLDC to formally submit its plans to the relevant state agencies for review. Upon obtaining state-level approval, the NLDC finalized an integrated development plan focused on 90 acres of the Fort Trumbull area. . . .

The NLDC intended the development plan to capitalize on the arrival of the Pfizer facility and the new commerce it was expected to attract. In addition to creating jobs, generating tax revenue, and helping to "build momentum for the revitalization of downtown New London," *id.*, at 92, the plan was also designed to make the City more attractive and to create leisure and recreational opportunities on the waterfront and in the park.

The city council approved the plan in January 2000, and designated the NLDC as its development agent in charge of implementation. See Conn. Gen. Stat. §8-188 (2005). The city council also authorized the NLDC to purchase property or to acquire property by exercising eminent domain in the City's name. §8-193. The NLDC successfully negotiated the purchase of most of the real estate in the 90-acre area, but its negotiations with petitioners failed. As a consequence, in November 2000, the NLDC initiated the condemnation proceedings that gave rise to this case.

II

Petitioner Susette Kelo has lived in the Fort Trumbull area since 1997. She has made extensive improvements to her house, which she prizes for its water view. Petitioner Wilhelmina Dery was born in her Fort Trumbull house in 1918 and has lived there her entire life. Her husband Charles (also a petitioner) has lived in the house since they married some 60 years ago. In all, the nine petitioners own 15 properties in Fort Trumbull—4 in parcel 3 of the development plan and 11 in parcel 4A. Ten of the parcels are occupied by the owner or a family member; the other five are held as investment properties. There is no allegation that any of these properties is blighted or otherwise in poor condition; rather, they were condemned only because they happen to be located in the development area. . . .

We granted certiorari to determine whether a city's decision to take property for the purpose of economic development satisfies the "public use" requirement of the Fifth Amendment. 542 U.S. 965, 125 S. Ct. 27, 159 L. Ed. 2d 857 (2004).

III

Two polar propositions are perfectly clear. On the one hand, it has long been accepted that the sovereign may not take the property of *A* for the sole purpose of transferring it to another private party *B*, even though *A* is paid just compensation. On the other hand, it is equally clear that a State may transfer property from one private party to another if future "use by the public" is the purpose of the taking; the condemnation of land for a railroad with common-carrier duties is a familiar example. Neither of these propositions, however, determines the disposition of this case.

As for the first proposition, the City would no doubt be forbidden from taking petitioners' land for the purpose of conferring a private benefit on a particular private party. See *Midkiff*, 467 U.S., at 245, 104 S. Ct. 2321 ("A purely private taking could not withstand the scrutiny of the public use requirement; it would serve no legitimate purpose of government and would thus be void"); *Missouri Pacific R. Co. v. Nebraska*, 164 U.S. 403, 17 S. Ct. 130, 41 L. Ed. 489 (1896). Nor would the City be allowed to take property under the mere pretext of a public purpose, when its actual purpose was to bestow a private benefit. The takings before us, however, would be executed pursuant to a "carefully considered" development plan. 268 Conn., at 54, 843 A.2d, at 536. The trial judge and all the members of the Supreme Court of Connecticut agreed that there was no evidence of an illegitimate purpose in this case. Therefore, as was true of the statute challenged in *Midkiff*, 467 U.S., at 245, 104 S. Ct. 2321, the City's development plan was not adopted "to benefit a particular class of identifiable individuals."

On the other hand, this is not a case in which the City is planning to open the condemned land—at least not in its entirety—to use by the general public. Nor will the private lessees of the land in any sense be required to operate like common carriers, making their services available to all comers. But although such a projected use would be sufficient to satisfy the public use requirement, this "Court long ago rejected any literal requirement that condemned property be put into use for the general public." *Id.*, at 244, 104 S. Ct. 2321. Indeed, while many state courts in the mid-19th century endorsed "use by the public" as the proper definition of public use, that narrow view steadily eroded over time. Not only was the "use by the public" test difficult to administer (*e.g.*, what proportion of the public need have access to the property? at what price?), but it proved to be impractical given the diverse and always evolving needs of society. Accordingly, when this Court began applying the Fifth Amendment to the States at the close of the 19th century, it embraced the broader and more natural interpretation of public use as "public purpose." See, *e.g., Fallbrook Irrigation Dist. v. Bradley*, 164 U.S. 112, 158-164, 17 S. Ct. 56, 41 L. Ed. 369 (1896). Thus, in a case upholding a mining company's use of an aerial bucket line to transport ore over property it did not own, Justice Holmes' opinion for the Court stressed "the inadequacy of use by the general public as a universal test." *Strickley v. Highland Boy Gold Mining Co.*, 200 U.S. 527, 531, 26 S. Ct. 301, 50 L. Ed. 581 (1906). We have repeatedly and consistently rejected that narrow test ever since.

The disposition of this case therefore turns on the question whether the City's development plan serves a "public purpose." Without exception, our cases have defined that concept broadly, reflecting our longstanding policy of deference to legislative judgments in this field.

In *Berman v. Parker*, 348 U.S. 26, 75 S. Ct. 98, 99 L. Ed. 27 (1954), this Court upheld a redevelopment plan targeting a blighted area of Washington, D.C., in which most of the housing for the area's 5,000 inhabitants was beyond repair. Under the plan, the area would be condemned and part of it utilized for the construction of streets, schools, and other public facilities. The remainder of the land would be leased or sold to private parties for the purpose of redevelopment, including the construction of low-cost housing.

The owner of a department store located in the area challenged the condemnation, pointing out that his store was not itself blighted and arguing that the creation of a "better balanced, more attractive community" was not a valid public use. *Id.*, at 31, 75 S. Ct. 98. Writing for a unanimous Court, Justice Douglas refused to evaluate this claim in isolation, deferring instead to the legislative and agency judgment that the area "must be planned as a whole" for the plan to be successful. *Id.*, at 34, 75 S. Ct. 98. The Court explained that "community redevelopment programs need not, by force of the Constitution, be on a piecemeal basis—lot by lot, building by building." *Id.*, at 35, 75 S. Ct. 98. The public use underlying the taking was unequivocally affirmed. . . .

In *Hawaii Housing Authority v. Midkiff*, 467 U.S. 229, 104 S. Ct. 2321, 81 L. Ed. 2d 186 (1984), the Court considered a Hawaii statute whereby fee title was taken from lessors and transferred to lessees (for just compensation) in order to reduce the concentration of land ownership. We unanimously upheld the statute and rejected the Ninth Circuit's view that it was "a naked attempt on the part of the state of Hawaii to take the property of A and transfer it to B solely for B's private use and benefit." *Id.*, at 235, 104 S. Ct. 2321 (internal quotation marks omitted). Reaffirming *Berman's* deferential approach to legislative judgments in this field, we concluded that the State's purpose of eliminating the "social and economic evils of a land oligopoly" qualified as a valid public use. 467 U.S., at 241-242, 104 S. Ct. 2321. Our opinion also rejected the contention that the mere fact that the State immediately transferred the properties to private individuals upon condemnation somehow diminished the public character of the taking. "[I]t is only the taking's purpose, and not its mechanics," we explained, that matters in determining public use. *Id.*, at 244, 104 S. Ct. 2321. . . .

Viewed as a whole, our jurisprudence has recognized that the needs of society have varied between different parts of the Nation, just as they have evolved over time in response to changed circumstances. Our earliest cases in particular embodied a strong theme of federalism, emphasizing the "great respect" that we owe to state legislatures and state courts in discerning local public needs. . . . For more than a century, our public use jurisprudence has wisely eschewed rigid formulas and intrusive scrutiny in favor of affording legislatures broad latitude in determining what public needs justify the use of the takings power.

IV

Those who govern the City were not confronted with the need to remove blight in the Fort Trumbull area, but their determination that the area was sufficiently distressed to justify a program of economic rejuvenation is entitled to our deference. The City has carefully formulated an economic development plan that it believes will provide appreciable benefits to the community, including—but by no means limited to—new jobs and increased tax revenue. As with other exercises in urban planning and development, the City is endeavoring to coordinate a variety of commercial, residential, and recreational uses of land, with the hope that they will form a whole greater than the sum of its parts. To effectuate this plan, the City has invoked a state statute that specifically authorizes the use of eminent domain to promote economic development. Given the comprehensive character of the plan, the thorough deliberation that preceded its adoption, and the limited scope of our review, it is appropriate for us, as it was in *Berman*, to resolve the challenges of the individual owners, not on a piecemeal basis, but rather in light of the entire plan. Because that plan unquestionably serves a public purpose, the takings challenged here satisfy the public use requirement of the Fifth Amendment. . . .

In affirming the City's authority to take petitioners' properties, we do not minimize the hardship that condemnations may entail, notwithstanding the payment of just compensation. . . . This Court's authority, however, extends only to determining whether the City's proposed condemnations are for a "public use" within the meaning of the Fifth Amendment to the Federal Constitution. Because over a century of our case law interpreting that provision dictates an affirmative answer to that question, we may not grant petitioners the relief that they seek.

The judgment of the Supreme Court of Connecticut is affirmed. *It is so ordered.*

CASE QUESTIONS

WEST COAST HOTEL v. PARRISH

1. How does the Court interpret the right to enter into a contract in the context of "liberty"?

2. On what grounds does the Court justify limiting the contractual rights of employers when it pertains to their employees?

3. How was the Court's holding potentially affected by the fact that the law at issue in this case pertained solely to women? Do you think the same rationale would apply if the case were decided today? Explain.

4. When considering the balancing of competing interests, which side does the Court support? How does this represent a shift from previous holdings of the Court?

5. What level of scrutiny (see Chapter 1) does the Court employ for determining if the Washington law is valid? What specific language in the Court's opinion supports your answer?

KELO v. CITY OF NEW LONDON, CONNECTICUT

1. What is the difference between a "public use" and a "public purpose"? Why is this an important distinction for the Court's holding?

2. According to the Court, what weight is the legislature's judgment to be given when determining if this taking was constitutional? Why?

HYPOTHETICAL WITH ACCOMPANYING ANALYSIS

Hypothetical

Sophie Schwimmer was Aquatown High School's swimming star. She is currently a senior in the state high school, and she has been on the school's swim team since her freshman year. Sophie has always been dedicated to swimming and has never let her team down at a meet. Recently, however, Sophie has experienced a bad case of "Senioritis," which resulted in her missing a number of practices. Because Sophie is such an extraordinary swimmer, Coach Waters has put up with her antics, but the last straw came when she missed a critical meet against Aquatown's arch rival, Poseidon Prep School. When Coach Waters investigated why Sophie had missed the swim meet, he learned that she went to an all-day bonfire and dance at another local high school. The following morning, the coach called Sophie into his office and confronted her about the situation. Sophie said she had missed the meet because she hadn't been feeling well, despite the fact that numerous students saw Sophie at the bonfire. At the end of the 15-minute meeting, Coach Waters told Sophie that, effectively immediately, she was off the swim team.

The following day, Sophie and her parents met with Coach Waters and the principal of Aquatown High School. Sophie explained that she was miserable for having been kicked off the team. She said that she had recently received a full scholarship to a prestigious college for her swimming and if she were dismissed from the high school team, she was concerned her scholarship might be revoked. Sophie said that she had every intention of going to the Olympics one day and being kicked off the team could mean the end of her life-long dream. Finally, she told the coach that he had "permanently tarnished her reputation" among her peers for kicking her off the team. After listening to everything Sophie had to say, the principal told Sophie that Coach Waters had to do what he felt was best for the team as a whole, which gave him a tremendous amount of discretion. Therefore, the principal supported Coach Waters' decision to remove Sophie from the team.

Sophie has filed suit against Coach Waters and the principal, claiming that her due process rights were violated because she was not given an adequate opportunity to refute the allegations against her or present evidence supporting her position. Analyze whether Sophie will likely succeed in her lawsuit.

Analysis

The right to due process of law encompasses a variety of legal principals, and the proper analysis of whether Sophie's lawsuit has merit will require the consideration of a number of factors. The first issue to be addressed is which Due Process Clause will be implicated in Sophie's case. Because Aquatown High School is a state school, the Fourteenth Amendment will govern our analysis of this issue. Next, it must be determined whether Sophie is asserting a challenge based on her substantive or procedural due process rights. Substantive due process deals with the ability of government to regulate certain areas of an individual's life. Procedural due process, on the other hand, requires a state to incorporate adequate or fair procedures when depriving an individual of life, liberty, or property. Sophie is not challenging the inherent ability of Coach Waters to dismiss her from the swim team, rather, she is challenging the *way* in which he did so. Sophie, therefore, is raising a procedural due process claim.

In order to establish a violation of procedural due process, Sophie must first show that she had a protected liberty or property interest at stake. If she can make such a showing, then she must demonstrate that she did not receive due process when considering a combination of (1) the private interest that will be affected by the official action; (2) the risk of an erroneous deprivation of the interest through the procedures used; (3) the probable value of additional or substitute procedural safeguards; and (4) the government's interest that the additional or substitute procedural safeguard would entail. Matthews v. Eldridge, 424 U.S. 319 (1976).

The main issue in this scenario centers around whether Sophie has a liberty or property interest in her membership on the swim team. The Supreme Court has never directly addressed whether participation in high school extracurricular activities gives rise to such an interest. The Court has, however, concluded that a student has a liberty interest in attending school. *See* Goss v. Lopez, 419 U.S. 545 (1975) (10-day suspension from school gave rise to protected liberty interest). In the instant case, the government could argue that a student has no right to participate in activities such as the swim team and thus no due process concerns arise when Sophie was dismissed from the team. Sophie, on the other hand, could argue that dismissal from the team could have serious repercussions on her future, such as the revocation of her college scholarship and lessened opportunities for a lucrative swimming career. Mere damage to her reputation, without more, will not be enough to give Sophie a property interest in remaining on the swim team. Paul v. Davis, 424 U.S. 693 (1976). Therefore, in order to meet the first requirement of a procedural due process claim, Sophie will have to show that she has a liberty interest in remaining on the team and failure to keep her on the team would have detrimental and measurable consequences.

If a court were to hold that Sophie has no protected property interest in remaining on the swim team, no further inquiry would be necessary as to whether Sophie was given adequate procedural protections. If, on the other hand, a court were to hold that Sophie did have a property or liberty interest, it would next examine the factors set forth in *Matthews* to determine whether the meeting among Sophie, her parents, the coach, and the principal of Aquatown High School adequately protected her due process right before being dismissed from the team. Since Sophie claimed that she should be entitled to refute Coach Waters' position and present evidence to support her position, a court may hold she was entitled to more than the 15-minute meeting, especially if doing so would impose little burden on the high school in order to protect her due process rights.

HYPOTHETICAL FOR STUDENT ANALYSIS

Dean Farmer owns 200 acres of wooded land in a mid-western state. Each year, Dean invites hunters onto his land to kill the grabbit, a small rodent which is a cross between a groundhog and a rabbit. Dean charges the hunters a flat fee for the ability to hunt on his land, and the money he makes is his only means of income. Unfortunately for the grabbit, however, the small critters have the awkwardness of a groundhog rather than the stealth of a rabbit, so they make very easy targets. The grabbit population has declined significantly in recent years, although they are still plentiful enough not to be put on an endangered species list. In order to protect the grabbit population, the state has decided to place certain limitations on grabbit hunting. The recently enacted Grabbit Protection Act ("GPA") provides that: (1) the grabbit hunting season shall be reduced from four months to two months each year; and (2) hunters are limited in the number of grabbits they can lawfully kill each season (prior to the law no such limits existed).

Dean is less than happy about the GPA because it will likely mean fewer hunters on his land and, in turn, less money in his wallet. He's concerned he won't be able to make ends meet if grabbit hunting declines due to the new law, so he has decided to challenge the law on three alternative grounds. First, Dean maintains that the law violates his substantive due process rights because it prevents him from earning income as he so chooses. Second, he argues that the law amounts to an unconstitutional taking under the Fifth Amendment. Third, he maintains that the GPA is a violation of the Contracts Clause because it restricts his ability to contract with hunters to use his land. Discuss Dean's likelihood of success on each of the alternative grounds.

DISCUSSION QUESTIONS

1. The state of New Freedom has recently enacted a law which requires business to recycle all paper products and bear any additional cost associated with the recycling. Care Less, Inc., a small business in the state, challenges the law as an unconstitutional restriction on its economic due process rights. New Freedom has responded by arguing that the Due Process Clause of the Fourteenth Amendment specifically applies to "persons" only, so Care Less is not permitted to bring suit on due process grounds. Will New Freedom's argument prevail? *See* Santa Clara County v. Southern Pacific R.R. Co., 118 U.S. 394 (1886).

2. From the early 1900s through the 1930s, the Supreme Court struck down well over 100 state laws which attempted to restrict economic liberties. Why do you think the Court looked so disfavorably upon the government's interference with businesses? What was going on in the nation during that time period that might have contributed to the Court's philosophy?

3. Research Challenge: Familiarize yourself with the basic premise of thought of philosopher John Locke and his Social Contract Theory. How did this theory play a role in the inclusion of various economic protections within the Constitution and the Amendments?

4. How might the Equal Protection Clause of the Fourteenth Amendment be implicated in the regulation of businesses? Can you think of any laws that arguably discriminate against one business over another? See Chapter 8, *infra*, and Yick Wo v. Hopkins, 118 U.S. 356 (1886), Truax v. Raich, 239 U.S. 33 (1915), and Morey v. Doud, 354 U.S. 457 (1957).

5. Billy Shoemaker bought a small parcel of land along Route 71, the main road running through the town of Roseville, because he planned on building a shoe repair store on the site. Right after he purchased the land, Roseville passed a zoning ordinance that prohibited any new commercial structures from being built along Route 71. Have Billy's Fifth Amendment rights under the Takings Clause been violated? Explain. *See* Agins v. City of Tiburon, 447 U.S. 255 (1980).

6. Wayne obtains title to land, knowing all the while that zoning restrictions on the land are already in place. Once he obtains title, he challenges the restrictions based on due process and Fifth Amendment violations. The town counterargues that Wayne waived his right to challenge the restrictions because he knew of the restrictions *before* purchasing the land. Will the town's argument prevail? *See* Palazzolo v. Rhode Island, 533 U.S. 606 (2001).

7. Research challenge: Track the progression of Supreme Court cases relying specifically on the Contracts Clause for its discussion of economic freedoms. What pattern do you see?

8. In the wake of the terrorist attacks of September 11, 2001, the federal government enacted the Authorization for Use of Military Forces (AUMF), which authorized the President to use all necessary force against anyone associated with the attacks. In November of 2001, Yaser Hamdi, an American citizen, was detained by U.S. military forces in Afghanistan. Because he was classified as an "enemy combatant," he was afforded no due process. Hamdi ultimately brought his habeas corpus suit before the Supreme Court, challenging his confinement. What was the result? Do you agree with the Court's holding? *See* Hamdi v. Rumsfeld, 542 U.S. 507 (2004).

9. Karyn is an unemployed mother of four young children who has been receiving state welfare benefits for over a year. One day out of the clear blue, the state terminated Karyn's benefits without giving her any reason why. Karen argues that her procedural due process rights have been violated, but the state counters that Karyn has no right to procedural due process because the receipt of welfare benefits is a privilege and not a right. Which side will prevail? What if Karyn had just applied for the welfare benefits but was summarily denied them, would she then be entitled to procedural due process? *See* Goldberg v. Kelly, 397 U.S. 254 (1970).

10. Research challenge: Familiarize yourself with the "*Dred Scott* case" (Scott v. Sandford, 60 U.S. 393 (1857)), now recognized as arguably one of the Court's most embarrassing judicial opinions. How did the Court in that case

recognize the economic property rights of southern landowners? What was the ultimate fate of the Court's decision in the *Dred Scott* case?

11. One of the issues that arises with regard to procedural due process challenges is whether the government may suspend or terminate without procedural protections certain *privileges* it has bestowed upon individuals. What examples of privileges can you think of that might fall under this category? Why do you think an individual would claim procedural due process rights before that privilege could be altered in any way? *See, e.g.,* Bell v. Burson, 402 U.S. 535 (1971).

12. Research challenge: Justice Roberts's alignment with the majority in *West Coast Hotel v. Parrish* is often referred to as the "switch in time that saved nine." What does that mean?

13. The City of Purity recently passed a law banning the world's oldest profession. Chastity is one of Purity's most infamous prostitutes. She is challenging the law as a violation of her substantive due process rights, arguing that she has a liberty interest in engaging in whatever occupation she chooses and the city cannot infringe upon her economic freedoms. Do you think Chastity will likely succeed in her argument? Why or why not?

True/False

1. An individual will never be entitled to procedural due process protections when the government seeks to restrict a privilege previously given to an individual.

2. Courts should apply the rational basis test when determining whether a government regulation impacting an individual's economic freedom violates substantive due process.

3. The Fifth Amendment Takings Clause will typically not be violated unless an individual is deprived of *all* economic use of his property by virtue of the taking.

4. A law can only violate either procedural or substantive due process; it can never violate both.

5. A law can only violate either the Fifth or the Fourteenth Amendment Due Process Clause; it can never violate both.

Multiple Choice

6. Pursuant to an economic revitalization plan, the City of Breighton has recently exercised its right of eminent domain over a parcel of land containing 20 dilapidated houses in a high-crime area. After compensating the homeowners, Breighton officials gave the parcel to Realty, Corp., a private land developer which is going to build low-rent apartments and a community center on the land in order to benefit Breighton city residents. The homeowners have challenged Breighton's actions on the Fifth Amendment grounds that the city unconstitutionally took their private property to give to another private company. Will their challenge prevail?

   A. Yes, because the power of eminent domain only allows the government to take private property for public use.
   B. Yes, because the taking amounted to a total economic loss of the homeowners' property.
   C. No, because Breighton permissibly exercised its power of eminent domain for public use since it would serve a public purpose.
   D. No, because the government did not actually take their property, Realty, Corp. did.

7. Which of the following statements about *West Coast Hotel v. Parrish* is false?

   A. It explicitly overruled one of its prior decisions.
   B. It applied a more rigorous level of scrutiny in evaluating substantive due process challenges than what had been used in previous cases.

    C. It upheld the validity of the minimum wage law at issue in that case.

    D. All of the above statements are false.

8. In which of the following scenarios would Betty most likely *not* be entitled to procedural due process protections?

    A. Betty has applied for welfare benefits; the state has denied her application without any explanation why.

    B. Betty has been receiving welfare benefits for over a year; the state has terminated her benefits without any explanation why.

    C. Betty has her driver's license suspended for alleged reckless driving habits.

    D. Betty would be entitled to procedural due process protections in all of the above scenarios.

9. In an effort to protect the environment, the State of New Greenland has recently passed a law banning any landowners in the state from cutting down trees on their own property. Timberco, Inc., a business located in New Greenland engaged in the logging industry, is forced to breach several contracts with homebuilding companies because it cannot provide the lumber in light of the new law. Timberco, therefore, wishes to challenge New Greenland's law. Which provision(s) could provide the mechanism for Timberco to make such a challenge?

    A. The Due Process Clause.

    B. The Due Process Clause and the Takings Clause.

    C. The Due Process Clause, the Takings Clause, and the Contracts Clause.

    D. None of the above.

10. Revisit the above question. Which of the following arguments, if made by New Greenland, *could* serve as a defense to its position that the law withstands a substantive due process challenge?

    A. Timberco has no standing to challenge the law because the Due Process Clause applies only to "persons," and Timberco is not a person.

    B. The law is rationally related to the legitimate state interest of protecting the environment.

    C. Timberco is not entitled to make a substantive due process challenge because a fundamental right is not at stake.

    D. Timberco does not have a valid substantive due process claim because the New Greenland law is not entirely prohibiting Timberco from logging; it is only prohibiting the company from logging in the State of New Greenland.

Chapter 6
The Right to Privacy

"At the heart of liberty is the right to define one's own concept of existence, of meaning, of the universe, and of the mystery of human life."

—Justice Sandra Day O'Connor
Planned Parenthood v. Casey, 505 U.S. 833 (1992)

INTRODUCTION

The right to privacy is considered to be a basic human right protected by the Constitution. However, if you read the Constitution and its Amendments, you won't find any plain statement that we have a right to privacy. So then, how can the Constitution guarantee a protection that isn't mentioned explicitly anywhere within it? The Supreme Court has explained that the Constitution and its Amendments must be read as a whole and has concluded that a right to privacy is a fundamental freedom that is implicitly protected from government infringement. The Supreme Court focused on the Fourth Amendment's protection from unreasonable searches and seizures and liberty interests protected in the due process provisions of the Fifth and Fourteenth Amendments in reaching this conclusion. Justice Brandeis has perhaps best characterized the nature of the right to privacy as, simply, "the right to be let alone."

There are many instances in which we expect our personal matters to be private and the government to keep its nose out of our business. Those instances include what intimate relationships we have and with whom, as well as whether or when to have a child. Some who are terminally ill may even wish to decide for themselves when to die. The Supreme Court has addressed the extent of the right to privacy in many different controversial cases ranging from birth control, to abortion, to homosexual relationships, to the right to die. Additionally, the body of law related to the right to privacy as it applies to gender, reproduction, and sexual intimacy has evolved from the Supreme Court's decisions related to birth control. Within this chapter we explore those sensitive issues and learn when the government may step in or when it must stay out of our lives.

STUDENT *Checklist*

The Right to Privacy

Except when a person's liberty is limited by incarceration or probation, when determining if a personal decision is protected from government infringement, consider the following questions in applying the **strict scrutiny** test:

- Is the decision a **fundamentally private matter**?

- Does the government have a **compelling purpose** for infringing on the private decision?

- Is there a no **less compelling way** to achieve the compelling government purpose without infringing on a person's privacy?

If a person is **incarcerated** or **on probation**, apply the **rational basis test** by answering the following questions:

- Is the plaintiff incarcerated or on probation as a result of a **criminal conviction**?

- Does the government have a **legitimate reason** for infringing on the private decision?

- Is the government's action **rationally related** to the legitimate reason for its actions?

SUPREME COURT CASES

ROE v. WADE, 410 U.S. 113 (1973)

[In this famous case, Jane Roe, a pregnant woman, wished to have a legal and safe abortion in Texas. Texas law made it a crime to "procure an abortion." Roe sought to have the statute declared unconstitutional because it violated her right of personal privacy.]

. . . The principal thrust of appellant's attack on the Texas statutes is that they improperly invade a right, said to be possessed by the pregnant woman, to choose to terminate her pregnancy. Appellant would discover this right in the concept of personal "liberty" embodied in the Fourteenth Amendment's Due Process Clause; or in personal marital, familial, and sexual privacy said to be protected by the Bill of Rights or its penumbras, see Griswold v. Connecticut, 381 U.S. 479, 85 S. Ct. 1678, 14 L. Ed. 2d 510 (1965); Eisenstadt v. Baird, 405 U.S. 438 (1972); id., at 460, 92 S. Ct. 1029, at 1042, 31 L. Ed. 2d 349 (White, J., concurring in result); or among those rights reserved to the people by the Ninth Amendment, Griswold v. Connecticut, 381 U.S., at 486, 85 S. Ct., at 1682 (Goldberg, J., concurring). Before addressing this claim, we feel it desirable briefly to survey, in several aspects, the history of abortion, for such insight as that history may afford us, and then to examine the state purposes and interests behind the criminal abortion laws. . . .

VI

It perhaps is not generally appreciated that the restrictive criminal abortion laws in effect in a majority of States today are of relatively recent vintage. Those laws, generally proscribing abortion or its attempt at any time during pregnancy except when necessary to preserve the pregnant woman's life, are not of ancient or even of common-law origin. Instead, they derive from statutory changes effected, for the most part, in the latter half of the 19th century. . . .

VIII

The Constitution does not explicitly mention any right of privacy. In a line of decisions, however, going back perhaps as far as Union Pacific R. Co. v. Botsford, 141 U.S. 250, 251, 11 S. Ct. 1000, 1001, 35 L. Ed. 734 (1891), the Court has recognized that a right of personal privacy, or a guarantee of certain areas or zones of privacy, does exist under the Constitution. In varying contexts, the Court or individual Justices have, indeed, found at least the roots of that right in the First Amendment, Stanley v. Georgia, 394 U.S. 557, 564, 89 S. Ct. 1243, 1247, 22 L. Ed. 2d 542 (1969); in the Fourth and Fifth Amendments, Terry v. Ohio, 392 U.S. 1, 8-9, 88 S. Ct. 1868, 1872-1873, 20 L. Ed. 2d 889 (1968), Katz v. United States, 389 U.S. 347, 350, 88 S. Ct. 507, 510, 19 L. Ed. 2d 576 (1967), Boyd v. United States, 116 U.S. 616, 6 S. Ct. 524, 29 L. Ed. 746 (1886), see Olmstead v. United States, 277 U.S. 438, 478, 48 S. Ct. 564, 572, 72 L. Ed. 944 (1928) (Brandeis, J., dissenting); in the penumbras of the Bill of Rights, Griswold v. Connecticut, 381 U.S., at 484-485, 85 S. Ct., at 1681-1682; in the Ninth Amendment, id., at 486, 85 S. Ct. at 1682 (Goldberg, J., concurring); or in the concept of liberty guaranteed by the first section of the Fourteenth Amendment, see Meyer v. Nebraska, 262 U.S. 390, 399, 43 S. Ct. 625, 626, 67 L. Ed. 1042 (1923). These decisions make it clear that only personal rights that can be deemed "fundamental" or "implicit in the concept of ordered liberty," Palko v. Connecticut, 302 U.S. 319, 325, 58 S. Ct. 149, 152, 82 L. Ed. 288 (1937), are included in this guarantee of personal privacy. They also make it clear that the right has some extension to activities relating to marriage, Loving v. Virginia, 388 U.S. 1, 12, 87 S. Ct. 1817, 1823, 18 L. Ed. 2d 1010 (1967); procreation, Skinner v. Oklahoma, 316 U.S. 535, 541-542, 62 S. Ct. 1110, 1113-1114, 86 L. Ed. 1655 (1942); contraception, Eisenstadt v. Baird, 405 U.S., at 453-454, 92 S. Ct., at 1038-1039; id., at 460, 463-465, 92 S. Ct. at 1042, 1043-1044 (White, J., concurring in result); family relationships, Prince v. Massachusetts, 321 U.S. 158, 166, 64 S. Ct. 438, 442, 88 L. Ed. 645 (1944); and child rearing and education, Pierce v. Society of Sisters, 268 U.S. 510, 535, 45 S. Ct. 571, 573, 69 L. Ed. 1070 (1925), Meyer v. Nebraska, supra.

This right of privacy, whether it be founded in the Fourteenth Amendment's concept of personal liberty and restrictions upon state action, as we feel it is, or, as the District Court determined, in the Ninth Amendment's reservation of rights to the people, is broad enough to encompass a woman's decision whether or not to terminate her pregnancy. The detriment that the State would impose upon the pregnant woman by denying this choice altogether is apparent. Specific and direct harm medically diagnosable even in early pregnancy may be involved. Maternity, or additional offspring, may force upon the woman a distressful life and future. Psychological harm may be imminent. Mental and physical health may be taxed by child care. There is also the distress, for all concerned, associated with the unwanted child, and there is the problem of bringing a child into a family already unable, psychologically and otherwise, to care for it. In other cases, as in this one, the additional difficulties and continuing stigma of unwed motherhood may be involved. All these are factors the woman and her responsible physician necessarily will consider in consultation.

On the basis of elements such as these, appellant and some amici argue that the woman's right is absolute and that she is entitled to terminate her pregnancy at whatever time, in whatever way, and for whatever reason she alone chooses. With this we do not agree. Appellant's arguments that Texas either has no valid interest at all in regulating the abortion decision, or no interest strong enough to support any limitation upon the woman's sole determination, are unpersuasive. The Court's decisions recognizing a right of privacy also acknowledge that some state regulation in areas protected by that right is appropriate. As noted above, a State may properly assert important interests in safeguarding health, in maintaining medical standards, and in protecting potential life. At some point in pregnancy, these respective interests become sufficiently compelling to sustain regulation of the factors that govern the abortion decision. The privacy right involved, therefore, cannot be said to be absolute. In fact, it is not clear to us that the claim asserted by some amici that one has an unlimited right to do with one's body as one pleases bears a close relationship to the right of privacy previously articulated in the Court's decisions. The Court has refused to recognize an unlimited right of this kind in the past. Jacobson v. Massachusetts, 197 U.S. 11, 25 S. Ct. 358, 49 L. Ed. 643 (1905) (vaccination); Buck v. Bell, 274 U.S. 200, 47 S. Ct. 584, 71 L. Ed. 1000 (1927) (sterilization).

We, therefore, conclude that the right of personal privacy includes the abortion decision, but that this right is not unqualified and must be considered against important state interests in regulation. We note that those federal and state courts that have recently considered abortion law challenges have reached the same conclusion. A majority, in addition to the District Court in the present case, have held state laws unconstitutional, at least in part, because of vagueness or because of overbreadth and abridgment of rights.

Others have sustained state statutes. . . . Although the results are divided, most of these courts have agreed that the right of privacy, however based, is broad enough to cover the abortion decision; that the right, nonetheless, is not absolute and is subject to some limitations; and that at some point the state interests as to protection of health, medical standards, and prenatal life, become dominant. We agree with this approach.

Where certain "fundamental rights" are involved, the Court has held that regulation limiting these rights may be justified only by a "compelling state interest," . . . and that legislative enactments must be narrowly drawn to express only the legitimate state interests at stake. In the recent abortion cases, cited above, courts have recognized these principles. Those striking down state laws have generally scrutinized the State's interests in protecting health and potential life, and have concluded that neither interest justified broad limitations on the reasons for which a physician and his pregnant patient might decide that she should have an abortion in the early stages of pregnancy. Courts sustaining state laws have held that the State's determinations to protect health or prenatal life are dominant and constitutionally justifiable.

IX

The District Court held that the appellee failed to meet his burden of demonstrating that the Texas statute's infringement upon Roe's rights was necessary to support a compelling state interest, and that, although the appellee presented "several compelling justifications for state presence in the area of abortions," the statutes outstripped these justifications and swept "far beyond any areas of compelling state interest." 314 F. Supp., at 1222-1223. Appellant and appellee both contest that holding. Appellant, as has been indicated, claims an absolute right that bars any state imposition of criminal penalties in the area. Appellee argues that the State's determination to recognize and protect prenatal life from and after conception constitutes a compelling state interest. As noted above, we do not agree fully with either formulation.

A. The appellee and certain amici argue that the fetus is a "person" within the language and meaning of the Fourteenth Amendment. In support of this, they outline at length and in detail the well-known facts of fetal development. If this suggestion of personhood is established, the appellant's case, of course, collapses, for the fetus' right to life would then be guaranteed specifically by the Amendment. The appellant conceded as much on reargument. On the other hand, the appellee conceded on reargument that no case could be cited that holds that a fetus is a person within the meaning of the Fourteenth Amendment.

The Constitution does not define "person" in so many words. Section 1 of the Fourteenth Amendment contains three references to "person." The first, in defining "citizens," speaks of "persons born or naturalized in the United States." The word also appears both in the Due Process Clause and in the Equal Protection Clause. "Person" is used in other places in the Constitution: in the listing of qualifications for Representatives and Senators, Art. I, §2, cl. 2, and §3, cl. 3; in the Apportionment Clause, Art. I, §2, cl. 3; in the Migration and Importation provision, Art. I, §9, cl. 1; in the Emoulument Clause, Art. I, §9, cl. 8; in the Electros provisions, Art. II, §1, cl. 2, and the superseded cl. 3; in the provision outlining qualifications for the office of President, Art. II, §1, cl. 5; in the Extradition provisions, Art. IV, §2, cl. 2, and the superseded Fugitive Slave Clause 3; and in the Fifth, Twelfth, and Twenty-second Amendments, as well as in §§ 2 and 3 of the Fourteenth Amendment. But in nearly all these instances, the use of the word is such that it has application only postnatally. None indicates, with any assurance, that it has any possible prenatal application.

There are other inconsistencies between Fourteenth Amendment status and the typical abortion statute. It has already been pointed out that in Texas the woman is not a principal or an accomplice with respect to an abortion upon her. If the fetus is a person, why is the woman not a principal or an accomplice? Further, the penalty for criminal abortion specified by Art. 1195 is significantly less than the maximum penalty for murder prescribed by Art. 1257 of the Texas Penal Code. If the fetus is a person, may the penalties be different?

All this, together with our observation, supra, that throughout the major portion of the 19th century prevailing legal abortion practices were far freer than they are today, persuades us that the word "person," as used in the Fourteenth Amendment, does not include the unborn. This is in accord with the results reached in those few cases where the issue has been squarely presented. Indeed, our decision in United States v. Vuitch, 402 U.S. 62, 91 S. Ct. 1294, 28 L. Ed. 2d 601 (1971), inferentially is to the same effect, for we there would not have indulged in statutory interpretation favorable to abortion in specified circumstances if the necessary consequence was the termination of life entitled to Fourteenth Amendment protection.

This conclusion, however, does not of itself fully answer the contentions raised by Texas, and we pass on to other considerations.

B. The pregnant woman cannot be isolated in her privacy. She carries an embryo and, later, a fetus, if one accepts the medical definitions of the developing young in the human uterus. See Dorland's Illustrated Medical Dictionary 478-479, 547 (24th ed. 1965). The situation therefore is inherently different from marital intimacy, or bedroom possession of obscene material, or marriage, or procreation, or education, with which *Eisenstadt* and *Griswold, Stanley, Loving, Skinner* and *Pierce* and *Meyer* were respectively concerned. As we have intimated above, it is reasonable and appropriate for a State to decide that at some point in time another interest, that of health of the mother or that of potential human life, becomes significantly involved. The woman's privacy is no longer sole and any right of privacy she possesses must be measured accordingly.

Texas urges that, apart from the Fourteenth Amendment, life begins at conception and is present throughout pregnancy, and that, therefore, the State has a compelling interest in protecting that life from and after conception. We need not resolve the difficult question of when life begins. When those trained in the respective disciplines of medicine, philosophy, and theology are unable to arrive at any consensus, the judiciary, at this point in the development of man's knowledge, is not in a position to speculate as to the answer.

It should be sufficient to note briefly the wide divergence of thinking on this most sensitive and difficult question. There has always been strong support for the view that life does not begin until live birth. This was the belief of the Stoics. It appears to be the predominant, though not the unanimous, attitude of the Jewish faith. It may be taken to represent also the position of a large segment of the Protestant community, insofar as that can be ascertained; organized groups that have taken a formal position on the abortion issue have generally regarded abortion as a matter for the conscience of the individual and her family. As we have noted, the common law found greater significance in quickening. Physicians and their scientific colleagues have regarded that event with less interest and have tended to focus either upon conception, upon live birth, or upon the interim point at which the fetus becomes "viable," that is, potentially able to live outside the mother's womb, albeit with artificial aid. Viability is usually placed at about seven months (28 weeks) but may occur earlier, even at 24 weeks. The Aristotelian theory of "mediate animation," that held sway throughout the Middle Ages and the Renaissance in Europe, continued to be official Roman Catholic dogma until the 19th century, despite opposition to this "ensoulment" theory from those in the Church who would recognize the existence of life from the moment of conception. The latter is now, of course, the official belief of the Catholic Church. As one brief amicus discloses, this is a view strongly held by many non-Catholics as well, and by many physicians. Substantial problems for precise definition of this view are posed, however, by new embryological data that purport to indicate that conception is a "process" over time, rather than an event, and by new medical techniques such as menstrual extraction, the "morning-after" pill, implantation of embryos, artificial insemination, and even artificial wombs.

In areas other than criminal abortion, the law has been reluctant to endorse any theory that life, as we recognize it, begins before life birth or to accord legal rights to the unborn except in narrowly defined situations and except when the rights are contingent upon life birth. For example, the traditional rule of tort law denied recovery for prenatal injuries even though the child was born alive. That rule has been changed in almost every jurisdiction. In most States, recovery is said to be permitted only if the fetus was viable, or at least quick, when the injuries were sustained, though few courts have squarely so held. In a recent development, generally opposed by the commentators, some States permit the parents of a stillborn child to maintain an action for wrongful death because of prenatal injuries. Such an action, however, would appear to be one to vindicate the parents' interest and is thus consistent with the view that the fetus, at most, represents only the potentiality of life. Similarly, unborn children have been recognized as acquiring rights or interests by way of inheritance or other devolution of property, and have been represented by guardians ad litem. Perfection of the interests involved, again, has generally been contingent upon live birth. In short, the unborn have never been recognized in the law as persons in the whole sense.

X

In view of all this, we do not agree that, by adopting one theory of life, Texas may override the rights of the pregnant woman that are at stake. We repeat, however, that the State does have an important and legitimate interest in preserving and protecting the health of the pregnant woman, whether she be a resident of the State or a non-resident who seeks medical consultation and treatment there, and that it has still another important and legitimate interest in protecting the potentiality of human life. These interests are separate and distinct. Each grows in substantiality as the woman approaches term and, at a point during pregnancy, each becomes "compelling."

With respect to the State's important and legitimate interest in the health of the mother, the "compelling" point, in the light of present medical knowledge, is at approximately the end of the first trimester. This is so because of the now-established medical fact, referred to above at 725, that until the end of the first trimester mortality in abortion may be less than mortality in normal childbirth. It follows that, from and after this point, a State may regulate the abortion procedure to the extent that the regulation reasonably relates to the preservation and protection of maternal health. Examples of permissible state regulation in this area are requirements as to the qualifications of the person who is to perform the abortion; as to the licensure of that person; as to the facility in which the procedure is to be performed, that is, whether it must be a hospital or may be a clinic or some other place of less-than-hospital status; as to the licensing of the facility; and the like.

This means, on the other hand, that, for the period of pregnancy prior to this "compelling" point, the attending physician, in consultation with his patient, is free to determine, without regulation by the State, that, in his medical judgment, the patient's pregnancy should be terminated. If that decision is reached, the judgment may be effectuated by an abortion free of interference by the State.

With respect to the State's important and legitimate interest in potential life, the "compelling" point is at viability. This is so because the fetus then presumably has the capability of meaningful life outside the mother's womb. State regulation protective of fetal life after viability thus has both logical and biological justifications. If the State is interested in protecting fetal life after viability, it may go so far as to proscribe abortion during that period, except when it is necessary to preserve the life or health of the mother.

Measured against these standards, Art. 1196 of the Texas Penal Code, in restricting legal abortions to those "procured or attempted by medical advice for the purpose of saving the life of the mother," sweeps too broadly. The statute makes no distinction between abortions performed early in pregnancy and those performed later, and it limits to a single reason, "saving" the mother's life, the legal justification for the procedure. The statute, therefore, cannot survive the constitutional attack made upon it here.

This conclusion makes it unnecessary for us to consider the additional challenge to the Texas statute asserted on grounds of vagueness. See United States v. Vuitch, 402 U.S., at 67-72, 91 S. Ct., at 1296-1299.

XI

To summarize and to repeat:

1. A state criminal abortion statute of the current Texas type, that excepts from criminality only a life-saving procedure on behalf of the mother, without regard to pregnancy stage and without recognition of the other interests involved, is violative of the Due Process Clause of the Fourteenth Amendment.

   (a) For the stage prior to approximately the end of the first trimester, the abortion decision and its effectuation must be left to the medical judgment of the pregnant woman's attending physician.

   (b) For the stage subsequent to approximately the end of the first trimester, the State, in promoting its interest in the health of the mother, may, if it chooses, regulate the abortion procedure in ways that are reasonably related to maternal health.

   (c) For the stage subsequent to viability, the State in promoting its interest in the potentiality of human life may, if it chooses, regulate, and even proscribe, abortion except where it is necessary, in appropriate medical judgment, for the preservation of the life or health of the mother.

2. The State may define the term "physician," as it has been employed in the preceding paragraphs of this Part XI of this opinion, to mean only a physician currently licensed by the State, and may proscribe any abortion by a person who is not a physician as so defined.

* * *

This holding, we feel, is consistent with the relative weights of the respective interests involved, with the lessons and examples of medical and legal history, with the lenity of the common law, and with the demands of the profound problems of the present day. The decision leaves the State free to place increasing restrictions on abortion as the period of pregnancy lengthens, so long as those restrictions are tailored to the recognized state interests. The decision vindicates the right of the physician to administer medical treatment according to his professional judgment up to the points where important state interests provide compelling justifications for intervention. Up to those points, the abortion decision in all its aspects is inherently, and primarily, a medical decision, and basic responsibility for it must rest with the physician. If an individual practitioner abuses the privilege of exercising proper medical judgment, the usual remedies, judicial and intra-professional, are available. . . .

It is so ordered. Affirmed in part and reversed in part.

LAWRENCE v. TEXAS, 539 U.S. 558 (2003)

[A Texas statute prohibited deviant sexual intercourse, which included "(A) any contact between any part of the genitals of one person and the mouth or anus of another person; . . ." Police arrested and charged two adult males for violating this statute by engaging in consensual sexual relations in a private dwelling. The men were convicted and appealed, asserting that, among other things, they had a constitutional right to privacy to engage in adult consensual sexual relations.]

. . . Liberty protects the person from unwarranted government intrusions into a dwelling or other private places. In our tradition the State is not omnipresent in the home. And there are other spheres of our lives and existence, outside the home, where the State should not be a dominant presence. Freedom extends beyond spatial bounds. Liberty presumes an autonomy of self that includes freedom of thought, belief, expression, and certain intimate conduct. The instant case involves liberty of the person both in its spatial and more transcendent dimensions.

* * *

We conclude the case should be resolved by determining whether the petitioners were free as adults to engage in the private conduct in the exercise of their liberty under the Due Process Clause of the Fourteenth Amendment to the Constitution. For this inquiry we deem it necessary to reconsider the Court's holding in *Bowers*.

There are broad statements of the substantive reach of liberty under the Due Process Clause in earlier cases, including *Pierce v. Society of Sisters*, 268 U.S. 510 (1925), and *Meyer v. Nebraska*, 262 U.S. 390 (1923); but the most pertinent beginning point is our decision in *Griswold v. Connecticut*, 381 U.S. 479 (1965).

In *Griswold* the Court invalidated a state law prohibiting the use of drugs or devices of contraception and counseling or aiding and abetting the use of contraceptives. The Court described the protected interest as a right to privacy and placed emphasis on the marriage relation and the protected space of the marital bedroom. *Id.*, at 485.

After *Griswold* it was established that the right to make certain decisions regarding sexual conduct extends beyond the marital relationship. In *Eisenstadt v. Baird*, 405 U.S. 438 (1972), the Court invalidated a law prohibiting the distribution of contraceptives to unmarried persons. The case was decided under the Equal Protection Clause, *id.*, at 454; but with respect to unmarried persons, the Court went on to state the fundamental proposition that the law impaired the exercise of their personal rights, *ibid*. It quoted from the statement of the Court of Appeals finding the law to be in conflict with fundamental human rights, and it followed with this statement of its own:

> "It is true that in *Griswold* the right of privacy in question inhered in the marital relationship. . . . If the right of privacy means anything, it is the right of the *individual*, married or single, to be free from unwarranted governmental intrusion into matters so fundamentally affecting a person as the decision whether to bear or beget a child." *Id.*, at 453.

The opinions in *Griswold* and *Eisenstadt* were part of the background for the decision in *Roe v. Wade*, 410 U.S. 113 (1973). As is well known, the case involved a challenge to the Texas law prohibiting abortions, but the laws of other States were affected as well. Although the Court held the woman's rights were not absolute, her right to elect an abortion did have real and substantial protection as an exercise of her liberty under the Due Process Clause. The Court cited cases that protect spatial freedom and cases that go well beyond it. *Roe* recognized the right of a woman to make certain fundamental decisions affecting her destiny and confirmed once more that the protection of liberty under the Due Process Clause has a substantive dimension of fundamental significance in defining the rights of the person.

In *Carey v. Population Services Int'l*, 431 U.S. 678 (1977), the Court confronted a New York law forbidding sale or distribution of contraceptive devices to persons under 16 years of age. Although there was no single opinion for the Court, the law was invalidated. Both *Eisenstadt* and *Carey*, as well as the holding and rationale in *Roe*, confirmed that the reasoning of *Griswold* could not be confined to the protection of rights of married adults. This was the state of the law with respect to some of the most relevant cases when the Court considered *Bowers v. Hardwick.*

The facts in *Bowers* had some similarities to the instant case. A police officer, whose right to enter seems not to have been in question, observed Hardwick, in his own bedroom, engaging in intimate sexual conduct with another adult male. The conduct was in violation of a Georgia statute making it a criminal offense to engage in sodomy. One difference between the two cases is that the Georgia statute prohibited the conduct whether or not the participants were of the same sex, while the Texas statute, as we have seen, applies only to participants of the same sex. Hardwick was not prosecuted, but he brought an action in federal court to declare the state statute invalid. He alleged he was a practicing homosexual and that the criminal prohibition violated rights guaranteed to him by the Constitution. The Court, in an opinion by Justice White, sustained the Georgia law. Chief Justice Burger and Justice Powell joined the opinion of the Court and filed separate, concurring opinions. Four Justices dissented. 478 U.S., at 199 (opinion of Blackmun, J., joined by Brennan, Marshall, and Stevens, JJ.); *id.*, at 214 (opinion of Stevens, J., joined by Brennan and Marshall, JJ.).

The Court began its substantive discussion in *Bowers* as follows: "The issue presented is whether the Federal Constitution confers a fundamental right upon homosexuals to engage in sodomy and hence invalidates the laws of the many States that still make such conduct illegal and have done so for a very long time." *Id.*, at 190. That statement, we now conclude, discloses the Court's own failure to appreciate the extent of the liberty at stake. To say that the issue in *Bowers* was simply the right to engage in certain sexual conduct demeans the claim the individual put forward, just as it would demean a married couple were it to be said marriage is simply about the right to have sexual intercourse. The laws involved in *Bowers* and here are, to be sure, statutes that purport to do no more than prohibit a particular sexual act. Their penalties and purposes, though, have more far-reaching consequences, touching upon the most private human conduct, sexual behavior, and in the most private of places, the home. The statutes do seek to control a personal relationship that, whether or not entitled to formal recognition in the law, is within the liberty of persons to choose without being punished as criminals.

This, as a general rule, should counsel against attempts by the State, or a court, to define the meaning of the relationship or to set its boundaries absent injury to a person or abuse of an institution the law protects. It suffices for us to acknowledge that adults may choose to enter upon this relationship in the confines of their homes and their own private lives and still retain their dignity as free persons. When sexuality finds overt expression in intimate conduct with another person, the conduct can be but one element in a personal bond that is more enduring. The liberty protected by the Constitution allows homosexual persons the right to make this choice.

Having misapprehended the claim of liberty there presented to it, and thus stating the claim to be whether there is a fundamental right to engage in consensual sodomy, the *Bowers* Court said: "Proscriptions against that conduct have ancient roots." *Id.*, at 192. In academic writings, and in many of the scholarly *amicus* briefs filed to assist the Court in this case, there are fundamental criticisms of the historical premises relied upon by the majority and concurring opinions in *Bowers.* Brief for Cato Institute as *Amicus Curiae* 16-17; Brief for American Civil Liberties Union et al. as *Amici Curiae* 15-21; Brief for Professors of History et al. as *Amici Curiae* 3-10. We need not enter this debate in the attempt to reach a definitive historical judgment, but the following considerations counsel against adopting the definitive conclusions upon which *Bowers* placed such reliance.

At the outset it should be noted that there is no longstanding history in this country of laws directed at homosexual conduct as a distinct matter. . . .

It was not until the 1970's that any State singled out same-sex relations for criminal prosecution, and only nine States have done so. . . .

In summary, the historical grounds relied upon in *Bowers* are more complex than the majority opinion and the concurring opinion by Chief Justice Burger indicate. Their historical premises are not without doubt and, at the very least, are overstated.

It must be acknowledged, of course, that the Court in *Bowers* was making the broader point that for centuries there have been powerful voices to condemn homosexual conduct as immoral. The condemnation has been shaped by religious beliefs, conceptions of right and acceptable behavior, and respect for the traditional family. For many persons these are not trivial concerns but profound and deep convictions accepted as ethical and moral principles to which they aspire and which thus determine the course of their lives. These considerations do not answer the question before us, however. The issue is whether the majority may use the power of the State to enforce these views on the whole society through operation of the criminal law. "Our obligation is to define the liberty of all, not to mandate our own moral code." *Planned Parenthood of Southeastern Pa. v. Casey*, 505 U.S. 833, 850 (1992). . . .

Two principal cases decided after *Bowers* cast its holding into even more doubt. In *Planned Parenthood of Southeastern Pa. v. Casey*, 505 U.S. 833 (1992), the Court reaffirmed the substantive force of the liberty protected by the Due Process Clause. The *Casey* decision again confirmed that our laws and tradition afford constitutional protection to personal decisions relating to marriage, procreation, contraception, family relationships, child rearing, and education. *Id.*, at 851. In explaining the respect the Constitution demands for the autonomy of the person in making these choices, we stated as follows:

> "These matters, involving the most intimate and personal choices a person may make in a lifetime, choices central to personal dignity and autonomy, are central to the liberty protected by the Fourteenth Amendment. At the heart of liberty is the right to define one's own concept of existence, of meaning, of the universe, and of the mystery of human life. Beliefs about these matters could not define the attributes of personhood were they formed under compulsion of the State." *Ibid.*

Persons in a homosexual relationship may seek autonomy for these purposes, just as heterosexual persons do. The decision in *Bowers* would deny them this right.

The second post-*Bowers* case of principal relevance is *Romer v. Evans*, 517 U.S. 620 (1996). There the Court struck down class-based legislation directed at homosexuals as a violation of the Equal Protection Clause. *Romer* invalidated an amendment to Colorado's constitution which named as a solitary class persons who were homosexuals, lesbians, or bisexual either by "orientation, conduct, practices or relationships," *id.*, at 624 (internal quotation marks omitted), and deprived them of protection under state antidiscrimination laws. We concluded that the provision was "born of animosity toward the class of persons affected" and further that it had no rational relation to a legitimate governmental purpose. *Id.*, at 634. . . .

The foundations of *Bowers* have sustained serious erosion from our recent decisions in *Casey* and *Romer*. When our precedent has been thus weakened, criticism from other sources is of greater significance. In the United States criticism of *Bowers* has been substantial and continuing, disapproving of its reasoning in all respects, not just as to its historical assumptions. *See, e.g.,* C. Fried, *Order and Law: Arguing the Reagan Revolution—A Firsthand Account* 81-84 (1991); R. Posner, *Sex and Reason* 341-350 (1992). The courts of five different States have declined to follow it in interpreting provisions in their own state constitutions parallel to the Due Process Clause of the Fourteenth Amendment. . . .

Bowers was not correct when it was decided, and it is not correct today. It ought not to remain binding precedent. *Bowers v. Hardwick* should be and now is overruled.

The present case does not involve minors. It does not involve persons who might be injured or coerced or who are situated in relationships where consent might not easily be refused. It does not involve public conduct or prostitution. It does not involve whether the government must give formal recognition to any relationship that homosexual persons seek to enter. The case does involve two adults who, with full and mutual consent from each other, engaged in sexual practices common to a homosexual lifestyle. The petitioners are entitled to respect for their private lives. The State cannot demean their existence or control their destiny by making their private sexual conduct a crime. Their right to liberty under the Due Process Clause gives them the full right to engage in their conduct without intervention of the government. "It is a promise of the Constitution that there is a realm of personal liberty which the government may not enter." *Casey, supra,* at 847. The Texas statute furthers no legitimate state interest which can justify its intrusion into the personal and private life of the individual.

Had those who drew and ratified the Due Process Clauses of the Fifth Amendment or the Fourteenth Amendment known the components of liberty in its manifold possibilities, they might have been more specific. They did not presume to have this insight. They knew times can blind us to certain truths and later generations can see that laws once thought necessary and proper in fact serve only to oppress. As the Constitution endures, persons in every generation can invoke its principles in their own search for greater freedom.

The judgment of the Court of Appeals for the Texas Fourteenth District is reversed, and the case is remanded for further proceedings not inconsistent with this opinion.

It is so ordered.

CASE QUESTIONS

ROE v. WADE

1. Why do you think the *Roe* Court made it a point to determine whether limitations on abortion were constitutional without considering philosophy, personal experiences, or religious training?

2. Which Amendments are at the root of the right to privacy? Explain.

3. How does the Constitution define a "person"? According to the *Roe* Court, is a fetus a person?

4. Why does the Court refuse to determine when a life begins?

5. During which trimester may a woman have an abortion unencumbered by governmental regulation? Is there any period in which the government can limit a right to an abortion? Why?

6. What level of constitutional scrutiny is applied in determining if government action unconstitutionally infringes on the right to privacy?

LAWRENCE v. TEXAS

1. What were the rulings in Griswold v. Connecticut, 381 U.S. 479 (1965), and Eisenstadt v. Baird, 405 U.S. 438 (1972)? Why were these rulings important to the *Lawrence* decision?

2. How did the *Romer v. Evans* and *Planned Parenthood of Southeastern Pa. v. Casey* cases influence the Court's decision to overturn *Bowers v. Hardwick*?

3. Does the *Lawrence* case give any formal recognition to homosexual relationships? Explain.

4. Explain why the Supreme Court has concluded that privacy is a component of liberty.

· HYPOTHETICAL WITH ACCOMPANYING ANALYSIS

Hypothetical

Daniel D. Linquent was a trucker and was on the road 25 days a month. Because he had no real roots, his relationships were fleeting. He would hang out at the truck stops along his route, drink beer with other truckers, and, on what he considered a good night, take a woman back to his cab for a little intimacy. Well, it turned out that in three years of trucking, Daniel fathered nine children, all with different women. The mothers always had trouble pinning Daniel down since he was always on the road, and Daniel never acted as a parent to any of his kids. In fact, he never even paid child support. Each mother filed a lawsuit against Daniel. The courts, on each occasion, ordered Daniel to pay support. However, Daniel never made a single payment and ended up owing a total of $25,000 in child support arrearages.

The prosecutor charged Daniel with a violation of state statute §1-234, which criminalizes the failure to pay child support under a valid court order. Daniel was convicted in the criminal proceeding, and the judge sentenced him to six months in jail along with five years probation. As conditions of his probation, the judge (1) ordered Daniel to become current on his support to the nine kids that he already had; and (2) stated that Daniel could have no additional children during his probationary period until and unless he became current on his support obligations. Daniel appealed the conditions of probation, arguing that limiting his ability to procreate violated his right to privacy. Analyze whether the condition of Daniel's probation is constitutional.

Analysis

The right to procreate is a fundamental privacy right protected by the penumbras of the Constitution. Skinner v. Oklahoma, 316 U.S. 535 (1942); *see also* Griswold v. Connecticut, 381 U.S. 479 (1965). In Daniel's case, the requirement that he not have any more children until he is current on his child support infringes on Daniel's fundamental rights and freedoms. As such, it initially appears that the strict scrutiny test should be applied to determine the constitutionality of the limitation on Daniel's ability to procreate. However, because Daniel has been convicted of a crime, he will first be constitutionally incarcerated and lose his right to liberty. Merely by being in jail, Daniel will not have the ability to procreate during those six months. It is logical then to conclude that the right to privacy and procreation is no longer a fundamental right upon conviction of a crime. As such, the rational basis test should be applied in determining whether the limitations on Daniel's ability to procreate during a five-year probationary period are constitutional.

In applying the rational basis test, a rational relationship must exist between limiting Daniel's ability to procreate and a legitimate government interest. The state will likely argue that it is a legitimate government purpose to ensure that children are supported by their parents. If parents don't support their children, these children become victims, and the burden of ensuring their support falls on taxpayers. As such, there would be a rational relationship in not allowing Daniel to procreate, because if he had more children, it would only further diminish his ability to provide for all of his kids.

Even if the strict scrutiny test were to be applied, it is likely that providing for the welfare of children is a compelling government interest and that the condition of probation is narrowly tailored to that interest. The limitation would not be too broad because the prohibition on procreation would be lifted if Daniel caught up on his past due child support, and the condition would cease to exist once his probationary period ended.

Since Daniel committed a crime, his liberty may be suspended. Because privacy is a component of liberty and because the government has a rational reason to ensure that Daniel provides for his children, the government can likely infringe on Daniel's privacy in issuing conditions of probation limiting his right to procreate.

Betty was a burglar who always struck in the night when no one was home. She was very timid and slinky, just like a cat. She could pick locks with the greatest of ease and slip out unnoticed with a stash of cash and jewelry mere minutes after entry. Betty's most recent mark was the Jacobs's mansion. She knew that the Jacobs spent the winters in the tropics and that the house was empty. She had cased the mansion for a week until she was sure no one was home. She had studied the wiring going into the house for the alarm system and knew how to dismantle it from the outside. So, she set upon her plan. She cut the wires to the alarm and was inside the mansion and back out with the loot in minutes. However, as she was making her getaway, the police apprehended her. Betty had not known that the alarm system was also connected to the Wi-Fi and the police had been alerted immediately.

Betty was charged with burglary. In the State of Dystopia, a new law had recently been passed requiring anyone charged with a crime of violence or burglary to submit a DNA sample for entry into the Dystopia database. Betty did not want the government to have information related to her genetic makeup, including whether she had or was susceptible to certain medical conditions or diseases. She believed that this new law was unconstitutional, and she sued to prevent the DNA collection. Analyze whether the new law violates Betty's right to privacy.

1. Dave and June wanted to have a child, but each time June got pregnant she miscarried. So, their friend Pat agreed to be a gestational carrier. Dave's sperm and June's eggs would be fertilized in vitro, and the resulting embryo would be transferred to Pat for gestation and delivery. Pat would then give the baby back to Dave and June. However, the State of Dystopia has a law prohibiting having a baby via a gestational carrier. Does this law infringe upon Dave and June's right to privacy? Does a right to privacy still exist when a third party is involved?

2. Do you believe that when the government "drew and ratified the Due Process Clauses of the Fifth Amendment or the Fourteenth Amendment" it intended that the liberty interests in those clauses be applied to issues such as consensual homosexual sodomy or the right to die? *See Lawrence.* Explain.

3. Research challenge: What is the current state of *Roe v. Wade?* Does the case still stand as decided in 1973, or have subsequent Supreme Court rulings made any modifications or additions to the ruling?

4. Is an absolute late term abortion ban, prohibiting all abortions during the third trimester of pregnancy, constitutional, even if the life of the mother is at stake?

5. Mary is pregnant and having complications. Her doctor tells her that the baby will die during a vaginal delivery and that a Cesarean section is necessary for the baby to survive. Mary doesn't want any scars from a surgery. So, she refuses the Cesarean section. Can the government force Mary to have a Cesarean section? Why or why not?

6. Clarice has terminal cancer. Two doctors have told her she only has six months or less to live. She is in a terrible amount of pain. Clarice decides she wants to die now and not suffer any longer. She asks her doctor to give her something that will take her life quickly and without pain. However, there is a law in Clarice's state preventing a doctor from assisting in a suicide. Does this law infringe on Clarice's right to privacy? Why or why not?

7. Derrick wants to smoke pot recreationally and in the privacy of his own home. He believes that he is not hurting anyone. Does he have the right to privacy to use marijuana for personal recreational use? Why or why not? *See* Ravin v. State, 537 P.2d 494 (Alaska 1975).

8. Buster had HIV. The government passed a law requiring that anyone with HIV be sterilized to prevent a child from being born who is also infected. Is it constitutional to require Buster to be sterilized? Explain. *See* Buck v. Bell, 274 U.S. 200 (1927).

9. Lisa and Leslie are same-sex partners who wish to have a child using a new technology in which the mitochondrial DNA of Lisa's egg will be implanted into Leslie's egg, thereby fertilizing Leslie's egg. Assume the law prohibits such a procedure. Is this an unconstitutional limitation on Lisa and Leslie's right to privacy?

10. Dr. Laurie Navratalova has perfected the science of cloning. She has made ten embryos which are clones of herself. They are frozen in the lab, and she has not transplanted them into her uterus for gestation because current federal law prohibits cloning a human being. Assume she files a lawsuit asking the court to invalidate the law, arguing that it unconstitutionally burdens her right to privacy. Who will win the lawsuit? Explain why you reached that conclusion.

11. Research challenge: In 1990, 26-year-old Terri Schiavo had a heart attack and suffered severe brain damage. She was in a persistent vegetative state, but was conscious, for 15 years. Terri's husband wanted her feeding tube removed, and Terri's parents did not. Determine who won this case and why. How was the right to privacy specifically implicated in her case?

12. Do you think laws prohibiting homosexuals from marrying violate the right to privacy? Why or why not?

13. Research challenge: Assume that there is a state law requiring a motorcyclist to wear a helmet. Gary does not want to wear a helmet, believing that deciding whether or not to wear a helmet should be an individual's decision and

not the government's decision. What level of constitutional scrutiny would the court apply to Gary's legal challenge to the statute? Why?

14. Bryan, who has a long history of mental illness, has been charged with three counts of murder. While awaiting trial, Bryan has steadfastly refused to take his anti-psychotic medication. The state wants to force Bryan to take the medication because that's the only way he will be competent to stand trial. Which side will win? Why? *See* Sell v. United States, 539 U.S. 166 (2003).

15. Research challenge: Read the Court's full opinion in *Roe v. Wade*. What issue did the Court grapple with prior to reaching the merits of the case that implicated concepts discussed in Chapter 2 of this book dealing with the courts?

True/False

1. The Ninth Amendment was never considered when concluding that the Constitution and its Amendments protected a person's privacy from government interference.

2. Privacy is a component of liberty.

3. A person's privacy rights may be constitutionally limited after being convicted of a crime.

4. The government may prohibit consensual sexual conduct between two adults of the same sex.

5. The Supreme Court has determined that because there is a right to privacy, homosexuals have the right to marry.

Multiple Choice

6. Major emphasis was given to which of the following when the Supreme Court determined that the Constitution and its Amendments protected an individual from governmental infringement on privacy?

   A. The Fourth Amendment
   B. The Fifth Amendment & Fourteenth Amendment Due Process Clauses
   C. The Ninth Amendment
   D. All of the above

7. The following limitation(s) on abortion are unconstitutional:

   A. Requiring a wife to notify the father of the fetus 24 hours before procuring an abortion.
   B. Requiring a 14-year-old to get parental consent or a court order before procuring an abortion.
   C. Requiring a clinic to provide educational information regarding abortion to a woman, and requiring a woman to wait 24 hours before being able to procure the abortion.
   D. All of the above.

8. Courts have generally declined to declare that a right to privacy has been unconstitutionally infringed in which of the following cases?

   A. Requiring motorists and passengers to wear seatbelts.
   B. Requiring motorcyclists to wear helmets.
   C. Prohibiting doctor-assisted suicide.
   D. All of the above.

9. The government has started a Web site listing the names and addresses of everyone who has tested positive for HIV.

   A. The posting of such names is constitutional because there is a compelling government interest in preventing the spread of HIV, and posting such names is narrowly tailored to a compelling government interest.
   B. The posting of such names is constitutional because there is no right to privacy when it comes to the spread of communicable diseases.
   C. The posting of such names is constitutional because there is a rational reason for doing so, and that rational reason is trying to prevent the spread of HIV.
   D. The posting of such names is unconstitutional because, although there may be a compelling interest in preventing the spread of HIV, the posting of names is not narrowly tailored to further that interest.

10. In *Roe v. Wade*, the Supreme Court:

   A. Decided that a fetus was a person.
   B. Decided that a fetus was not a person.
   C. Did not decide if a fetus was or was not a person.
   D. Decided that the fetus was a person only after the first trimester of pregnancy.

Chapter 7
Equal Protection

> "No state shall make or enforce any law which shall abridge the privileges or immunities of citizens of the United States . . . nor deny to any person within its jurisdiction the equal protection of the laws."
>
> **—Amendment XIV**

INTRODUCTION

On July 4, 1776, in the Declaration of Independence, the Continental Congress declared, "We hold these truths to be self-evident, that all men are created equal, that they are endowed by their Creator with certain unalienable Rights, that among these are Life, Liberty and the pursuit of Happiness." Although the desire for equality significantly motivated the colonies to declare independence from England, in 1789, the states ratified the United States Constitution, a document which did not expressly capture the concept of equality. In fact, the right to equal protection of the laws was not made explicit in our Constitution until the Fourteenth Amendment was passed in 1868 with the hope of extinguishing the practices of slavery. From our country's infancy until well into the twentieth century, the concept that "all men are created equal" really only applied to white men. Women and racial minorities were excluded from equal protection of the laws.

The body of law emanating from the Supreme Court and explaining what equal protection is and how it should be applied under certain circumstances has evolved quite a bit since the Fourteenth Amendment was passed. We have gone from a nation of slavery, to a nation that allowed for segregation under Plessy v. Ferguson, 163 U.S. 537 (1896), and its "separate but equal" doctrine that condoned separate public facilities for African Americans and Caucasians, such as separate water fountains, separate schools, and separate seats on the bus, to a nation where, under a strict scrutiny standard, separate can never be equal in racial matters.

Often, we traditionally think of equal protection in the context of racial discrimination, but the protection extends to any circumstance in which the government classifies people and treats that class differently. Courts are still addressing issues related to equal protection of the laws in numerous other

103

circumstances, ranging from national origin discrimination, gender discrimination, sexual orientation discrimination, age discrimination, wealth discrimination, and so on. The bottom line is that under equal protection, two similarly situated people must be treated the same. But, if two people are situated differently, then they can be treated differently.

The Supreme Court has established a framework for equal protection analysis in the form of the levels of constitutional scrutiny discussed in Chapter 1. Discrimination against members of a suspect class and denial of fundamental rights to any class are subjected to strict scrutiny, while gender and illegitimacy discrimination are subjected to middle level scrutiny, and discrimination against those of a non-suspect class is reviewed under the rational basis test.

In addition to these levels of constitutional scrutiny that are essential to equal protection analysis, there are some additional things that you should note in your study of equal protection. First, the Fourteenth Amendment only applies to state action—not federal action and not to private action. Does that mean that the federal government does not have to provide citizens equal protection of the laws? No, it does not. The Supreme Court has interpreted the substantive due process provisions of the Fifth Amendment to afford the same equal protection at the federal level. Bolling v. Sharpe, 347 U.S. 497 (1954). Second, state constitutions can provide greater protections under state laws than the U.S. Constitution. For instance, the federal government never passed an Equal Rights Amendment guaranteeing women and men the same protections under the laws. However, many states have amended their constitutions to guaranty such protections. For example, under Maryland's Equal Rights Amendment, gender is a suspect class, and strict scrutiny is applied when the state makes a classification based upon gender and discriminates against that class. Whereas, the Supreme Court only applies middle-level scrutiny to a gender discrimination analysis under the U.S. Constitution.

STUDENT *Checklist*

Equal Protection

1. Determine if the **government** made a **classification**.

2. Determine if the **government** is **discriminating against a class** per the language of a statute or in its application of a law.

3. Determine if it is a **state** government or **federal** government that is discriminating against the class.

■ If a **state** government is discriminating, then the **Equal Protection Clause of the Fourteenth Amendment** applies.

■ If the **federal** government is discriminating, then the equal protection analysis must be made under the **Due Process Clause of the Fifth Amendment**.

4. Choose the appropriate level of constitutional scrutiny:

■ Apply **strict scrutiny** when the classification is based upon a **suspect class (race or national origin)** or when any class is unable to exercise a **fundamental right**.

■ Apply **middle-level scrutiny** when the classification is based upon **gender** or **illegitimacy**.

■ Apply **lower-level scrutiny** when the classification is **not** based upon gender, illegitimacy or suspect class or does not impose on the class' ability to exercise a fundamental right.

SUPREME COURT CASES

BROWN v. BOARD OF EDUCATION OF TOPEKA, KANSAS, 347 U.S. 483 (1954)

[African-American students, seeking admission to whites-only public schools, challenged Kansas's segregation in public schools. Kansas asserted that it treated both races equally because it provided similar facilities and resources to white and non-white schools. The African-American students asserted that separate can never be equal and that such segregation was unconstitutional.]

Mr. CHIEF JUSTICE WARREN delivered the opinion of the Court.

. . . In the South, the movement toward free common schools, supported by general taxation, had not yet taken hold. Education of white children was largely in the hands of private groups. Education of Negroes was almost non-existent, and practically all of the race were illiterate. In fact, any education of Negroes was forbidden by law in some states. Today, in contrast, many Negroes have achieved outstanding success in the arts and sciences as well as in the business and professional world. It is true that public school education at the time of the Amendment had advanced further in the North, but the effect of the Amendment on Northern States was generally ignored in the congressional debates. Even in the North, the conditions of public education did not approximate those existing today. The curriculum was usually rudimentary; ungraded schools were common in rural areas; the school term was but three months a year in many states; and compulsory school attendance was virtually unknown. As a consequence, it is not surprising that there should be so little in the history of the Fourteenth Amendment relating to its intended effect on public education.

In the first cases in this Court construing the Fourteenth Amendment, decided shortly after its adoption, the Court interpreted it as proscribing all state-imposed discriminations against the Negro race. The doctrine of "separate but equal" did not make its appearance in this Court until 1896 in the case of *Plessy v. Ferguson*, supra, involving not education but transportation. American courts have since labored with the doctrine for over half a century. In this Court, there have been six cases involving the "separate but equal" doctrine in the field of public education. . . .

In the instant cases, that question is directly presented. Here, . . . there are findings below that the Negro and white schools involved have been equalized, or are being equalized, with respect to buildings, curricula, qualifications and salaries of teachers, and other "tangible" factors. Our decision, therefore, cannot turn on merely a comparison of these tangible factors in the Negro and white schools involved in each of the cases. We must look instead to the effect of segregation itself on public education.

In approaching this problem, we cannot turn the clock back to 1868 when the Amendment was adopted, or even to 1896 when *Plessy v. Ferguson* was written. We must consider public education in the light of its full development and its present place in American life throughout the Nation. Only in this way can it be determined if segregation in public schools deprives these plaintiffs of the equal protection of the laws.

* * *

We come then to the question presented: Does segregation of children in public schools solely on the basis of race, even though the physical facilities and other "tangible" factors may be equal, deprive the children of the minority group of equal educational opportunities? We believe that it does.

In *Sweatt v. Painter*, supra, in finding that a segregated law school for Negroes could not provide them equal educational opportunities, this Court relied in large part on "those qualities which are incapable of objective measurement but which make for greatness in a law school." In *McLaurin v. Oklahoma State Regents*, supra, the Court, in requiring that a Negro admitted to a white graduate school be treated like all other students, again resorted to intangible considerations: ". . . his ability to study, to engage in discussions and exchange views with other students, and, in general, to learn his profession." Such considerations apply with added force to children in grade and high schools. To separate them from others of similar age and qualifications solely because of their race generates a feeling of inferiority as to their status in the community that may affect their hearts and minds in a way unlikely ever to be undone. The effect of this separation on their educational opportunities was well stated by a finding in the Kansas case by a court which nevertheless felt compelled to rule against the Negro plaintiffs:

> "Segregation of white and colored children in public schools has a detrimental effect upon the colored children. The impact is greater when it has the sanction of the law; for the policy of separating the races is usually interpreted as denoting the inferiority of the negro group. A sense of inferiority affects the motivation of a child to learn. Segregation with the sanction of law, therefore, has a tendency to [retard] the educational and mental development of negro children and to deprive them of some of the benefits they would receive in a racial[ly] integrated school system."

Whatever may have been the extent of psychological knowledge at the time of *Plessy v. Ferguson*, this finding is amply supported by modern authority. Any language in *Plessy v. Ferguson* contrary to this finding is rejected.

We conclude that in the field of public education the doctrine of "separate but equal" has no place. Separate educational facilities are inherently unequal. Therefore, we hold that the plaintiffs and others similarly situated for whom the actions have been brought are, by reason of the segregation complained of, deprived of the equal protection of the laws guaranteed by the Fourteenth Amendment. This disposition makes unnecessary any discussion whether such segregation also violates the Due Process Clause of the Fourteenth Amendment.

Because these are class actions, because of the wide applicability of this decision, and because of the great variety of local conditions, the formulation of decrees in these cases presents problems of considerable complexity. On reargument, the consideration of appropriate relief was necessarily subordinated to the primary question—the constitutionality of segregation in public education. We have now announced that such segregation is a denial of the equal protection of the laws. . . .

It is so ordered.

GRUTTER v. BOLLINGER, 539 U.S. 306 (2003)

[A Caucasian student who was denied admission to the University of Michigan School of Law challenged the law school's affirmative-action based admission policy. The admission policy focused on academic ability and allowed race, among many other things, to be considered in admitting a student into the law school. The affirmative action policy was designed to help increase diversity in law school classes and overall student success. The plaintiff believed that other less-qualified students were admitted and that race was a "predominant factor" in her not being admitted. School officials testified that there were no racial quotas but that statistics were reviewed daily to "to ensure that a critical mass of underrepresented minority students would be reached so as to realize the educational benefits of a diverse student body." The officials also testified that the critical mass could not be reached simply by admitting on the basis of GPA and LSAT scores.]

Justice O'CONNOR delivered the opinion of the Court.

This case requires us to decide whether the use of race as a factor in student admissions by the University of Michigan Law School (Law School) is unlawful.

* * *

We granted certiorari . . . to resolve the disagreement among the Courts of Appeals on a question of national importance: Whether diversity is a compelling interest that can justify the narrowly tailored use of race in selecting applicants for admission to public universities. . . .

We last addressed the use of race in public higher education over 25 years ago. In the landmark [Regents of the University of California v.] *Bakke* [, 438 U.S. 265 (1978)] case, we reviewed a racial set-aside program that reserved 16 out of 100 seats in a medical school class for members of certain minority groups. . . . The decision produced six separate opinions, none of which commanded a majority of the Court. . . . The only holding for the Court in *Bakke* was that a "State has a substantial interest that legitimately may be served by a properly devised admissions program involving the competitive consideration of race and ethnic origin." Thus, we reversed that part of the lower court's judgment that enjoined the university "from any consideration of the race of any applicant."

Since this Court's splintered decision in *Bakke*, Justice Powell's opinion announcing the judgment of the Court has served as the touchstone for constitutional analysis of race-conscious admissions policies. Public and private universities across the Nation have modeled their own admissions programs on Justice Powell's views on permissible race-conscious policies. . . .

[F]or the reasons set out below, today we endorse Justice Powell's view that student body diversity is a compelling state interest that can justify the use of race in university admissions.

The Equal Protection Clause provides that no State shall "deny to any person within its jurisdiction the equal protection of the laws." U.S. Const.,

Amdt. 14, §2. Because the Fourteenth Amendment "protect[s] *persons*, not *groups*," all "governmental action based on race—a *group* classification long recognized as in most circumstances irrelevant and therefore prohibited— should be subjected to detailed judicial inquiry to ensure that the *personal* right to equal protection of the laws has not been infringed." We are a "free people whose institutions are founded upon the doctrine of equality." It follows from that principle that "government may treat people differently because of their race only for the most compelling reasons."

We have held that all racial classifications imposed by government "must be analyzed by a reviewing court under strict scrutiny." This means that such classifications are constitutional only if they are narrowly tailored to further compelling governmental interests. "Absent searching judicial inquiry into the justification for such race-based measures," we have no way to determine what "classifications are 'benign' or 'remedial' and what classifications are in fact motivated by illegitimate notions of racial inferiority or simple racial politics." We apply strict scrutiny to all racial classifications to "smoke out" illegitimate uses of race by assuring that [government] is pursuing a goal important enough to warrant use of a highly suspect tool."

Strict scrutiny is not "strict in theory, but fatal in fact." Although all governmental uses of race are subject to strict scrutiny, not all are invalidated by it. As we have explained, "whenever the government treats any person unequally because of his or her race, that person has suffered an injury that falls squarely within the language and spirit of the Constitution's guarantee of equal protection." But that observation "says nothing about the ultimate validity of any particular law; that determination is the job of the court applying strict scrutiny." Then race-based action is necessary to further a compelling governmental interest, such action does not violate the constitutional guarantee of equal protection so long as the narrow-tailoring requirement is also satisfied.

Context matters when reviewing race-based governmental action under the Equal Protection Clause. . . . Not every decision influenced by race is equally objectionable and strict scrutiny is designed to provide a framework for carefully examining the importance and the sincerity of the reasons advanced by the governmental decisionmaker for the use of race in that particular context.

With these principles in mind, we turn to the question whether the Law School's use of race is justified by a compelling state interest. . . . [T]he Law School asks us to recognize, in the context of higher education, a compelling state interest in student body diversity.

We first wish to dispel the notion that the Law School's argument has been foreclosed, either expressly or implicitly, by our affirmative-action cases decided since *Bakke*. . . . Today, we hold that the Law School has a compelling interest in attaining a diverse student body.

* * *

Even in the limited circumstance when drawing racial distinctions is permissible to further a compelling state interest, government is still "constrained in how it may pursue that end: [T]he means chosen to accomplish the [government's] asserted purpose must be specifically and narrowly framed to accomplish that purpose." The purpose of the narrow tailoring requirement is to ensure that "the means chosen 'fit' . . . th[e] compelling goal so closely that there is little or no possibility that the motive for the classification was illegitimate racial prejudice or stereotype."

Since *Bakke*, we have had no occasion to define the contours of the narrow-tailoring inquiry with respect to race-conscious university admissions programs. That inquiry must be calibrated to fit the distinct issues raised by the use of race to achieve student body diversity in public higher education. . . .

To be narrowly tailored, a race-conscious admissions program cannot use a quota system—it cannot "insulat[e] each category of applicants with certain desired qualifications from competition with all other applicants." Instead, a university may consider race or ethnicity only as a " 'plus' in a particular applicant's file," without "insulat[ing] the individual from comparison with all other candidates for the available seats." In other words, an admissions program must be "flexible enough to consider all pertinent elements of diversity in light of the particular qualifications of each applicant, and to place them on the same footing for consideration, although not necessarily according them the same weight."

We find that the Law School's admissions program bears the hallmarks of a narrowly tailored plan. As Justice Powell made clear in *Bakke*, truly individualized consideration demands that race be used in a flexible, nonmechanical way. It follows from this mandate that universities cannot establish quotas for members of certain racial groups or put members of those groups on separate admissions tracks. Nor can universities insulate applicants who belong to certain racial or ethnic groups from the competition for admission. Universities can, however, consider race or ethnicity more flexibly as a "plus" factor in the context of individualized consideration of each and every applicant.

We are satisfied that the Law School's admissions program, like the Harvard plan described by Justice Powell, does not operate as a quota. Properly understood, a "quota" is a program in which a certain fixed number or proportion of opportunities are "reserved exclusively for certain minority groups." Quotas " 'impose a fixed number or percentage which must be attained, or which cannot be exceeded,' " and "insulate the individual from comparison with all other candidates for the available seats."

The Law School's goal of attaining a critical mass of underrepresented minority students does not transform its program into a quota. As the Harvard plan described by Justice Powell recognized, there is of course "some relationship between numbers and achieving the benefits to be derived from a diverse student body, and between numbers and providing a reasonable environment for those students admitted." "[S]ome attention to numbers," without more, does not transform a flexible admissions system into a rigid quota. Nor, as Justice Kennedy posits, does the Law School's consultation of the "daily reports," which keep track of the racial and ethnic composition of the class (as well as of residency and gender), "suggest[ ] there was no further attempt at individual review save for race itself" during the final stages of the admissions process. See *post*, at 6 (dissenting opinion). To the contrary, the Law School's admissions officers testified without contradiction that they never gave race any more or less weight based on the information contained in these reports. Moreover, as Justice Kennedy concedes, see *post*, at 4, between 1993 and 2000, the number of African-American, Latino, and Native-American students in each class at the Law School varied from 13.5 to 20.1 percent, a range inconsistent with a quota.

The Chief Justice believes that the Law School's policy conceals an attempt to achieve racial balancing, and cites admissions data to contend that the Law School discriminates among different groups within the critical mass. But, as The Chief Justice concedes, the number of underrepresented minority students who ultimately enroll in the Law School differs substantially from their representation in the applicant pool and varies considerably for each group from year to year.

That a race-conscious admissions program does not operate as a quota does not, by itself, satisfy the requirement of individualized consideration. When using race as a "plus" factor in university admissions, a university's admissions program must remain flexible enough to ensure that each applicant is evaluated as an individual and not in a way that makes an applicant's race or ethnicity the defining feature of his or her application. The importance of this individualized consideration in the context of a race-conscious admissions program is paramount.

Here, the Law School engages in a highly individualized, holistic review of each applicant's file, giving serious consideration to all the ways an applicant might contribute to a diverse educational environment. The Law School affords this individualized consideration to applicants of all races. There is no policy, either *de jure* or *de facto*, of automatic acceptance or rejection based on any single "soft" variable. Unlike the program at issue in *Gratz* v. *Bollinger, ante*, the Law School awards no mechanical, predetermined diversity "bonuses" based on race or ethnicity. Like the Harvard plan, the Law School's admissions policy "is flexible enough to consider all pertinent elements of diversity in light of the particular qualifications of each applicant, and to place them on the same footing for consideration, although not necessarily according them the same weight."

We also find that, like the Harvard plan Justice Powell referenced in *Bakke*, the Law School's race-conscious admissions program adequately ensures that all factors that may contribute to student body diversity are meaningfully considered alongside race in admissions decisions. With respect to the use of race itself, all underrepresented minority students admitted by the Law School have been deemed qualified. By virtue of our Nation's struggle with racial inequality, such students are both likely to have experiences of particular importance to the Law School's mission, and less likely to be admitted in meaningful numbers on criteria that ignore those experiences.

The Law School does not, however, limit in any way the broad range of qualities and experiences that may be considered valuable contributions to student body diversity. To the contrary, the 1992 policy makes clear "[t]here are many possible bases for diversity admissions," and provides examples of admittees who have lived or traveled widely abroad, are fluent in several languages, have overcome personal adversity and family hardship, have exceptional records of extensive community service, and have had successful careers in other fields. The Law School seriously considers each "applicant's promise of making a notable contribution to the class by way of a particular strength, attainment, or characteristic—*e.g.*, an unusual intellectual achievement, employment experience, nonacademic performance, or personal background." All applicants have the opportunity to highlight their own potential diversity contributions through the submission of a personal statement, letters of recommendation, and an essay describing the ways in which the applicant will contribute to the life and diversity of the Law School.

What is more, the Law School actually gives substantial weight to diversity factors besides race. The Law School frequently accepts nonminority applicants with grades and test scores lower than underrepresented minority applicants (and other nonminority applicants) who are rejected. . . . This shows that the Law School seriously weighs many other diversity factors besides race that can make a real and dispositive difference for nonminority applicants as well. By this flexible approach, the Law School sufficiently takes into account, in practice as well as in theory, a wide variety of characteristics besides race and ethnicity that contribute to a diverse student body. Justice Kennedy speculates that "race is likely outcome determinative for many members of minority groups" who do not fall within the upper range of LSAT scores and grades. But the same could be said of the Harvard plan discussed approvingly by Justice Powell in *Bakke*, and indeed of any plan that uses race as one of many factors.

Petitioner and the United States argue that the Law School's plan is not narrowly tailored because race-neutral means exist to obtain the educational benefits of student body diversity that the Law School seeks. We disagree. Narrow tailoring does not require exhaustion of every conceivable race-neutral alternative. Nor does it require a university to choose between maintaining a reputation for excellence or fulfilling a commitment to provide educational opportunities to members of all racial groups. . . . Narrow tailoring does, however, require serious, good faith consideration of workable race-neutral alternatives that will achieve the diversity the university seeks. . . .

We agree with the Court of Appeals that the Law School sufficiently considered workable race-neutral alternatives. The District Court took the Law School to task for failing to consider race-neutral alternatives such as "using a lottery system" or "decreasing the emphasis for all applicants on undergraduate GPA and LSAT scores." But these alternatives would require a dramatic sacrifice of diversity, the academic quality of all admitted students, or both.

The Law School's current admissions program considers race as one factor among many, in an effort to assemble a student body that is diverse in ways broader than race. Because a lottery would make that kind of nuanced judgment impossible, it would effectively sacrifice all other educational values, not to mention every other kind of diversity. So too with the suggestion that the Law School simply lower admissions standards for all students, a drastic remedy that would require the Law School to become a much different institution and sacrifice a vital component of its educational mission. The United States advocates "percentage plans," recently adopted by public undergraduate institutions in Texas, Florida, and California to guarantee admission to all students above a certain class-rank threshold in every high school in the State. The United States does not, however, explain how such plans could work for graduate and professional schools. Moreover, even assuming such plans are race-neutral, they may preclude the university from conducting the individualized assessments necessary to assemble a student body that is not just racially diverse, but diverse along all the qualities valued by the university. We are satisfied that the Law School adequately considered race-neutral alternatives currently capable of producing a critical mass without forcing the Law School to abandon the academic selectivity that is the cornerstone of its educational mission.

We acknowledge that "there are serious problems of justice connected with the idea of preference itself." Narrow tailoring, therefore, requires that a race-conscious admissions program not unduly harm members of any racial group. Even remedial race-based governmental action generally "remains subject to continuing oversight to assure that it will work the least harm possible to other innocent persons competing for the benefit." To be narrowly tailored, a race-conscious admissions program must not "unduly burden individuals who are not members of the favored racial and ethnic groups."

We are satisfied that the Law School's admissions program does not. Because the Law School considers "all pertinent elements of diversity," it can (and does) select nonminority applicants who have greater potential to enhance student body diversity over underrepresented minority applicants. As Justice Powell recognized in *Bakke*, so long as a race-conscious admissions program uses race as a "plus" factor in the context of individualized consideration, a rejected applicant "will not have been foreclosed from all consideration for that seat simply because he was not the right color or had the wrong surname. . . . His qualifications would have been weighed fairly and competitively, and he would have no basis to complain of unequal treatment under the Fourteenth Amendment."

We agree that, in the context of its individualized inquiry into the possible diversity contributions of all applicants, the Law School's race-conscious admissions program does not unduly harm nonminority applicants.

We are mindful, however, that "[a] core purpose of the Fourteenth Amendment was to do away with all governmentally imposed discrimination based on race." Accordingly, race-conscious admissions policies must be limited in time. This requirement reflects that racial classifications, however compelling their goals, are potentially so dangerous that they may be employed no more broadly than the interest demands. Enshrining a permanent justification for racial preferences would offend this fundamental equal protection principle. We see no reason to exempt race-conscious admissions programs from the requirement that all governmental use of race must have a logical end point. The Law School, too, concedes that all "race-conscious programs must have reasonable durational limits."

In the context of higher education, the durational requirement can be met by sunset provisions in race-conscious admissions policies and periodic reviews to determine whether racial preferences are still necessary to achieve student body diversity. . . .

The requirement that all race-conscious admissions programs have a termination point "assure[s] all citizens that the deviation from the norm of equal treatment of all racial and ethnic groups is a temporary matter, a measure taken in the service of the goal of equality itself."

We take the Law School at its word that it would "like nothing better than to find a race-neutral admissions formula" and will terminate its race-conscious admissions program as soon as practicable. It has been 25 years since Justice Powell first approved the use of race to further an interest in student body diversity in the context of public higher education. Since that time, the number of minority applicants with high grades and test scores has indeed increased. We expect that 25 years from now, the use of racial preferences will no longer be necessary to further the interest approved today.

In summary, the Equal Protection Clause does not prohibit the Law School's narrowly tailored use of race in admissions decisions to further a compelling interest in obtaining the educational benefits that flow from a diverse student body. . . . The judgment of the Court of Appeals for the Sixth Circuit, accordingly, is affirmed.

It is so ordered.

CASE QUESTIONS

BROWN v. BOARD OF EDUCATION

1. When determining whether segregation in schools was constitutional, why did the Court not consider the state of education in the United States when the Fourteenth Amendment was passed or when *Plessy v. Ferguson* was decided?

2. Per the Court's decision, why is the government's role in providing education to the public so important?

3. Explain what the Court considered to be the detrimental effects of separating children by race in education.

4. Explain the basis for the Court's decision to overturn *Plessy v. Ferguson.*

5. Why can separate never be equal?

GRUTTER v. BOLLINGER

1. Did the Supreme Court determine that racial diversity in the student body is a compelling government interest? Why or why not?

2. How did the *Grutter* Court treat the *Bakke* decision?

3. Why did the Court determine that the law school's admissions program did not operate as a quota?

4. What diversity factors did the law school consider other than race?

5. What is the core purpose of the Fourteenth Amendment?

6. Why did the law school have a compelling government interest to enroll a critical mass of minority students?

HYPOTHETICAL WITH ACCOMPANYING ANALYSIS

Hypothetical

Only males have to register for the military draft. Assume that the military has begun conscripting those registered for the draft. Some of those conscripted serve in non-combat areas and some serve in combat areas. All of those drafted have had to put their education and careers on hold while serving two-year tours of duty. Assume that 20 percent of those drafted have either died during their military service or suffered significant and permanent war injuries. Women are not required to register for the draft and are not subject to conscription. Analyze whether the male-only military draft is constitutional.

Analysis

Although there are strong arguments that women and men should be treated equally, under Supreme Court precedent, gender discrimination in military matters will not violate equal protection as there is an important governmental interest being advanced by conscripting only men. As this is a federal action, the equal protection principles of the Substantive Due Process Clause of the Fifth Amendment would apply. Also, because this is a matter involving gender classification, the issue should be analyzed using middle-level scrutiny. Notably, in the case of Rostker v. Goldberg, 453 U.S. 57 (1981), which reviewed draft registration but not actual conscription, the Court was not explicit in the level of scrutiny it employed. Rather, it implied that it was using middle-level scrutiny as established in Craig v. Boren, 429 U.S. 190 (1976).

The Court has traditionally given great deference to Congress in areas related to national security and military affairs. It has even limited the application of due process in such matters. *Rostker, supra.* The important government interest is to protect national security in wartime by mobilizing a combat force and replacing combat forces. By statute, women may not serve on combat missions. As such, women and men are not similarly situated and equal protection would not apply. Even if it did apply, there would be at least an important, if not compelling interest in national security that would be served by an all-male draft.

Of course, there are strong arguments against such a conclusion, which impeach rationality of the position that women cannot serve in combat. Some of the current day facts that undermine this position are that some women are as physically strong and able as men and that combat eligibility standards should be gender-neutral and based only on demonstrated physical ability. Also, any arguments that women are not mentally prepared for battle situations can be contravened by examples of women who were not serving in combat positions but were engaged in combat and earned medals of honor for their performance in such situations. Another argument that women should be allowed to serve in combat positions is that because of today's technology and mechanization of war, physical strength is no longer necessary to be an effective military combatant.

Even if the Court were to conclude that women could perform equally, because of such deference to the government in dealing with military and security issues and because strict scrutiny is not applicable, it is still possible that the Court would continue to conclude that male-only conscription does not violate equal protection and is constitutional.

The Human Genome Project has revealed genetic markers that will indicate a person's likelihood of being afflicted with certain physical and mental health conditions. The Maine State Police Department had a high turnover rate in its employees because of medical conditions that prevented officers from working in their jobs, which required them to be physically able to pursue and subdue violent criminals. This high turnover rate caused the state to incur high training costs for replacement officers. At the time, training cost the state approximately $500,000 per officer. Assume that the State of Maine has issued a law requiring all persons applying for jobs as police officers to submit to genetic testing and that the Maine State Police Department must reject all candidates for whom such tests reveal a certainty or strong likelihood that a candidate will become afflicted by a laundry list of health conditions. Schizophrenia, a mental disease, was on the list. It was included because, in the recent past, a police officer suffering from undiagnosed schizophrenia had a psychotic breakdown and shot numerous innocent civilians with his service weapon. Four well-qualified candidates were denied employment because they had genetic markers for schizophrenia. They filed suit, alleging that denial of employment violated their due process rights. Experts at trial uniformly testified that the genetic marker for schizophrenia meant that a person was likely, though not certain, to suffer from the disease, and that the severity of the symptoms may vary. Analyze the candidates' likelihood of success in their lawsuit.

DISCUSSION QUESTIONS

1. Research challenge: The *Brown* case that you read above is considered by legal scholars as "*Brown 1*." What is "*Brown 2*"? What was the Supreme Court's ruling in "*Brown 2*"?

2. Assume that the State of Alabama passed a law prohibiting anyone who has had sex reassignment surgery from being employed as a public school teacher. This law caused several school districts to fire teachers who had had the surgery in the past. Analyze this law to determine if it violates the Equal Protection Clause.

3. Research challenge: What is the Harvey Milk School in New York City? Do you think that it is constitutional or unconstitutional for the local government to create such a school for this special class of students? What level of constitutional scrutiny should be applied in your analysis of constitutionality? See *Brown v. Board of Education of Topeka Kansas*, above, and *United States v. Virginia*, 518 U.S. 515 (1986), for guidance.

4. With regard to the Harvey Milk School, irrespective of whether such a school is constitutional, do you think that such a school is a good idea?

5. Does it violate the Equal Protection Clause for a state's statutory rape statute to only hold adult males criminally responsible for having sexual intercourse with minor females and not to hold adult females criminally responsible for having sexual intercourse with minor males? Why or why not?

6. Is it constitutional for a state to establish an alcohol drinking age of 21? Why or why not?

7. Research challenge: Prior to becoming a lawyer and then a Supreme Court Justice, Thurgood Marshall was denied admission to what law school on the basis of his race?

8. Do you think that the Court has appropriately determined that gender is not a suspect classification and that strict scrutiny should not be applied to gender discrimination by the government?

9. The federal government has passed the Defense of Marriage Act (DOMA). One provision of the act refuses to recognize legally valid same-sex marriages from states that allow such marriages. So, for example, a same-sex spouse would not be entitled to his or her spouse's federal Social Security benefits. Analyze the constitutionality of DOMA. What level of constitutional scrutiny should be applied to your analysis and why?

10. Research challenge: What is the difference between "de jure" and "de facto" discrimination?

11. Assume that the State of Utopia allows a doctor to "pull the plug" on a terminally ill patient but not to administer a lethal dose of medication to hasten the death of a terminally ill patient. Is this an equal protection violation? Why or why not? What level of constitutional scrutiny did you apply to your analysis?

12. Some states require police officers to retire at age 50. Would there be a sufficient correlation between the trait of age and the anticipated harm to make the rule constitutional or is the statute over-inclusive or under-inclusive?

13. Research challenge: What was the last case in which a racial classification survived strict scrutiny by the Supreme Court? What was that case about, and why did the court allow for such racial discrimination?

14. Research challenge: What is miscegenation? Did anti-miscegenation statutes violate equal protection? What Supreme Court case supports your conclusion?

15. Read the case of Bush v. Gore, 531 U.S. 98 (2000). Explain how equal protection was a basis for the Court's decision. Do you agree with the majority or the dissent?

16. The military will not allow women to hold combat positions. Explain why you think this prohibition does or does not violate equal protection.

17. Does your state have an Equal Rights Amendment to its constitution? What level of scrutiny is applied to gender discrimination issues under your state's constitution?

18. Because of bad economic times, the State of Massachusetts has cut back on its commuter train service. The cutback has adversely impacted blind commuters who have no other alternative means of transportation. Is this de jure or de facto discrimination? Does the state's action violate the Equal Protection Clause?

True/False

1. It does not violate equal protection for a private country club to refuse membership to females.

2. According to the Supreme Court, separating students in public education on the basis of race imposes a badge of inferiority on those in the racial minority.

3. If a classification is not a suspect classification but is a classification of a non-suspect group that burdens a fundamental right, strict scrutiny will apply to an equal protection analysis.

4. A legislature passes a statute requiring all potential voters to pass an English fluency test to be registered to vote. The purpose for creating this statute is to ensure that voters properly understand the ballot, which is written in English. However, the effect of such statute is to prevent native Spanish speakers who would otherwise be eligible to vote from voting. The strict scrutiny test would apply to determining if there is an equal protection violation because there is a fundamental right at issue.

5. A legislature passes a statute requiring all potential voters to pass an English fluency test to be registered to vote. The purpose for creating this statute is to ensure that voters properly understand the ballot, which is written in English. However, the effect of such statute is to prevent native Spanish speakers who would otherwise be eligible to vote from voting. The statute would not violate the Equal Protection Clause because the government was never motivated by animosity toward native Spanish speakers and was actually motivated by the desire to have a well-informed electorate.

Multiple Choice

6. Autoworks Unlimited, a corporation organized under the laws of the State of Maryland, has a policy in which it will not hire anyone with a physical handicap.

   A. The Equal Protection Clause of the Fourteenth Amendment would apply because it is state discrimination.
   B. The Due Process Clause of the Fifth Amendment would apply because it is federal discrimination.
   C. There are no constitutional implications because it is a private company that is discriminating.
   D. None of the above.

7. Key State Prison is afflicted with gang violence. Specifically, a gang comprised of Latin Americans battles a gang comprised of African Americans.

   A. The prison warden may segregate the African-American and Latin-American prisoners into different wings of the prison and never allow the prisoners of different races to commingle to prevent gang violence without violating the Equal Protection Clause because there is a compelling government interest.

   B. The prison warden may not segregate the African-American and Latin-American prisoners because there are less restrictive means of preventing gang violence in prisons. Therefore, racial segregation would violate the Equal Protection Clause.

   C. Prisoners are not entitled to Equal Protection of the laws.

8. Gerrymandering is the process of drawing district lines for the purposes of electing congressional representatives. For years, the district lines have been drawn in such a way so as to dilute the African-American population, so that African Americans could not form a recognizable majority. As such, the state has never had an African-American representative in Congress. To remedy this problem, the state redrew one of its districts so that it would be comprised mostly of African-American voters. Caucasian voters file a lawsuit against the state alleging that such racial gerrymandering violates the Equal Protection Clause.

   A. There is no violation because the plaintiffs do not have standing.

   B. There is likely no violation because the state is attempting to remedy prior discrimination.

   C. There is likely a violation because race is the only motivation for such gerrymandering and it would not survive strict scrutiny, which is the appropriate test for this type of discrimination.

   D. There is likely no violation because, although race is the only motivation for such gerrymandering, it would likely survive the rational basis test, which is the appropriate test for this type of discrimination.

9. The federal government bans homosexuals from military service.

   A. The constitutionality of such a law that treats homosexuals differently from heterosexuals would be determined by an equal protection analysis under the Due Process Clause of the Fifth Amendment.

   B. The constitutionality of such a law that treats homosexuals differently from heterosexuals would be determined by an equal protection analysis under the Equal Protection Clause of the Fourteenth Amendment.

   C. The constitutionality of such a law that treats homosexuals differently from heterosexuals would be determined by an equal protection analysis under the provisions of the Third Amendment regarding soldiers.

   D. The constitutionality of such a law would not be at issue because the military is not required to provide equal protection under the law to soldiers.

10. Assume a state law only requires a father of a child born in wedlock to pay child support for a child when the parents become divorced, but that a father of a child born out of wedlock never has to pay child support for that child. Which level of constitutional scrutiny should be applied to determining if such a law violates the Equal Protection Clause?

    A. Minimal Scrutiny/Rational Basis Test
    B. Middle-Level Scrutiny
    C. Heightened/Strict Scrutiny
    D. Both A and B

8

Chapter

Freedom of Expression

"Congress shall make no law ... abridging the freedom of speech, or of the press; or the right of the people peaceably to assemble ..."

—The First Amendment

INTRODUCTION

Speech is not just verbal communication. Any "expressive conduct" is considered speech. This includes written communications, wearing of clothing and symbols, associating with members of a group, and even marching in a parade.

Some consider free speech to be the most important protection in the Bill of Rights since, without free speech, citizens cannot be free from government oppression. The Supreme Court has generally interpreted the First Amendment's free speech protections very broadly and limited government suppression of speech. Therefore, the Court applies the strict scrutiny test to content-based regulations of protected types of speech, such as political speech, and will only allow limitations when there is a compelling government interest, when the regulation limiting speech is narrowly tailored to furthering that interest, and when further speech will not better serve to meet the government's compelling need. When the government imposes a content-neutral regulation on protected speech, the Court applies middle-level scrutiny and will allow time, place, and manner restrictions on speech if it is necessary to serve an important government interest.

However, the Court has determined that some types of speech are more valuable than other types, and not all speech is protected by the First Amendment. Non-valued, and thus unprotected, speech includes: 1) obscenity; 2) fighting words; 3) fraud/misrepresentation; 4) advocacy of imminent lawless conduct; and 5) defamation. The government can limit or completely ban these unprotected forms of speech. The Court has also determined that commercial speech is more valuable than those types of non-protected speech listed above but not as important as other types of speech, such as political

121

speech. As such, the Court has determined that even content-based regulation on commercial speech only deserves middle-level scrutiny.

The forum is important in determining whether speech can be limited. Generally, there is no free speech right on another's private property. So, a speaker would not be allowed to go to a car dealer's lot and speak to potential customers about a lemon that the speaker purchased from the dealer. The car dealer has the right to only communicate its message on its own property. On the other hand, locations such as the courthouse steps or the Mall in Washington, D.C., are traditionally public forums, and the government does not have the power to restrict speech based upon its content or viewpoint at these locations. So, the government could not limit war protests on the Mall but permit a rally to support the troops. The government would be allowed to impose content-neutral regulations related to the time, place, and manner of the speech on the Mall. An example of a constitutional, content-neutral regulation would be only allowing speech of any viewpoint or of any protected content on the Mall after obtaining a permit with the intent that the information provided on the permit application would enable the city to prepare for law enforcement, lavatory facilities, and trash collection.

In addition to these other restrictions on government infringement on speech, the Supreme Court has also determined that regulations which are overly broad, vague, or impose prior restraints on (most) speech are unconstitutional. Overbreadth exists when the regulation limits legitimate speech in addition to the intended speech. An example would be a statute intending to protect children from exposure to pornography on the Internet prohibits the depiction of a female breast on the Internet. In that instance, not only does the regulation limit depictions that would be pornographic, but it also has a chilling effect on legitimate speech by preventing a speaker from posting important medical information regarding breast cancer or breast feeding on the Internet. A regulation would be void for vagueness if the speaker does not know exactly what he/she can say without fear of punishment. Compare two statutes: a) prohibiting the distribution of leaflets that advocate for abortion; and b) prohibiting the distribution of all leaflets. Statute "a" is vague in that it is difficult to tell when the contents of a leaflet advocate abortion or simply provide information related to abortion. With regard to statute "b," there is no question as to what is prohibited. Statute "a" would be unconstitutional. (See Chapter 5, Due Process and Economic Freedoms). Prior restraint is also not permitted. Essentially, the government can't prohibit or censor speech before it is uttered. So, the government could not prohibit a newspaper from publishing information related to banks collapsing to prevent public panic.

STUDENT *Checklist*

Free Speech

1. Determine if the **conduct** is **speech**.
2. Determine if the **speech** is **protected**.

- ■ If the speech is **not protected**, the government may **limit** or **ban** the speech.

- ■ If the speech is **protected**, **continue** to step 3, below.

3. Determine if the **forum** is **public** or **private**.

- ■ If the forum is private, there is no First Amendment right.

- ■ If the forum is public, continue to step 4, below.

4. Determine if the government's regulation is **content-based** or **content-neutral**.

- ■ For **content-based** regulation, apply **strict scrutiny** test to determine if there is a **compelling government interest**, that the regulation limiting speech is **narrowly tailored** to furthering that interest, and that **further speech** will not better serve to meet the government's compelling need.

- ■ For **content-neutral** regulation, apply **middle-level scrutiny** test to determine if the regulation of the **time, place, or manner** of the speech furthers an **important government interest**. *Note*: Even content-neutral regulations that result in a full ban of protected speech are not permitted.

5. Determine if the regulation is **overly broad**. If the regulation limits other legitimate speech in addition to the targeted speech, the regulation is unconstitutional.

6. Determine if the regulation is **vague**. If a speaker cannot determine what type of speech is actually limited, then the regulation is unconstitutionally **void for vagueness**.

7. Determine if the regulation imposes **prior restraint** on the speech, which is essentially censorship of the speech **prior to the actual utterance**. If there is prior restraint, it is likely that the regulation is unconstitutional except in rare cases of **national security**.

SUPREME COURT CASES

NEW YORK TIMES v. UNITED STATES, 403 U.S. 713 (1971)

[This case is a *per curiam* opinion, also known as an opinion by the whole court and not just one or several judges. In this case, the United States government sought an injunction against the *New York Times* and *Washington Post* to prevent the newspapers from publishing a classified study regarding the U.S. Decision-Making Process on Viet Nam. The Supreme Court ruled that issuing an injunction would be an unconstitutional restraint on free speech and affirmed the lower courts' decisions denying the injunction. Because this was a *per curiam* opinion, the actual court decision is short. Therefore, the concurring opinion is presented below to illustrate the history of the First Amendment.]

. . . Mr. Justice BLACK, with whom Mr. Justice DOUGLAS joins, concurring.

* * *

Our Government was launched in 1789 with the adoption of the Constitution. The Bill of Rights, including the First Amendment, followed in 1791. Now, for the first time in the 182 years since the founding of the Republic, the federal courts are asked to hold that the First Amendment does not mean what it says, but rather means that the Government can halt the publication of current news of vital importance to the people of this country.

. . . When the Constitution was adopted, many people strongly opposed it because the document contained no Bill of Rights to safeguard certain basic freedoms. They especially feared that the new powers granted to a central government might be interpreted to permit the government to curtail freedom of religion, press, assembly, and speech. In response to an overwhelming public clamor, James Madison offered a series of amendments to satisfy citizens that these great liberties would remain safe and beyond the power of government to abridge. Madison proposed what later became the First Amendment in three parts, two of which are set out below, and one of which proclaimed: "The people shall not be deprived or abridged of their right to speak, to write, or to publish their sentiments; *and the freedom of the press, as one of the great bulwarks of liberty, shall be inviolable.*" (Emphasis added.) The amendments were offered to curtail and restrict the general powers granted to the Executive, Legislative, and Judicial Branches two years before in the original Constitution. The Bill of Rights changed the original Constitution into a new charter under which no branch of government could abridge the people's freedoms of press, speech, religion, and assembly. . . . Madison and the other Framers of the First Amendment, able men that they were, wrote in language they earnestly believed could never be misunderstood: "Congress shall make no law . . . abridging the freedom . . . of the press. . . ." Both the history and language of the First Amendment support the view that the press must be left free to publish news, whatever the source, without censorship, injunctions, or prior restraints.

In the First Amendment the Founding Fathers gave the free press the protection it must have to fulfill its essential role in our democracy. The press was to serve the governed, not the governors. The Government's power to censor the press was abolished so that the press would remain forever free to censure the Government. The press was protected so that it could bare the secrets of government and inform the people. Only a free and unrestrained press can effectively expose deception in government. And paramount among the responsibilities of a free press is the duty to prevent any part of the government from deceiving the people and sending them off to distant lands to die of foreign fevers and foreign shot and shell. . . .

The Government's case here is based on premises entirely different from those that guided the Framers of the First Amendment. The Solicitor General has carefully and emphatically stated:

> "Now, Mr. Justice [BLACK], your construction of . . . [the First Amendment] is well known, and I certainly respect it. You say that no law means no law, and that should be obvious. I can only say, Mr. Justice, that to me it is equally obvious that 'no law' does not mean 'no law', and I would seek to persuade the Court that is true. . . . [T]here are other parts of the Constitution that grant powers and responsibilities to the Executive, and . . . the First Amendment was not intended to make it impossible for the Executive to function or to protect the security of the United States."

And the Government argues in its brief that in spite of the First Amendment, "[t]he authority of the Executive Department to protect the nation against publication of information whose disclosure would endanger the national security stems from two interrelated sources: the constitutional power of the President over the conduct of foreign affairs and his authority as Commander-in-Chief."

In other words, we are asked to hold that despite the First Amendment's emphatic command, the Executive Branch, the Congress, and the Judiciary can make laws enjoining publication of current news and abridging freedom of the press in the name of "national security." The Government does not even attempt to rely on any act of Congress. Instead it makes the bold and dangerously far-reaching contention that the courts should take it upon themselves to "make" a law abridging freedom of the press in the name of equity, presidential power and national security, even when the representatives of the people in Congress have adhered to the command of the First Amendment and refused to make such a law. . . . To find that the President has "inherent power" to halt the publication of news by resort to the courts would wipe out the First Amendment and destroy the fundamental liberty and security of the very people the Government hopes to make "secure." No one can read the history of the adoption of the First Amendment without being convinced beyond any doubt that it was injunctions like those sought here that Madison and his collaborators intended to outlaw in this Nation for all time.

The word "security" is a broad, vague generality whose contours should not be invoked to abrogate the fundamental law embodied in the First Amendment. The guarding of military and diplomatic secrets at the expense of informed representative government provides no real security for our Republic. The Framers of the First Amendment, fully aware of both the need to defend a new nation and the abuses of the English and Colonial governments, sought to give this new society strength and security by providing that freedom of speech, press, religion, and assembly should not be abridged. This thought was eloquently expressed in 1937 by Mr. Chief Justice Hughes—great man and great Chief Justice that he was—when the Court held a man could not be punished for attending a meeting run by Communists.

> "The greater the importance of safeguarding the community from incitements to the overthrow of our institutions by force and violence, the more imperative is the need to preserve inviolate the constitutional rights of free speech, free press and free [403 U.S. 713, 720] assembly in order to maintain the opportunity for free political discussion, to the end that government may be responsive to the will of the people and that changes, if desired, may be obtained by peaceful means. Therein lies the security of the Republic, the very foundation of constitutional government."

Mr. Justice Douglas, with whom Mr. Justice Black joins, concurring.

* * *

It should be noted at the outset that the First Amendment provides that "Congress shall make no law . . . abridging the freedom of speech, or of the press." That leaves, in my view, no room for governmental restraint on the press.

* * *

The Government says that it has inherent powers to go into court and obtain an injunction to protect the national interest, which in this case is alleged to be national security.

Near v. Minnesota, 283 U.S. 697, repudiated that expansive doctrine in no uncertain terms.

The dominant purpose of the First Amendment was to prohibit the wide-spread practice of governmental suppression of embarrassing information. It is common knowledge that the First Amendment was adopted against the wide-spread use of the common law of seditious libel to punish the dissemination of material that is embarrassing to the powers-that-be. . . . The present cases will, I think, go down in history as the most dramatic illustration of that principle. A debate of large proportions goes on in the Nation over our posture in Vietnam. That debate antedated the disclosure of the contents of the present documents. The latter are highly relevant to the debate in progress.

Secrecy in government is fundamentally anti-democratic, perpetuating bureaucratic errors. Open debate and discussion of public issues are vital to our national health. On public questions there should be "uninhibited, robust, and wide-open" debate.

Mr. Justice BRENNAN, concurring.

II

The error that has pervaded these cases from the outset was the granting of any injunctive relief whatsoever, interim or otherwise. The entire thrust of the Government's claim throughout these cases has been that publication of the material sought to be enjoined "could," or "might," or "may" prejudice the national interest in various ways. But the First Amendment tolerates absolutely no prior judicial restraints of the press predicated upon surmise or conjecture that untoward consequences may result. Our cases, it is true, have indicated that there is a single, extremely narrow class of cases in which the First Amendment's ban on prior judicial restraint may be overridden. Our cases have thus far indicated that such cases may arise only when the Nation "is at war," Schenck v. United States, 249 U.S. 47, 52 (1919), during which times "[n]o one would question but that a government might prevent actual obstruction to its recruiting service or the publication of the sailing dates of transports or the number and location of troops." Near v. Minnesota, 283 U.S. 697, 716 (1931). Even if the present world situation were assumed to be tantamount to a time of war, or if the power of presently available armaments would justify even in peacetime the suppression of information that would set in motion a nuclear holocaust, in neither of these actions has the Government presented or even alleged that publication of items from or based upon the material at issue would cause the happening of an event of that nature. "[T]he chief purpose of [the First Amendment's] guaranty [is] to prevent previous restraints upon publication." Near v. Minnesota, supra, at 713. Thus, only governmental allegation and proof that publication must inevitably, directly, and immediately cause the occurrence of an event kindred to imperiling the safety of a transport already at sea can support even the issuance of an interim restraining order. In no event may mere conclusions be sufficient: for if the Executive Branch seeks judicial aid in preventing publication, it must inevitably submit the basis upon which that aid is sought to scrutiny by the judiciary. And therefore, every restraint issued in this case, whatever its form, has violated the First Amendment—and not less so because that restraint was justified as necessary to afford the courts an opportunity to examine the claim more thoroughly. Unless and until the Government has clearly made out its case, the First Amendment commands that no injunction may issue. . . .

ASHCROFT v. FREE SPEECH COALITION, 535 U.S. 234 (2002)

[This case determines the constitutionality of the Child Pornography Prevention Act of 1996 (CPPA). The statute was challenged by a group of plaintiffs, ranging from artists to a coalition supporting free speech. CPPA prohibits possessing or distributing virtual child pornography, material that appeared to depict a child engaged in sexually explicit conduct but was made without any real children. Virtual child pornography can be created through computer generated images of children or by using adults who look like minors. The Court recognized that there could be circumstances when the material generated was neither obscene or child pornography, two instances when such speech would not be constitutionally protected. Therefore, the Court had to determine if CPPA was constitutional as it applied to such non-obscene and non-child pornographic material.]

* * *

The First Amendment commands, "Congress shall make no law ... abridging the freedom of speech." The government may violate this mandate in many ways, but a law imposing criminal penalties on protected speech is a stark example of speech suppression. ... The Constitution gives significant protection from overbroad laws that chill speech within the First Amendment's vast and privileged sphere. Under this principle, the CPPA is unconstitutional on its face if it prohibits a substantial amount of protected expression. The sexual abuse of a child is a most serious crime and an act repugnant to the moral instincts of a decent people. In its legislative findings, Congress recognized that there are subcultures of persons who harbor illicit desires for children and commit criminal acts to gratify the impulses. ... Congress also found that surrounding the serious offenders are those who flirt with these impulses and trade pictures and written accounts of sexual activity with young children.

Congress may pass valid laws to protect children from abuse, and it has. The prospect of crime, however, by itself does not justify laws suppressing protected speech. ("Among free men, the deterrents ordinarily to be applied to prevent crime are education and punishment for violations of the law, not abridgment of the rights of free speech") (internal quotation marks and citation omitted)). It is also well established that speech may not be prohibited because it concerns subjects offending our sensibilities. ... ("[T]he fact that society may find speech offensive is not a sufficient reason for suppressing it"); see also *Reno* v. *American Civil Liberties Union*, 521 U.S. 844, 874 (1997) ("In evaluating the free speech rights of adults, we have made it perfectly clear that '[s]exual expression which is indecent but not obscene is protected by the First Amendment' ").

As a general principle, the First Amendment bars the government from dictating what we see or read or speak or hear. The freedom of speech has its limits; it does not embrace certain categories of speech, including defamation, incitement, obscenity, and pornography produced with real children. While these categories may be prohibited without violating the First Amendment, none of them includes the speech prohibited by the CPPA. In his dissent from the opinion of the Court of Appeals, Judge Ferguson recognized this to be the law and proposed that virtual child pornography should be regarded as an additional category of unprotected speech. See 198 F.3d, at 1101. It would be necessary for us to take this step to uphold the statute.

As we have noted, the CPPA is much more than a supplement to the existing federal prohibition on obscenity. Under *Miller* v. *California*, 413 U.S. 15 (1973), the Government must prove that the work, taken as a whole, appeals to the prurient interest, is patently offensive in light of community standards, and lacks serious literary, artistic, political, or scientific value. *Id.*, at 24. The CPPA, however, extends to images that appear to depict a minor engaging in sexually explicit activity without regard to the *Miller* requirements. The materials need not appeal to the prurient interest. Any depiction of sexually explicit activity, no matter how it is presented, is proscribed. The CPPA applies to a picture in a psychology manual, as well as a movie depicting the horrors of sexual abuse. It is not necessary, moreover, that the image be patently offensive. Pictures of what appear to be 17-year-olds engaging in sexually explicit activity do not in every case contravene community standards.

The CPPA prohibits speech despite its serious literary, artistic, political, or scientific value. The statute proscribes the visual depiction of an idea—that of teenagers engaging in sexual activity—that is a fact of modern society and has been a theme in art and literature throughout the ages. Under the CPPA, images are prohibited so long as the persons appear to be under 18 years of age. 18 U.S.C. §2256(1). This is higher than the legal age for marriage in many States, as well as the age at which persons may consent to sexual relations. . . . It is, of course, undeniable that some youths engage in sexual activity before the legal age, either on their own inclination or because they are victims of sexual abuse.

Both themes—teenage sexual activity and the sexual abuse of children—have inspired countless literary works. William Shakespeare created the most famous pair of teenage lovers, one of whom is just 13 years of age. See *Romeo and Juliet*, act I, sc. 2, l. 9 ("She hath not seen the change of fourteen years"). In the drama, Shakespeare portrays the relationship as something splendid and innocent, but not juvenile. The work has inspired no less than 40 motion pictures, some of which suggest that the teenagers consummated their relationship. *E.g.*, *Romeo and Juliet* (B. Luhrmann director, 1996). Shakespeare may not have written sexually explicit scenes for the Elizabethean audience, but were modern directors to adopt a less conventional approach, that fact alone would not compel the conclusion that the work was obscene.

Contemporary movies pursue similar themes. Last year's Academy Awards featured the movie, *Traffic*, which was nominated for Best Picture. See *Predictable and Less So, the Academy Award Contenders*, N.Y. Times, Feb. 14, 2001, p. E11. The film portrays a teenager, identified as a 16-year-old, who becomes addicted to drugs. The viewer sees the degradation of her addiction, which in the end leads her to a filthy room to trade sex for drugs. The year before, *American Beauty* won the Academy Award for Best Picture. See *"American Beauty" Tops the Oscars*, N.Y. Times, Mar. 27, 2000, p. E1. In the course of the movie, a teenage girl engages in sexual relations with her teenage boyfriend, and another yields herself to the gratification of a middle-aged man. The film also contains a scene where, although the movie audience understands the act is not taking place, one character believes he is watching a teenage boy performing a sexual act on an older man.

Our society, like other cultures, has empathy and enduring fascination with the lives and destinies of the young. Art and literature express the vital interest we all have in the formative years we ourselves once knew, when wounds can be so grievous, disappointment so profound, and mistaken choices so tragic, but when moral acts and self-fulfillment are still in reach. Whether or not the films we mention violate the CPPA, they explore themes within the wide sweep of the statute's prohibitions. If these films, or hundreds of others of lesser note that explore those subjects, contain a single graphic depiction of sexual activity within the statutory definition, the possessor of the film would be subject to severe punishment without inquiry into the work's redeeming value. This is inconsistent with an essential First Amendment rule: The artistic merit of a work does not depend on the presence of a single explicit scene. ("[T]he social value of the book can neither be weighed against nor canceled by its prurient appeal or patent offensiveness"). Under *Miller*, the First Amendment requires that redeeming value be judged by considering the work as a whole. Where the scene is part of the narrative, the work itself does not for this reason become obscene, even though the scene in isolation might be offensive. For this reason, and the others we have noted, the CPPA cannot be read to prohibit obscenity, because it lacks the required link between its prohibitions and the affront to community standards prohibited by the definition of obscenity.

The Government seeks to address this deficiency by arguing that speech prohibited by the CPPA is virtually indistinguishable from child pornography, which may be banned without regard to whether it depicts works of value. Where the images are themselves the product of child sexual abuse, *Ferber* recognized that the State had an interest in stamping it out without regard to any judgment about its content. The production of the work, not its content, was the target of the statute. The fact that a work contained serious literary, artistic, or other value did not excuse the harm it caused to its child participants. It was simply "unrealistic to equate a community's toleration for sexually oriented materials with the permissible scope of legislation aimed at protecting children from sexual exploitation."

* * *

In contrast to the speech in *Ferber*, speech that itself is the record of sexual abuse, the CPPA prohibits speech that records no crime and creates no victims by its production. Virtual child pornography is not "intrinsically related" to the sexual abuse of children, as were the materials in *Ferber*. While the Government asserts that the images can lead to actual instances of child abuse, see *infra*, at 13-16, the causal link is contingent and indirect. The harm does not necessarily follow from the speech, but depends upon some unquantified potential for subsequent criminal acts. . . .

The second flaw in the Government's position is that *Ferber* did not hold that child pornography is by definition without value. On the contrary, the Court recognized some works in this category might have significant value . . . but relied on virtual images—the very images prohibited by the CPPA—as an alternative and permissible means of expression: "[I]f it were necessary for literary or artistic value, a person over the statutory age who perhaps looked younger could be utilized. Simulation outside of the prohibition of the statute could provide another alternative." *Ferber*, then, not only referred to the distinction between actual and virtual child pornography, it relied on it as a reason supporting its holding. *Ferber* provides no support for a statute that eliminates the distinction and makes the alternative mode criminal as well.

III

The CPPA, for reasons we have explored, is inconsistent with *Miller* and finds no support in *Ferber*. The Government seeks to justify its prohibitions in other ways. It argues that the CPPA is necessary because pedophiles may use virtual child pornography to seduce children. There are many things innocent in themselves, however, such as cartoons, video games, and candy, that might be used for immoral purposes, yet we would not expect those to be prohibited because they can be misused. . . . The precedents establish, however, that speech within the rights of adults to hear may not be silenced completely in an attempt to shield children from it. In *Butler* v. *Michigan* . . . [a] unanimous Court agreed upon the important First Amendment principle that the State could not "reduce the adult population . . . to reading only what is fit for children." We have reaffirmed this holding. See *United States* v. *Playboy Entertainment Group, Inc.*, 529 U. S. 803, 814 (2000) ("[T]he objective of shielding children does not suffice to support a blanket ban if the protection can be accomplished by a less restrictive alternative"). . . .

Here, the Government wants to keep speech from children not to protect them from its content but to protect them from those who would commit other crimes. The principle, however, remains the same: The Government cannot ban speech fit for adults simply because it may fall into the hands of children. The evil in question depends upon the actor's unlawful conduct, conduct defined as criminal quite apart from any link to the speech in question. This establishes that the speech ban is not narrowly drawn. The objective is to prohibit illegal conduct, but this restriction goes well beyond that interest by restricting the speech available to law-abiding adults.

The Government submits further that virtual child pornography whets the appetites of pedophiles and encourages them to engage in illegal conduct. This rationale cannot sustain the provision in question. The mere tendency of speech to encourage unlawful acts is not a sufficient reason for banning it. The government "cannot constitutionally premise legislation on the desirability of controlling a person's private thoughts." First Amendment freedoms are most in danger when the government seeks to control thought or to justify its laws for that impermissible end. The right to think is the beginning of freedom, and speech must be protected from the government because speech is the beginning of thought.

. . . The Government has shown no more than a remote connection between speech that might encourage thoughts or impulses and any resulting child abuse. Without a significantly stronger, more direct connection, the Government may not prohibit speech on the ground that it may encourage pedophiles to engage in illegal conduct.

* * *

Finally, the Government says that the possibility of producing images by using computer imaging makes it very difficult for it to prosecute those who produce pornography by using real children. Experts, we are told, may have difficulty in saying whether the pictures were made by using real children or by using computer imaging. The necessary solution, the argument runs, is to prohibit both kinds of images. The argument, in essence, is that protected speech may be banned as a means to ban unprotected speech. This analysis turns the First Amendment upside down.

The Government may not suppress lawful speech as the means to suppress unlawful speech. Protected speech does not become unprotected merely because it resembles the latter. . . . The overbreadth doctrine prohibits the Government from banning unprotected speech if a substantial amount of protected speech is prohibited or chilled in the process.

In sum, [CPPA] covers materials beyond the categories recognized in *Ferber* and *Miller*, and the reasons the Government offers in support of limiting the freedom of speech have no justification in our precedents or in the law of the First Amendment. The provision abridges the freedom to engage in a substantial amount of lawful speech. For this reason, it is overbroad and unconstitutional. . . .

CASE QUESTIONS

NEW YORK TIMES v. UNITED STATES

1. Do you think secrecy in government is anti-democratic? Explain why or why not.

2. What is the essential purpose and history of the First Amendment?

3. Why are prior restraints presumed to be invalid?

4. Why did the Court reject the Solicitor General's argument that the "President has 'inherent power' to halt the publication of news"?

5. Based upon this *per curiam* opinion, can the government ever restrain the press from printing a newsworthy story?

ASHCROFT v. FREE SPEECH COALITION

1. What did CPPA prohibit and what portions are challenged in this case?

2. The Court frequently refers to Miller v. California, 413 U.S. 15 (1973), and New York v. Ferber, 458 U.S. 747 (1982). What is the relevant precedent established by these two cases?

3. Why did the Court conclude that pornography depicting virtual images of children was not constitutionally prohibited child pornography?

4. Explain why the Court determined that CPPA's provisions were overbroad?

5. Why is it unconstitutional to limit protected speech in an effort to limit unprotected speech?

HYPOTHETICAL WITH ACCOMPANYING ANALYSIS

Hypothetical

The Klu Klux Klan decided to have a parade on Halloween. The idea was to promote its message of racial superiority. It intended to peacefully carry signs with words and symbols on them. It received a permit from the City of Grace to march on Main Street from 8:00–10:00 P.M. on October 31. The Klan accepted applications to march in the parade from 30 other groups, including the Neo Nazi's for Supremacy (a white supremacist group), Down with Mohammad (an anti-Islam group) and the Westboro Baptist Church (a homophobic group). The Southern Poverty Law Center (SPLC), an organization that opposes hate groups, also applied to march in the parade. However, the Klan refused to allow SPLC to march in the parade because the SPLC's message was directly opposed to the Klan's message. The SPLC filed a lawsuit against the Klan, seeking an injunction requiring the Klan to allow them to march in a parade on public streets. May the injunction be granted under the First Amendment?

Analysis

It is likely that it would be unconstitutional for a court to order the Klan to include SPLC in the parade, as to do so would violate the Klan's First Amendment rights. A parade is a form of speech because it is intended to garner public attention and communicate a message. Hurley v. Irish-American Gay Group of Boston, 515 U.S. 557 (1995). In this case, the organizer's message is one of intolerance and hate against various minorities. The SPLC's message is one of tolerance and is directly opposed to the organizer's message. The SPLC's proposed participation in the parade was to communicate that different message.

For a court to require the organizer to include a group such as the SPLC, it would have the effect of declaring the organizer's parade a public forum. However, this is not a public forum, as the government is not hosting it but rather a private entity is hosting it. As such, that private entity organizer has a right to decide what message it would like to communicate and what message it does not want to communicate. Even if the SPLC message of tolerance may be much more desirable to a court than the organizer's message of intolerance, the government may not interfere to encourage one message over another's message. *Id.*

The State of Elation had several incidents in which 10,000 free copies of University of Elation's newspaper, *Happy Times*, were taken from help-yourself newsstands and replaced with signs indicating someone's discontent with the contents of the paper, asserting that it was racist. The police never got involved, saying that "you can't steal something that is free." So, the State of Elation made it a misdemeanor, punishable by three months in jail and a $5,000 fine to take free newspapers in bulk with the intent to prevent others from reading the paper. After the law was enacted, Bobby, a homophobe, took 15,000 copies of the free "Gay Blade" newspaper and placed signs on the newsstand that said "Gays will go to hell." Bobby was charged with a violation of the above-referenced statute. May Bobby be constitutionally prosecuted under this statute or does the statute violate the First Amendment?

DISCUSSION QUESTIONS

1. Research challenge: Read Near v. Minnesota, 283 U.S. 697 (1931). Explain how this case repudiates the concept that the President has inherent powers to go into court and obtain an injunction to protect the national interest.

2. For years, the government prevented news agencies from photographing flag-draped coffins of soldiers who died in war and refused to grant media access to the coffins. The Obama administration reversed this practice. Explain why you think this practice is good or bad. Did the ban on photographing coffins and denial of access violate the First Amendment?

3. Many states and federal law have imposed enhanced penalties for "hate crimes." The FBI has defined a hate crime as a "criminal offense committed against a person, property, or society which is motivated, in whole or in part, by the offender's bias against a race, religion, disability, sexual orientation, or ethnicity/national origin," available at http://www.fbi.gov/ucr/cius_02/html/web/offreported/02-nhatecrime12.html Do you believe that enhanced penalties for hate crimes are constitutional or do you believe that enhanced penalties for hate crimes violate a defendant's First Amendment rights? Explain your answer.

4. Many law schools embrace a spirit of equality in society. As such, several law schools refused to allow military recruiters on campus or to participate in law school–sponsored job fairs because of its rules against allowing homosexuals in the military. The government has argued that any law school, including a private school, that receives federal funds must allow military recruiters on campus. If a law school prohibits the military from recruiting on its campus, the law school then forfeits any and all federal funding. May the government make funding contingent on allowing the military to recruit

on campuses, or does such contingency violate the law schools' First Amendment rights? *See* Rumsfeld v. Forum for Academic and Institutional Rights, Inc., 547 U.S. 47 (2006).

5. Research Challenge: New York passed the "Son of Sam" statute. What did that statute say? Did the Supreme Court hold such statute to be constitutional? Why or why not?

6. The University of Elation, a state university funded by taxpayer dollars, has numerous university-sponsored student organizations. Such organizations receive funding from the university for activities, and the organizations regularly post fliers and meet on campus. To become a university-sponsored student organization, the student group must submit an application for formal recognition as a university-sponsored student organization, along with bylaws and a mission statement. Of five groups that applied this semester, one was denied recognition as a university-sponsored student organization and the funding that accompanied such formal recognition. That group was the National Man Boy Love Association Student Chapter. The university denied the application because the stated mission was to share among the student body at the University of Elation the idea that sexual relations between men and boys is not evil and is, in fact, good. The bylaws provided that the group would not facilitate in any way any type of criminal activity and any member who violated the law would be kicked out of the chapter. Is the university's denial of formal recognition and funding unconstitutional? Explain why or why not.

7. See number 6, above. Assume that the University of Elation denied another group, the Students of the Church of the Lukumi Babalu Aye, formal recognition and funding. The denial was because the mission and bylaws advocated animal sacrifices in accordance with the church's religious beliefs. Would such denial be unconstitutional? Why or why not? How do the First Amendment's provisions related to the free exercise and non-establishment of religions factor into the constitutionality of the university's action? See Chapter 9.

8. How does one know if a work is obscene? What is the *Miller* test and is it still applicable to First Amendment obscenity analysis today?

9. Why can the government regulate commercial speech more than political speech?

10. Identify conduct other than oral communications that constitute speech.

11. Research challenge: What words does the FCC prohibit from being aired on network television because they are considered indecent?

12. At the Golden Globe Awards aired on the Fox network, Cher uttered the F-Word and Nicole Richie uttered the S-Word. The Federal Communications Commission brought action against Fox for broadcasting indecent language in violation of federal law. The matter was appealed to the Supreme Court in Federal Communications Commission v. Fox Televisions Stations, Inc., 2009 WL 1118715. In this case, the Supreme Court declined to rule on the First Amendment question and instead reversed and remanded the case on procedural grounds. Read the facts of this case. Then assume that

you are a member of the Supreme Court and that you were deciding the case on the constitutional merits. Do you believe that the FCC's action against Fox for these statements violates the First Amendment? Explain why or why not.

13. Read Boy Scouts of America v. Dale, 530 U.S. 640 (2000). Do the Boy Scouts have to allow homosexual scout leaders? Why or why not? In answering, explain how the First Amendment influences the Supreme Court's decision.

14. Assume federal law requires a political candidate to disclose the identities of campaign contributors. Does such law impermissibly infringe upon a candidate's right to freely associate? *See* McConnell v. Federal Elections Commission, 540 U.S. 93 (2003).

15. A group, Citizens United, made a film entitled *Hillary: The Movie*, which expressed opinions about whether Hillary Clinton would have made a good president. Because the movie was scheduled to be aired during Hillary Clinton's presidential campaign, the Federal Election Commission revented its showing, asserting that the campaign finance law, the Bipartisan Campaign Reform Act, prohibited such movie as a high dollar campaign advertisement. Citizens United has challenged the case in the Supreme Court. Is this movie political speech or campaign speech? Does campaign speech deserve any greater or less First Amendment protection than political speech? What was the Supreme Court's conclusion in this case? Clinton v. Federal Election Commission, Docket No. 08-205.

16. According to the *Baltimore Sun*, "Undercover Maryland State Police officers repeatedly spied on peace activists and anti-death penalty groups . . . and entered the names of some in a law-enforcement database of people thought to be terrorists or drug traffickers. . . . Despite the fact that the Maryland infiltrators' reports consistently said the activists acted lawfully, agents continued to recommend that the spying continue. Reports of the surveillance were sent to at least seven federal, state and local law enforcement agencies, including the National Security Agency. . . ." *Spying Uncovered* (July 18, 2008). Is such spying activity in violation of the First Amendment's free association provision?

True/False

1. Speech may be regulated if the viewpoint of the speaker is undesirable to the community as a whole.

2. Content-based regulation of untruthful speech is as equally unconstitutional as content-based regulation of truthful speech.

3. The strict scrutiny test is applied when content-based regulation of protected speech is challenged.

4. Government regulation of speech is unconstitutional if it is a prior restraint on speech.

5. The government can constitutionally regulate the time, place, and manner of speech in a public forum, if such regulation is content-neutral.

Multiple Choice

6. Which of the following is not a protected form of speech?

   A. Commercial speech
   B. Political speech
   C. Pornographic speech
   D. Obscene speech
   E. All but B

7. Which of the following is a non-public forum?

   A. Airport terminal
   B. Street
   C. Military base
   D. Inside a courthouse
   E. All but B

8. For a work to be obscene, the work as a whole must:

   A. Appeal to the prurient interest.
   B. Describe or depict sexual conduct.
   C. Lack serious literary, political, artistic, or scientific value.
   D. All of the above

9. Viewpoint-based restrictions on speech are analyzed under which standard?

   A. Strict scrutiny
   B. Middle-level scrutiny
   C. Rational basis

10. Assume that the City of Grace denied all permits for rallies opposing the war in Iraq but granted permits to those supporting the war because the Mayor of Grace is ardently anti-Muslim. Such action would be:

   A. Unconstitutional because the regulation is content-based.
   B. Unconstitutional because the regulation is viewpoint-based.
   C. Constitutional because the Mayor is advancing a message embraced by the majority of voters that elected her.
   D. Constitutional because the city has unquestionable authority to allow or disallow permits for rallies for any rational reason.

Chapter 9

Freedom of Religion

> "Congress shall make no law respecting an establishment of religion, or prohibiting the free exercise thereof[.]"
>
> **—The First Amendment**

INTRODUCTION

Over 200 years ago, James Monroe explained, "The religion of every man must be left to the conviction and conscience of every man; and it is the right of every man to exercise it as these may dictate." Given the nature of the very subject, it comes as no surprise that the twin clauses of the First Amendment dealing with freedom of religion have received much attention as well as controversy from courts, legislatures, and the public alike.

The first of the two clauses, the Establishment Clause, prevents government from establishing or endorsing one religion over another, or religion over non-religion generally. Its purpose is to erect a "wall of separation" between church and state. However, when analyzing establishment issues under the First Amendment, the Supreme Court has offered a number of tests for determining violations of the clause, but it has never adequately explained when one test should be employed over another, or whether *all* of its various tests should be used. You'll find a perfect example of this very confusion in *McCreary County v. ACLU of Kentucky* and the *Van Orden v. Perry* case excerpted within this chapter. So how do you proceed to analyze whether a particular governmental action violates the Establishment Clause? Simple. Play it safe, and analyze it as thoroughly as possible using as much guidance from the Court as possible. You may not have a concrete answer by the time it's all said and done, but at least you'll have a thorough analysis and a good solid educated guess.

The second clause, the Free Exercise Clause, restricts the government's regulation of religious beliefs, and even more importantly, individual *actions* that are a result of those religious beliefs. Only when government regulations seek to impose limits on conduct that are directly attributable to those religious beliefs do we get into Free Exercise issues. The regulation might intentionally affect religious-based conduct, or it might not. Either way, the Free Exercise Clause applies.

Of course, at times *both* clauses might be implicated in a single scenario. Suppose, for example, that a religious group applies for a county permit to construct a temple on a particular site. Arguably, granting the permit could create an Establishment Clause problem because the government would be perceived as advancing that particular religion by allowing it to construct the temple. On the other hand, withholding the permit could violate the Free Exercise Clause because it would prohibit the group from worshiping. So the question then becomes, which clause "wins" so to speak? Again, the Supreme Court has never explicitly answered this question, and it might be because each case must be considered and analyzed separately, but the majority of the time when the two clauses conflict, the Free Exercise Clause will prevail.

STUDENT

Freedom of Religion

1. Did the challenged law pertain to **religion**?

■ Did the individual **subjectively** possess **non-secular beliefs**?

■ Were those beliefs **sincere**?

■ Did those beliefs occupy a **central place** in the individual's life?

■ Were the beliefs more than just **philosophical** or **political** in nature?

2. Establishment Clause

■ Does the Establishment Clause **apply**?

■ Was the Establishment Clause **violated**?
   Under the *Lemon* **test**
      ❑ Did the law have a **secular** (non-religious) **purpose**?
      ❑ Was the **primary effect** of the law **neutral** in that it **neither advanced nor inhibited** religion?
      ❑ Did the law result in an **excessive entanglement** between religion and government?
   Under the **coercion test**, did the government compel participation of individuals in a religious exercise to which they objected?
   Under the **endorsement test**, did the government endorse religion by conveying or attempting to convey the message that religion was preferred over non-religion?

3. Free Exercise Clause

■ Does the Free Exercise Clause **apply**?
   Did the government infringe upon an individual's religious **beliefs** or
   Did the government infringe upon an individual's religious-based **conduct** by
      ❑ **Prohibiting** or **discouraging** conduct **required** by someone's religious beliefs; or

> ❏ **Compelling** or **encouraging** conduct **forbidden** by someone's religious beliefs?
>
> ▪ Was the Free Exercise Clause **violated**?
>
>   Did the government infringe upon an individual's religious **beliefs**?
>
>   If the government sought to regulate religious-based **conduct**, did the government fail to meet **strict scrutiny** by showing
>
>   ❏ It had a **compelling government interest** in the regulation; and
>
>   ❏ **No less restrictive means** could accomplish the interest?

SUPREME COURT CASES

VAN ORDEN v. PERRY, 545 U.S. 677 (2005)

The question here is whether the Establishment Clause of the First Amendment allows the display of a monument inscribed with the Ten Commandments on the Texas State Capitol grounds. We hold that it does.

The 22 acres surrounding the Texas State Capitol contain 17 monuments and 21 historical markers commemorating the "people, ideals, and events that compose Texan identity." Tex. H. Con. Res. 38, 77th Leg., Reg. Sess. (2001). The monolith challenged here stands 6-feet high and 3 1/2-feet wide. It is located to the north of the Capitol building, between the Capitol and the Supreme Court building. Its primary content is the text of the Ten Commandments. An eagle grasping the American flag, an eye inside of a pyramid, and two small tablets with what appears to be an ancient script are carved above the text of the Ten Commandments. Below the text are two Stars of David and the superimposed Greek letters Chi and Rho, which represent Christ. The bottom of the monument bears the inscription "PRE-SENTED TO THE PEOPLE AND YOUTH OF TEXAS BY THE FRATERNAL ORDER OF EAGLES OF TEXAS 1961." App. to Pet. for Cert. 21.

The legislative record surrounding the State's acceptance of the monument from the Eagles—a national social, civic, and patriotic organization—is limited to legislative journal entries. After the monument was accepted, the State selected a site for the monument based on the recommendation of the state organization responsible for maintaining the Capitol grounds. The Eagles paid the cost of erecting the monument, the dedication of which was presided over by two state legislators.

Petitioner Thomas Van Orden is a native Texan and a resident of Austin. At one time he was a licensed lawyer, having graduated from Southern Methodist Law School. Van Orden testified that, since 1995, he has encountered the Ten Commandments monument during his frequent visits to the Capitol grounds. His visits are typically for the purpose of using the law library in the Supreme Court building, which is located just northwest of the Capitol building.

Forty years after the monument's erection and six years after Van Orden began to encounter the monument frequently, he sued numerous state officials in their official capacities under Rev. Stat. §1979, 42 U.S.C. §1983, seeking both a declaration that the monument's placement violates the Establishment Clause and an injunction requiring its removal. . . .

Our cases, Januslike, point in two directions in applying the Establishment Clause. One face looks toward the strong role played by religion and religious traditions throughout our Nation's history. . . .

The other face looks toward the principle that governmental intervention in religious matters can itself endanger religious freedom.

This case, like all Establishment Clause challenges, presents us with the difficulty of respecting both faces. Our institutions presuppose a Supreme Being, yet these institutions must not press religious observances upon their citizens. One face looks to the past in acknowledgment of our Nation's heritage, while the other looks to the present in demanding a separation between church and state. Reconciling these two faces requires that we neither abdicate our responsibility to maintain a division between church and state nor evince a hostility to religion by disabling the government from in some ways recognizing our religious heritage. . . .

These two faces are evident in representative cases both upholding and invalidating laws under the Establishment Clause. Over the last 25 years, we have sometimes pointed to *Lemon v. Kurtzman,* 403 U.S. 602, 91 S. Ct. 2105, 29 L. Ed. 2d 745 (1971), as providing the governing test in Establishment Clause challenges. . . . Yet, just two years after *Lemon* was decided, we noted that the factors identified in *Lemon* serve as "no more than helpful signposts." *Hunt v. McNair,* 413 U.S. 734, 741, 93 S. Ct. 2868, 37 L. Ed. 2d 923 (1973). Many of our recent cases simply have not applied the *Lemon* test. . . . Others have applied it only after concluding that the challenged practice was invalid under a different Establishment Clause test.

Whatever may be the fate of the *Lemon* test in the larger scheme of Establishment Clause jurisprudence, we think it not useful in dealing with the sort of passive monument that Texas has erected on its Capitol grounds. Instead, our analysis is driven both by the nature of the monument and by our Nation's history. . . .

In this case we are faced with a display of the Ten Commandments on government property outside the Texas State Capitol. Such acknowledgments of the role played by the Ten Commandments in our Nation's heritage are common throughout America. We need only look within our own Courtroom. Since 1935, Moses has stood, holding two tablets that reveal portions of the Ten Commandments written in Hebrew, among other lawgivers in the south frieze. Representations of the Ten Commandments adorn the metal gates lining the north and south sides of the Courtroom as well as the doors leading into the Courtroom. Moses also sits on the exterior east facade of the building holding the Ten Commandments tablets. . . .

Our opinions, like our building, have recognized the role the Decalogue plays in America's heritage. *See, e.g., McGowan v. Maryland,* 366 U.S., at 442, 81 S. Ct. 1101; *id.,* at 462, 81 S. Ct. 1101 (separate opinion of Frankfurter, J.). The Executive and Legislative Branches have also acknowledged the historical role of the Ten Commandments. *See, e.g.,* Public Papers of the Presidents, Harry S. Truman, 1950, p. 157 (1965); S. Con. Res. 13, 105th Cong., 1st Sess. (1997); H. Con. Res. 31, 105th Cong., 1st Sess. (1997). These displays and recognitions of the Ten Commandments bespeak the rich American tradition of religious acknowledgments.

Of course, the Ten Commandments are religious—they were so viewed at their inception and so remain. The monument, therefore, has religious significance. According to Judeo-Christian belief, the Ten Commandments were given to Moses by God on Mt. Sinai. But Moses was a lawgiver as well as a religious leader. And the Ten Commandments have an undeniable historical meaning, as the foregoing examples demonstrate. Simply having religious content or promoting a message consistent with a religious doctrine does not run afoul of the Establishment Clause. . . .

There are, of course, limits to the display of religious messages or symbols. For example, we held unconstitutional a Kentucky statute requiring the posting of the Ten Commandments in every public schoolroom. *Stone v. Graham,* 449 U.S. 39, 101 S. Ct. 192, 66 L. Ed. 2d 199 (1980) (*per curiam*). In the classroom context, we found that the Kentucky statute had an improper and plainly religious purpose. *Id.,* at 41, 101 S. Ct. 192. As evidenced by *Stone's* almost exclusive reliance upon two of our school prayer cases, *id.,* at 41-42, 101 S. Ct. 192 (citing *School Dist. of Abington Township v. Schempp,* 374 U.S. 203, 83 S. Ct. 1560, 10 L. Ed. 2d 844 (1963), and *Engel v. Vitale,* 370 U.S. 421, 82 S. Ct. 1261, 8 L. Ed. 2d 601 (1962)), it stands as an example of the fact that we have "been particularly vigilant in monitoring compliance with the Establishment Clause in elementary and secondary schools," *Edwards v. Aguillard,* 482 U.S. 578, 583-584, 107 S. Ct. 2573, 96 L. Ed. 2d 510 (1987). . . . Indeed, *Edwards v. Aguillard* recognized that *Stone*—along with *Schempp* and *Engel*—was a consequence of the "particular concerns that arise in the context of public elementary and secondary schools." 482 U.S., at 584-585, 107 S. Ct. 2573. Neither *Stone* itself nor subsequent opinions have indicated that *Stone's* holding would extend to a legislative chamber, see *Marsh v. Chambers, supra,* or to capitol grounds.

The placement of the Ten Commandments monument on the Texas State Capitol grounds is a far more passive use of those texts than was the case in *Stone,* where the text confronted elementary school students every day. Indeed, Van Orden, the petitioner here, apparently walked by the monument for a number of years before bringing this lawsuit. The monument is therefore also quite different from the prayers involved in *Schempp* and *Lee v. Weisman.* Texas has treated its Capitol grounds monuments as representing the several strands in the State's political and legal history. The inclusion of the Ten Commandments monument in this group has a dual significance, partaking of both religion and government. We cannot say that Texas' display of this monument violates the Establishment Clause of the First Amendment.

The judgment of the Court of Appeals is affirmed. *It is so ordered.*

GONZALES v. O CENTRO ESPIRITA BENEFICENTE UNIAO DO VEGETAL, 546 U.S. 418 (2006)

A religious sect with origins in the Amazon Rainforest receives communion by drinking a sacramental tea, brewed from plants unique to the region, that contains a hallucinogen regulated under the Controlled Substances Act by the Federal Government. The Government concedes that this practice is a sincere exercise of religion, but nonetheless sought to prohibit the small American branch of the sect from engaging in the practice, on the ground that the Controlled Substances Act bars all use of the hallucinogen. The sect sued to block enforcement against it of the ban on the sacramental tea, and moved for a preliminary injunction.

It relied on the Religious Freedom Restoration Act of 1993, which prohibits the Federal Government from substantially burdening a person's exercise of religion, unless the Government "demonstrates that application of the burden to the person" represents the least restrictive means of advancing a compelling interest. 42 U.S.C. §2000bb-1(b). The District Court granted the preliminary injunction, and the Court of Appeals affirmed. We granted the Government's petition for certiorari. Before this Court, the Government's central submission is that it has a compelling interest in the *uniform* application of the Controlled Substances Act, such that no exception to the ban on use of the hallucinogen can be made to accommodate the sect's sincere religious practice. We conclude that the Government has not carried the burden expressly placed on it by Congress in the Religious Freedom Restoration Act, and affirm the grant of the preliminary injunction.

I

In *Employment Div., Dept. of Human Resources of Ore. v. Smith,* 494 U.S. 872, 110 S. Ct. 1595, 108 L. Ed. 2d 876 (1990), this Court held that the Free Exercise Clause of the First Amendment does not prohibit governments from burdening religious practices through generally applicable laws. In *Smith,* we rejected a challenge to an Oregon statute that denied unemployment benefits to drug users, including Native Americans engaged in the sacramental use of peyote. *Id.,* at 890, 110 S. Ct. 1595. In so doing, we rejected the interpretation of the Free Exercise Clause announced in *Sherbert v. Verner,* 374 U.S. 398, 83 S. Ct. 1790, 10 L. Ed. 2d 965 (1963), and, in accord with earlier cases, see *Smith,* 494 U.S., at 879-880, 884-885, 110 S. Ct. 1595, held that the Constitution does not require judges to engage in a case-by-case assessment of the religious burdens imposed by facially constitutional laws. *Id.,* at 883-890, 110 S. Ct. 1595.

Congress responded by enacting the Religious Freedom Restoration Act of 1993 (RFRA), 107 Stat. 1488, as amended, 42 U.S.C. §§ 2000bb *et seq.,* which adopts a statutory rule comparable to the constitutional rule rejected in *Smith.* Under RFRA, the Federal Government may not, as a statutory matter, substantially burden a person's exercise of religion, "even if the burden results from a rule of general applicability." §2000bb-1(a). The only exception recognized by the statute requires the Government to satisfy the compelling interest test—to "demonstrat[e] that application of the burden to the person—(1) is in furtherance of a compelling governmental interest; and (2) is the least restrictive means of furthering that compelling governmental interest." §2000bb-1(b). A person whose religious practices are burdened in violation of RFRA "may assert that violation as a claim or defense in a judicial proceeding and obtain appropriate relief." §2000bb-1(c).

The Controlled Substances Act, 84 Stat. 1242, as amended, 21 U.S.C. §§ 801 *et seq.* (2000 ed. and Supp. I), regulates the importation, manufacture, distribution, and use of psychotropic substances. The Act classifies substances into five schedules based on their potential for abuse, the extent to which they have an accepted medical use, and their safety. See §812(b) (2000 ed.). Substances listed in Schedule I of the Act are subject to the most comprehensive restrictions, including an outright ban on all importation and use, except pursuant to strictly regulated research projects. See §§823, 960(a)(1). The Act authorizes the imposition of a criminal sentence for simple possession of Schedule I substances, see §844(a), and mandates the imposition of a criminal sentence for possession "with intent to manufacture, distribute, or dispense" such substances, see §§841(a), (b).

O Centro Espírita Beneficente União do Vegetal (UDV) is a Christian Spiritist sect based in Brazil, with an American branch of approximately 130 individuals. Central to the UDV's faith is receiving communion through *hoasca* (pronounced "wass-ca"), a sacramental tea made from two plants unique to the Amazon region. One of the plants, *psychotria viridis,* contains dimethyltryptamine (DMT), a hallucinogen whose effects are enhanced by alkaloids from the other plant, *banisteriopsis caapi.* DMT, as well as "any material, compound, mixture, or preparation, which contains any quantity of [DMT]," is listed in Schedule I of the Controlled Substances Act. §812(c), Schedule I(c).

In 1999, United States Customs inspectors intercepted a shipment to the American UDV containing three drums of *hoasca*. A subsequent investigation revealed that the UDV had received 14 prior shipments of *hoasca*. The inspectors seized the intercepted shipment and threatened the UDV with prosecution.

The UDV filed suit against the Attorney General and other federal law enforcement officials, seeking declaratory and injunctive relief. The complaint alleged, *inter alia,* that applying the Controlled Substances Act to the UDV's sacramental use of *hoasca* violates RFRA. . . .

. . . RFRA requires the Government to demonstrate that the compelling interest test is satisfied through application of the challenged law "to the person"—the particular claimant whose sincere exercise of religion is being substantially burdened. 42 U.S.C. §2000bb-1(b). RFRA expressly adopted the compelling interest test "as set forth in *Sherbert v. Verner,* 374 U.S. 398, 83 S. Ct. 1790, 10 L. Ed. 2d 965 (1963) and *Wisconsin v. Yoder,* 406 U.S. 205, 92 S. Ct. 1526, 32 L. Ed. 2d 15 (1972)." 42 U.S.C. §2000bb(b)(1). In each of those cases, this Court looked beyond broadly formulated interests justifying the general applicability of government mandates and scrutinized the asserted harm of granting specific exemptions to particular religious claimants. In *Yoder,* for example, we permitted an exemption for Amish children from a compulsory school attendance law. We recognized that the State had a "paramount" interest in education, but held that "despite its admitted validity in the generality of cases, we must searchingly examine the interests that the State seeks to promote . . . and the impediment to those objectives that would flow from recognizing *the claimed Amish exemption.*" 406 U.S., at 213, 221, 92 S. Ct. 1526 (emphasis added). The Court explained that the State needed "to show with more particularity how its admittedly strong interest . . . would be adversely affected by granting an exemption *to the Amish.*" *Id.,* at 236, 92 S. Ct. 1526 (emphasis added).

In *Sherbert,* the Court upheld a particular claim to a religious exemption from a state law denying unemployment benefits to those who would not work on Saturdays, but explained that it was not announcing a constitutional right to unemployment benefits for "*all* persons whose religious convictions are the cause of their unemployment." 374 U.S., at 410, 83 S. Ct. 1790 (emphasis added). The Court distinguished the case "in which an employee's religious convictions serve to make him a nonproductive member of society." *Ibid.; see also Smith,* 494 U.S., at 899, 110 S. Ct. 1595 (O'Connor, J., concurring in judgment) (strict scrutiny "at least requires a case-by-case determination of the question, sensitive to the facts of each particular claim"). Outside the Free Exercise area as well, the Court has noted that "[c]ontext matters" in applying the compelling interest test, *Grutter v. Bollinger,* 539 U.S. 306, 327, 123 S. Ct. 2325, 156 L. Ed. 2d 304 (2003), and has emphasized that "strict scrutiny *does* take 'relevant differences' into account—indeed, that is its fundamental purpose," *Adarand Constructors, Inc. v. Peña,* 515 U.S. 200, 228, 115 S. Ct. 2097, 132 L. Ed. 2d 158 (1995).

B

Under the more focused inquiry required by RFRA and the compelling interest test, the Government's mere invocation of the general characteristics of Schedule I substances, as set forth in the Controlled Substances Act, cannot carry the day. It is true, of course, that Schedule I substances such as DMT are exceptionally dangerous. *See, e.g., Touby v. United States,* 500 U.S. 160, 162, 111 S. Ct. 1752, 114 L. Ed. 2d 219 (1991). Nevertheless, there is no indication that Congress, in classifying DMT, considered the harms posed by the particular use at issue here—the circumscribed, sacramental use of *hoasca* by the UDV. The question of the harms from the sacramental use of *hoasca* by the UDV *was* litigated below. Before the District Court found that the Government had not carried its burden of showing a compelling interest in preventing such harms, the court noted that it could not "ignore that the legislative branch of the government elected to place materials containing DMT in Schedule I of the [Act], reflecting findings that substances containing DMT have 'a high potential for abuse,' and 'no currently accepted medical use in treatment in the United States,' and that '[t]here is a lack of accepted safety for use of [DMT] under medical supervision.'" 282 F. Supp. 2d, at 1254. But Congress' determination that DMT should be listed under Schedule I simply does not provide a categorical answer that relieves the Government of the obligation to shoulder its burden under RFRA.

This conclusion is reinforced by the Controlled Substances Act itself. The Act contains a provision authorizing the Attorney General to "waive the requirement for registration of certain manufacturers, distributors, or dispensers if he finds it consistent with the public health and safety." 21 U.S.C. §822(d). The fact that the Act itself contemplates that exempting certain people from its requirements would be "consistent with the public health and safety" indicates that congressional findings with respect to Schedule I substances should not carry the determinative weight, for RFRA purposes, that the Government would ascribe to them.

And in fact an exception has been made to the Schedule I ban for religious use. For the past 35 years, there has been a regulatory exemption for use of peyote—a Schedule I substance—by the Native American Church. See 21 CFR §1307.31 (2005). In 1994, Congress extended that exemption to all members of every recognized Indian Tribe. *See* 42 U.S.C. §1996a(b)(1). Everything the Government says about the DMT in *hoasca*—that, as a Schedule I substance, Congress has determined that it "has a high potential for abuse," "has no currently accepted medical use," and has "a lack of accepted safety for use . . . under medical supervision," 21 U.S.C. §812(b)(1)—applies in equal measure to the mescaline in peyote, yet both the Executive and Congress itself have decreed an exception from the Controlled Substances Act for Native American religious use of peyote. If such use is permitted in the face of the congressional findings in §812(b)(1) for hundreds of thousands of Native Americans practicing their faith, it is difficult to see how those same findings alone can preclude any consideration of a similar exception for the 130 or so American members of the UDV who want to practice theirs. . . .

C

The well-established peyote exception also fatally undermines the Government's broader contention that the Controlled Substances Act establishes a closed regulatory system that admits of no exceptions under RFRA. The Government argues that the effectiveness of the Controlled Substances Act will be "necessarily . . . undercut" if the Act is not uniformly applied, without regard to burdens on religious exercise. Brief for Petitioners 18. The peyote exception, however, has been in place since the outset of the Controlled Substances Act, and there is no evidence that it has "undercut" the Government's ability to enforce the ban on peyote use by non-Indians. . . .

Here the Government's argument for uniformity is different; it rests not so much on the particular statutory program at issue as on slippery-slope concerns that could be invoked in response to any RFRA claim for an exception to a generally applicable law. The Government's argument echoes the classic rejoinder of bureaucrats throughout history: If I make an exception for you, I'll have to make one for everybody, so no exceptions. But RFRA operates by mandating consideration, under the compelling interest test, of exceptions to "rule[s] of general applicability." 42 U.S.C. §2000bb-1(a). Congress determined that the legislated test "is a workable test for striking sensible balances between religious liberty and competing prior governmental interests." §2000bb(a)(5). This determination finds support in our cases; in *Sherbert,* for example, we rejected a slippery-slope argument similar to the one offered in this case, dismissing as "no more than a possibility" the State's speculation "that the filing of fraudulent claims by unscrupulous claimants feigning religious objections to Saturday work" would drain the unemployment benefits fund. 374 U.S., at 407, 83 S. Ct. 1790.

We reaffirmed just last Term the feasibility of case-by-case consideration of religious exemptions to generally applicable rules. In *Cutter v. Wilkinson,* 544 U.S. 709, 125 S. Ct. 2113, 161 L. Ed. 2d 1020 (2005), we held that the Religious Land Use and Institutionalized Persons Act of 2000, which allows federal and state prisoners to seek religious accommodations pursuant to the same standard as set forth in RFRA, does not violate the Establishment Clause. We had "no cause to believe" that the compelling interest test "would not be applied in an appropriately balanced way" to specific claims for exemptions as they arose. *Id.,* at 2122-23. Nothing in our opinion suggested that courts were not up to the task.

We do not doubt that there may be instances in which a need for uniformity precludes the recognition of exceptions to generally applicable laws under RFRA. But it would have been surprising to find that this was such a case, given the longstanding exemption from the Controlled Substances Act for religious use of peyote, and the fact that the very reason Congress enacted RFRA was to respond to a decision denying a claimed right to sacramental use of a controlled substance. See 42 U.S.C. §2000bb(a)(4). . . .

* * *

The Government repeatedly invokes Congress' findings and purposes underlying the Controlled Substances Act, but Congress had a reason for enacting RFRA, too. Congress recognized that "laws 'neutral' toward religion may burden religious exercise as surely as laws intended to interfere with religious exercise," and legislated "the compelling interest test" as the means for the courts to "strik[e] sensible balances between religious liberty and competing prior governmental interests." 42 U.S.C. §§2000bb(a)(2), (5).

We have no cause to pretend that the task assigned by Congress to the courts under RFRA is an easy one. Indeed, the very sort of difficulties highlighted by the Government here were cited by this Court in deciding that the approach later mandated by Congress under RFRA was not required as a matter of constitutional law under the Free Exercise Clause. *See Smith,* 494 U.S., at 885-890, 110 S. Ct. 1595. But Congress has determined that courts should strike sensible balances, pursuant to a compelling interest test that requires the Government to address the particular practice at issue. Applying that test, we conclude that the courts below did not err in determining that the Government failed to demonstrate, at the preliminary injunction stage, a compelling interest in barring the UDV's sacramental use of *hoasca.*

The judgment of the United States Court of Appeals for the Tenth Circuit is affirmed, and the case is remanded for further proceedings consistent with this opinion.

It is so ordered.

CASE QUESTIONS

VAN ORDEN v. PERRY

1. What weight, if any, did *Van Orden* give the Court's precedent of Lemon v. Kurtzman, 403 U.S. 602 (1971)?

2. Research challenge: Read the case of McCreary County v. ACLU of Kentucky, 545 U.S. 844 (2005), which was decided the same day as *Van Orden*. In your opinion, are the two opinions consistent or inconsistent with one another? Explain.

3. In what other cases did the Court address whether the posting of the Ten Commandments on public property violated the First Amendment? What were the respective holdings of those cases?

GONZALES v. O CENTRO ESPIRITA BENEFICENTE UNIAO DO VEGETAL

1. What impact did Employment Division v. Smith, 494 U.S. 872 (1990), have on Sherbert v. Verner, 374 U.S. 398 (1963)?

2. What impact did the Religious Freedom Restoration Act (RFRA) have on *Employment Division, Department of Human Resources of Oregon v. Smith*? Who does this law apply to?

3. What impact did *Gonzales* have on the RFRA?

4. What generalizations about the law can you make after answering the previous questions?

HYPOTHETICAL WITH ACCOMPANYING ANALYSIS

Hypothetical

Courtney is an 18-year-old high school dropout who has struggled with her identity over the past several years. She has recently become involved with a group of individuals who call themselves "The Light." It is headed by a charismatic leader who refers to himself only as "The Chosen One," and he claims to be the next "prophet of this and all other worlds to come." The group was founded only six months ago and currently has less than 50 members, comprised mostly of runaway teenagers similar to Courtney who are trying to "find themselves."

After studying the doctrines and beliefs of The Light for approximately six weeks, The Chosen One informed Courtney that she was ready for a formal induction into The Light. The Chosen One explained to Courtney that the central belief of members is that "the body, soul, and spirit must be cleansed of all things material." In order to prove her sincerity of beliefs, Courtney was required to give up all of her material possessions and "willingly show the world her condemnation of materialism." As part of an induction ceremony to be held at a state park, Courtney would be required to rid herself of all clothing and lift up her spirit to The Chosen One for acceptance into The Light. Courtney realized, however, that disrobing in a public park would violate the state's law against indecent exposure, a criminal misdemeanor which was enacted decades ago. According to Legislative notes from the time the law was enacted, the indecent exposure law sought to prohibit "inappropriate bodily exposure in a public place which is not merely a nuisance to society but is also potentially offensive, alarming, or harmful to any individual member of that society." Courtney has petitioned the state for an exemption from the law, arguing that enforcing the law against her would violate her religious rights. Discuss and analyze all issues relevant to the First Amendment's Right to Freedom of Religion.

Analysis

The First Amendment provides that "Congress shall make no law respecting an establishment of religion or prohibiting the free exercise thereof[.]" Both the Establishment Clause and the Free Exercise Clause have been held applicable to the states through the Supreme Court's decisions in Everson v. Board of Education, 330 U.S. 1 (1947), and Cantwell v. Connecticut, 310 U.S. 296 (1940), respectively. When confronted with a potential issue related to the two clauses within the First Amendment, it first must be determined whether the challenged law pertained to a religion. If so, then it must be determined which clause of the First Amendment is triggered, and in some cases the answer may be both. Then, by engaging in a detailed analysis of the appropriate clause, it can be determined whether an individual's constitutional rights were violated.

In order for the First Amendment to be triggered, "religion" must somehow be involved. Although reluctant to offer an express definition of religion, the Supreme Court has provided some guidance on the subject. In an early case the Court explained that "religion" referred to "one's view of his relations to his Creator, and the obligations they impose of reverence for His being and character, and obedience to His will." Davis v. Beason, 133 U.S. 333 (1890). Later clarifications by the Court stated that a person's system of beliefs need not necessarily recognize a "supreme being," *see, e.g.*, Torasco v. Watkins, 367 U.S. 488 (1961), and it need not be considered an "organized religion." In fact, a person could be entitled to religious protection under the First Amendment even if those beliefs are held by *only* that person. Frazee v. Illinois Dep't of Soc. Sec., 489 U.S. 829 (1989). However, the individual's beliefs must be sincere, United States v. Ballard, 322 U.S. 78 (1944), and a belief claimed to be in conflict with governmental action must occupy a central part of the individual's religion. Religion does not include "essentially political, sociological, or philosophical views." United States v. Seeger, 380 U.S. 163 (1965). Given the previous guidance from the Court, there is some doubt as to whether "The Light" would qualify as a religion without knowing more details about its central tenants and beliefs. The group has been in existence for only six months, it has very few followers, and its leader claims to be the next prophet. Although the Court has recognized that the number of members or lack thereof will not prevent something from being recognized as a valid religion, those members still must have a sincere system of beliefs, and those beliefs must be central to any conflicting law. The Light does claim to have a central belief of condemning anything materialistic. However, such a belief appears as more of a philosophical view, which is not considered the same as a religious belief. In sum, in order to determine with certainty if The Light would be recognized as a religion, additional information about its practices and beliefs would be needed. Based only on the information in the hypothetical, however, a large degree of doubt exists that a court would recognize The Light as a religion entitled to protection under the First Amendment.

Assuming, however, that The Light does constitute a religion, it next must be determined which clause of the First Amendment is implicated. Courtney maintains that the state's criminal law prohibiting indecent exposure infringes upon her right to worship in accordance with her beliefs. Thus she is challenging the law on free exercise grounds. The Free Exercise Clause is implicated in two opposing circumstances, when either (1) the government prohibits or discourages conduct that is required by someone's religious beliefs; or (2) the government compels or encourages conduct that is forbidden by someone's religious beliefs. *See* Sherbert v. Verner, 374 U.S. 398 (1963). In our scenario, only the former circumstance is present because Courtney is forbidden from disrobing in public by the criminal law against indecent exposure. Next, the purpose of the law must be examined. If the law was enacted with the direct purpose of regulating religious conduct, it will be analyzed under strict scrutiny principles and will almost always be invalidated. *See, e.g.,* Church of the Lukumi Babalu Aye, Inc. v. Hialeah, 508 U.S. 520 (1993). No such motive appears in our case, since according to Legislative notes from the time of enactment, the law is aimed at all individuals who engage in potentially offensive or disruptive conduct. Therefore, it need only be determined whether the law has a burdensome effect on Courtney's exercise of her religious beliefs. In Employment Division v. Smith, 494 U.S. 872 (1990), the Court held that states can, but are not required to, give exemptions to individuals whose religious beliefs are in conflict with neutral state laws. *Smith* generally stands for the proposition that if a state law is neutral it will likely be upheld, even if consequentially it negatively impacts upon an individual's religious beliefs. In the instant scenario it has already been established that the indecent exposure law was enacted without pertaining to religion. Therefore, Courtney need not be given an exemption from the law in order to protect her First Amendment religious rights.

In conclusion, serious doubt exists as to whether Courtney would even be able to assert violations of her First Amendment religious freedoms since it is doubtful as to whether The Light would qualify as a "religion." However, even if it were determined that The Light did qualify as a religion entitled to First Amendment protection, she would likely not be entitled to an exemption from the religiously neutral indecent exposure law.

The school boards in two neighboring counties have recently established similar programs for graduating seniors. The purpose of the programs, county executives explained, was "to instill in students who will soon be entering higher education, the work force, and the world at large a sense of superior moral character, good citizenship, and a commitment to truthfulness, respect, and integrity."

In Diablo County, the program is called "Morals Matter." It consists of an hour-long session each weekday afternoon during the last class period of the school day, and it is held in the school's cafeteria. Morals Matter is open to all seniors regardless of their religious beliefs or lack thereof. Participation by the students is purely voluntary. The session consists of a non-denominational prayer service led by local clergy of a variety of religious faiths. School officials do not participate in the sessions in any way. In adjacent Lucifren County, the program is called "Creating Character." This program, unlike the one in Diablo County, takes place immediately after the school day has ended. During the hour-long weekly "spiritual sessions" located in the school's gymnasium, local clergy discuss concepts related to faith, morality, and sin. All seniors are required to attend at least six sessions in order to graduate. School guidance counselors are present during each session to facilitate discussion.

Damian Detwater, an atheist, is a graduating senior attending a Diablo County public school. He has sought an injunction in court prohibiting the Morals Matter program from continuing, arguing it violates his First Amendment rights. Angelica Attenburgh, a senior in Lucifren County, is a devout fundamentalist, and she too is seeking an injunction against the Creating Character program in her county based on religious grounds. Discuss the likelihood that each student will succeed in their respective challenges.

1. Research challenge: Chronicle the major Supreme Court decisions with regard to religious worship within the nation's public schools, including the holding of each case. After researching those cases, consider President Reagan's remark during his 1983 State of the Union Address that "God never should have been expelled from America's classrooms." Do you agree with his statement? Explain.

2. Revisit the *Newdow* case, excerpted in Chapter 2, dealing with the courts. Assuming Newdow had standing to bring the lawsuit, do you think the Court would have held that the Pledge of Allegiance, as written, violates the Establishment Clause? Explain.

3. Aside from the recitation of the Pledge of Allegiance discussed in Question 2 above, in what other subtle ways can you think of that religion is interwoven

into the operations of government? Do you think they violate the First Amendment? Explain.

4. Sally, an eight-year-old girl, was recently diagnosed with a potentially fatal disease. With a bone marrow transfusion she has relatively good likelihood of survival. Without the transfusion she will most certainly die. Sally and her family are members of a religious sect which adamantly oppose any medical treatment and believe that only God should determine Sally's fate. Sally does not want the medical treatment, nor do her parents want her to have it. The state, however, wants to intervene and force her to have the treatment in an effort to save her life. Who will win? What if, instead of being eight, Sally were 18. Would your answer change? *See* Jacobsen v. Massachusetts, 197 U.S. 11 (1905).

5. Marley Roberts is a member of the Reggae Resurrection, a small religion based out of the Caribbean. As part of his religious beliefs, he wears dreadlocks to honor his gods. Marley joins the U.S. military and is ordered to shave his head as all new recruits are. Marley argues that being forced to shave his head violates his right to free exercise of religion. Will Marley prevail? *See* Goldman v. Weinberger, 475 U.S. 503 (1986).

6. Camden County Community College allows its facilities to be used as a meeting place for numerous community groups, including Alcoholics Anonymous and Weight Watchers. The college also allows religious groups to meet on its campus. How would this practice potentially present a conflict between the Free Exercise Clause and the Establishment Clause? Which clause would likely prevail and why?

7. Revisit the Hypothetical with Accompanying Analysis from this chapter. How would the analysis of the scenario be different if it had dealt with a federal law rather than a state law? *See Gonzales, supra.* Would the state have any credible arguments that Courtney's claim is not yet ripe for review? See Chapter 2, The Courts.

8. Our nation has recently entered into an extremely controversial war against the nation of South Stratavaria. The draft was reinstated due to the vast number of soldiers needed to fight the war. Kevin and Joey were both drafted. Kevin refuses to participate in the war, claiming that violence goes against all of his religious beliefs. Joey also refuses to participate in the war, claiming that although not opposed to war in general, this particular war goes against his religious beliefs. Assuming the men's beliefs are sincere, will either of them succeed in challenging their service based on First Amendment grounds? Do you think they *should* succeed? Explain. *Compare* Gillette v. United States, 401 U.S. 437 (1971), *with* United States v. Seeger, 380 U.S. 163 (1965).

Read the below hypothetical and then answer the True/False questions that follow.

The town council of Saintville recently enacted a law proclaiming June as the "Month of Spiritualism." The law provides that "during the entire month any spiritual or religious organization may display on the grounds of the Saintville Town Hall any symbol representing their organization." The purpose of the law, as researched in the legislative history of the law, is to "encourage a celebration of different religions, denominations, and beliefs, and to promote the education and acceptance of all backgrounds and belief systems."

True/False

1. Saintville's law probably does not violate the Establishment Clause because it accommodates *all* religions and it does not endorse one religion over another.

2. Saintville's law is constitutional because it gives individuals the opportunity to express their religious beliefs in accordance with the Free Exercise Clause.

3. Saintville's law is constitutional under the two religious clauses of the First Amendment because part of the underlying purpose of the law was to "promotion education and acceptance," which is secular in nature.

4. If the Saintville law were challenged as unconstitutional under the First Amendment, a court would most likely reach the same result as in *McCreary County v. ACLU.*

5. Any constitutional challenge to the Saintville law based on the religion clauses of the First Amendment would be evaluated based on strict scrutiny.

Multiple Choice

6. In celebration of the upcoming Easter holiday, the State of Purity has erected a ten-foot cross on the front lawn of the Governor's mansion that is to be displayed for two weeks. Arnold, an atheist, claims that the display violates his First Amendment rights because the display is an establishment of religion. Will Arnold's claim likely succeed?

   A. No, because the cross is only a temporary and not a permanent fixture.
   B. No, because the governor's mansion is a private residence.
   C. No, because Arnold is an atheist, which is not recognized as a religion.
   D. Yes.

7. Which of the following would most likely constitute a violation of the Free Exercise Clause?

   A. A federal law prohibiting members of a small religious sect from believing in cannibalism as their path to salvation.
   B. A federal law prohibiting members of a small religious sect from practicing cannibalism as their path to salvation.
   C. Both A and B.
   D. Neither A nor B.

8. Which of the following statements is TRUE?

   A. The Free Exercise Clause has been applied to the states via the Fourteenth Amendment but the Establishment Clause has not.
   B. The Establishment Clause has been applied to the states via the Fourteenth Amendment but the Free Exercise Clause has not.
   C. If there is a conflict between the two clauses, the Free Exercise Clause will usually prevail over the Establishment Clause.
   D. If there is a conflict between the two clauses, the Establishment Clause will usually prevail over the Free Exercise Clause.

9. Masonville Middle School, a public school, currently incorporates all of the following activities into a typical school day for its students. Which of those activities will most likely violate the First Amendment?

   A. A moment of silence at the beginning of each school day for the purpose of either prayer or meditation.
   B. A one-hour religion class taught during the school day by privately employed religious teachers in which participation by students is purely voluntary.
   C. A five-minute announcement session at the end of each school day that is delivered by a student, broadcast over the school's public address system, and includes a blessing that students depart and be safe.
   D. All of the above likely violate the First Amendment.

10. Lemon v. Kurtzman, 403 U.S. 602 (1970), established a three-part test that is frequently cited by courts when deciding whether a law violates the Establishment Clause. Which of the following is NOT part of the *Lemon* test?

    A. The law must not create an excessive government entanglement with religion.
    B. The law must have a non-secular legislative purpose.
    C. The primary effect of the law must neither advance nor inhibit religion.
    D. All of the above are part of the *Lemon* three-part test.

Chapter 10

The Right to Bear Arms

"A well regulated Militia, being necessary to the security of a free State, the right of the people to keep and bear Arms, shall not be infringed."

—The Second Amendment

INTRODUCTION

The Second Amendment's right to bear arms doesn't *only* pertain to guns, but the controversy over the right to bear arms commonly boils down to an issue of gun control. On the one hand, proponents of an individual's right to bear arms use catch phrases like, "Guns don't kill people. People kill people." On the other hand, advocates of stricter gun laws remind us that it's all about "Crime control, not gun control." The heart of the debate centers on the language of the amendment itself. Should the two clauses be read *together*, so that the right to bear arms is protected only in the context of maintaining a militia? Or, do the clauses stand separate from one another, making the right to bear arms an individual right entirely independent of the formation or preservation of a militia? There are two sides to every coin, but those two sides have never been so diametrically opposed to one another as they have in this centuries-old debate.

When studying the issues in this chapter, keep two things in mind. First, the Second Amendment is one of the few remaining portions of the Bill of Rights that has not been incorporated against the states via the Fourteenth Amendment. What significance does that have? It means that the protections of the Second Amendment apply *only* to the federal government. The states are free to regulate the ability to bear arms as they see fit. Congress, however, is kept in constant check by both the Second Amendment and the fact that, without some specific constitutional authority (typically found in the Commerce Clause of Article I, §8), it cannot infringe upon rights traditionally reserved to the states. Second, understanding the Second Amendment can be particularly challenging, simply because there isn't a whole lot of case law on the subject. For starters, state case law won't offer us any help since the amendment applies only to the federal government. However, even within federal authority, the Second

155

Amendment is arguably one of the *least* discussed provisions within the Constitution or the Bill of Rights. Try doing a search on issues such as the Commerce Clause, freedom of speech, or equal protection (just to name a few). You will likely get hundreds if not thousands of cases—far too many to read without first narrowing down your search. But not the Second Amendment. Comparatively speaking, the law is sparse. That will all likely change as lower courts scramble to make heads or tails of the Supreme Court's opinion in *District of Columbia v. Heller* (excerpted within this chapter). For the moment, though, our authority is limited.

As you work your way through this chapter to becoming the resident expert on an often overlooked portion of the Bill of Rights, see on which side of the coin you fall. And as the debate rages on, remember that it's highly unlikely the two sides will call a cease-fire any time soon.

STUDENT *Checklist*

Second Amendment Right to Bear Arms

1. Is the Second Amendment **applicable**?

■ Was a **federal law** enacted;

■ that restricts an **individual's right** to bear arms?

2. Is the law a **permissible restriction** of the right to bear arms, including

■ **who** may possess the weapon;

■ **where** the weapon may be possessed, such as **"sensitive areas"**;

■ **what type** of weapons may be possessed, such as **dangerous and unusual weapons** that are **not typically possessed by law-abiding citizens for lawful purposes**; and/or

■ the **commercial sale** of arms?

3. Is the law regulating the right to bear arms in **violation** of the Constitution?

■ Did the law infringe upon the **states' rights** guaranteed by the **Tenth Amendment**?

■ Did the law **exceed Congress's authority** under its **enumerated powers**?

■ Did the law violate an individual's rights to keep and bear arms under the **Second Amendment**?

SUPREME COURT CASES

UNITED STATES v. MILLER, 307 U.S. 174 (1939)

[After being convicted of transporting a firearm in interstate commerce, the Court examined whether the Second Amendment protected an individual's right to keep and bear arms.]

. . . In the absence of any evidence tending to show that possession or use of a "shotgun having a barrel of less than eighteen inches in length" at this time has some reasonable relationship to the preservation or efficiency of a well regulated militia, we cannot say that the Second Amendment guarantees the right to keep and bear such an instrument. Certainly it is not within judicial notice that this weapon is any part of the ordinary military equipment or that its use could contribute to the common defense. Aymette v. State of Tennessee, 2 Humph., Tenn., 154, 158.

The Constitution as originally adopted granted to the Congress power—"To provide for calling forth the Militia to execute the Laws of the Union, suppress Insurrections and repel Invasions; To provide for organizing, arming, and disciplining, the Militia, and for governing such Part of them as may be employed in the Service of the United States, reserving to the States respectively, the Appointment of the Officers, and the Authority of training the Militia according to the discipline prescribed by Congress." U.S.C.A. Const. art. 1, §8. With obvious purpose to assure the continuation and render possible the effectiveness of such forces the declaration and guarantee of the Second Amendment were made. It must be interpreted and applied with that end in view.

The Militia which the States were expected to maintain and train is set in contrast with Troops which they were forbidden to keep without the consent of Congress. The sentiment of the time strongly disfavored standing armies; the common view was that adequate defense of country and laws could be secured through the Militia—civilians primarily, soldiers on occasion.

The signification attributed to the term Militia appears from the debates in the Convention, the history and legislation of Colonies and States, and the writings of approved commentators. These show plainly enough that the Militia comprised all males physically capable of acting in concert for the common defense. "A body of citizens enrolled for military discipline." And further, that ordinarily when called for service these men were expected to appear bearing arms supplied by themselves and of the kind in common use at the time. . . .

"The American Colonies In The 17th Century," Osgood, Vol. 1, ch. XIII, affirms in reference to the early system of defense in New England—

> "In all the colonies, as in England, the militia system was based on the principle of the assize of arms. This implied the general obligation of all adult male inhabitants to possess arms, and, with certain exceptions, to cooperate in the work of defence." "The possession of arms also implied the possession of ammunition, and the authorities paid quite as much attention to the latter as to the former." "A year later (1632) it was ordered that any single man who had not furnished himself with arms might be put out to service, and this became a permanent part of the legislation of the colony (Massachusetts)."

Also,

> "Clauses intended to insure the possession of arms and ammunition by all who were subject to military service appear in all the important enactments concerning military affairs. Fines were the penalty for delinquency, whether of towns or individuals. According to the usage of the times, the infantry of Massachusetts consisted of pikemen and musketeers. The law, as enacted in 1649 and thereafter, provided that each of the former should be armed with a pike, corselet, head-piece, sword, and knapsack. The musketeer should carry a 'good fixed musket,' not under bastard musket bore, not less than three feet, nine inches, nor more than four feet three inches in length, a priming wire, scourer, and mould, a sword, rest, bandoleers, one pound of powder, twenty bullets, and two fathoms of match. The law also required that two-thirds of each company should be musketeers."

The General Court of Massachusetts, January Session 1784 (Laws and Resolves 1784, c. 55, pp. 140, 142), provided for the organization and government of the Militia. It directed that the Train Band should "contain all able bodied men, from sixteen to forty years of age, and the Alarm List, all other men under sixty years of age . . . ." Also, "That every non-commissioned officer and private soldier of the said militia not under the control of parents, masters or guardians, and being of sufficient ability therefor in the judgment of the Selectmen of the town in which he shall dwell, shall equip himself, and be constantly provided with a good fire arm, &c."

By an Act passed April 4, 1786 (Laws 1786, c. 25), the New York Legislature directed:

> "That every able-bodied Male Person, being a Citizen of this State, or of any of the United States, and residing in this State, (except such Persons as are herein after excepted) and who are of the Age of Sixteen, and under the Age of Forty-five Years, shall, by the Captain or commanding Officer of the Beat in which such Citizens shall reside, within four Months after the passing of this Act, be enrolled in the Company of such Beat. . . . That every Citizen so enrolled and notified, shall, within three Months thereafter, provide himself, at his own Expense, with a good Musket or Firelock, a sufficient Bayonet and Belt, a Pouch with a Box therein to contain not less than Twenty-four Cartridges suited to the Bore of his Musket or Firelock, each Cartridge containing a proper Quantity of Powder and Ball, two spare Flints, a Blanket and Knapsack. . . ."

The General Assembly of Virginia, October, 1785 (12 Hening's Statutes c. 1, p. 9 et seq.), declared: "The defense and safety of the commonwealth depend upon having its citizens properly armed and taught the knowledge of military duty."

It further provided for organization and control of the Militia and directed that "All free male persons between the ages of eighteen and fifty years," with certain exceptions, "shall be inrolled or formed into companies." "There shall be a private muster of every company once in two months."

Also that

> "Every officer and soldier shall appear at his respective muster-field on the day appointed, by eleven o'clock in the forenoon, armed, equipped, and accoutred, as follows: . . . every non-commissioned officer and private with a good, clean musket carrying an ounce ball, and three feet eight inches long in the barrel, with a good bayonet and iron ramrod well fitted thereto, a cartridge box properly made, to contain and secure twenty cartridges fitted to his musket, a good knapsack and canteen, and moreover, each non-commissioned officer and private shall have at every muster one pound of good powder, and four pounds of lead, including twenty blind cartridges; and each serjeant shall have a pair of moulds fit to cast balls for their respective companies, to be purchased by the commanding officer out of the monies arising on delinquencies. Provided, That the militia of the counties westward of the Blue Ridge, and the counties below adjoining thereto, shall not be obliged to be armed with muskets, but may have good rifles with proper accoutrements, in lieu thereof. And every of the said officers, non-commissioned officers, and privates, shall constantly keep the aforesaid arms, accoutrements, and ammunition, ready to be produced whenever called for by his commanding officer. If any private shall make it appear to the satisfaction of the court hereafter to be appointed for trying delinquencies under this act that he is so poor that he cannot purchase the arms herein required, such court shall cause them to be purchased out of the money arising from delinquents."

Most if not all of the States have adopted provisions touching the right to keep and bear arms. Differences in the language employed in these have naturally led to somewhat variant conclusions concerning the scope of the right guaranteed. But none of them seem to afford any material support for the challenged ruling of the court below. . . .

We are unable to accept the conclusion of the court below and the challenged judgment must be reversed. The cause will be remanded for further proceedings.

Reversed and remanded.

DISTRICT OF COLUMBIA v. HELLER, 128 S. CT. 2783 (2008)

[*Heller* marked the first time the Supreme Court directly addressed the Second Amendment since *Miller* was decided almost 70 years earlier.]

We consider whether a District of Columbia prohibition on the possession of usable handguns in the home violates the Second Amendment to the Constitution. . . .

Respondent Dick Heller is a D.C. special police officer authorized to carry a handgun while on duty at the Federal Judicial Center. He applied for a registration certificate for a handgun that he wished to keep at home, but the District refused. He thereafter filed a lawsuit in the Federal District Court for the District of Columbia seeking, on Second Amendment grounds, to enjoin the city from enforcing the bar on the registration of handguns, the licensing requirement insofar as it prohibits the carrying of a firearm in the home without a license, and the trigger-lock requirement insofar as it prohibits the use of "functional firearms within the home." App. 59a. The District Court dismissed respondent's complaint, see *Parker v. District of Columbia*, 311 F. Supp. 2d 103, 109 (2004). The Court of Appeals for the District of Columbia Circuit, construing his complaint as seeking the right to render a firearm operable and carry it about his home in that condition only when necessary for self-defense, reversed, see *Parker v. District of Columbia*, 478 F.3d 370, 401 (2007). . . .

The Second Amendment provides: "A well regulated Militia, being necessary to the security of a free State, the right of the people to keep and bear Arms, shall not be infringed." In interpreting this text, we are guided by the principle that "[t]he Constitution was written to be understood by the voters; its words and phrases were used in their normal and ordinary as distinguished from technical meaning." *United States v. Sprague*, 282 U.S. 716, 731, 51 S. Ct. 220, 75 L. Ed. 640 (1931); see also *Gibbons v. Ogden*, 9 Wheat. 1, 188, 6 L. Ed. 23 (1824). Normal meaning may of course include an idiomatic meaning, but it excludes secret or technical meanings that would not have been known to ordinary citizens in the founding generation.

The two sides in this case have set out very different interpretations of the Amendment. Petitioners and today's dissenting Justices believe that it protects only the right to possess and carry a firearm in connection with militia service. See Brief for Petitioners 11-12; *post*, at — (Stevens, J., dissenting). Respondent argues that it protects an individual right to possess a firearm unconnected with service in a militia, and to use that arm for traditionally lawful purposes, such as self-defense within the home. See Brief for Respondent 2-4.

The Second Amendment is naturally divided into two parts: its prefatory clause and its operative clause. The former does not limit the latter grammatically, but rather announces a purpose. The Amendment could be rephrased, "Because a well regulated Militia is necessary to the security of a free State, the right of the people to keep and bear Arms shall not be infringed." See J. Tiffany, A Treatise on Government and Constitutional Law §585, p. 394 (1867); Brief for

Professors of Linguistics and English as *Amici Curiae* 3 (hereinafter Linguists' Brief). Although this structure of the Second Amendment is unique in our Constitution, other legal documents of the founding era, particularly individual-rights provisions of state constitutions, commonly included a prefatory statement of purpose. . . .

Logic demands that there be a link between the stated purpose and the command. The Second Amendment would be nonsensical if it read, "A well regulated Militia, being necessary to the security of a free State, the right of the people to petition for redress of grievances shall not be infringed." That requirement of logical connection may cause a prefatory clause to resolve an ambiguity in the operative clause. . . . But apart from that clarifying function, a prefatory clause does not limit or expand the scope of the operative clause. See F. Dwarris, A General Treatise on Statutes 268-269 (P. Potter ed. 1871) (hereinafter Dwarris); T. Sedgwick, The Interpretation and Construction of Statutory and Constitutional Law 42-45 (2d ed. 1874). " 'It is nothing unusual in acts . . . for the enacting part to go beyond the preamble; the remedy often extends beyond the particular act or mischief which first suggested the necessity of the law.' " J. Bishop, Commentaries on Written Laws and Their Interpretation §51, p. 49 (1882) (quoting *Rex v. Marks*, 3 East, 157, 165 (K.B. 1802)). Therefore, while we will begin our textual analysis with the operative clause, we will return to the prefatory clause to ensure that our reading of the operative clause is consistent with the announced purpose.

1. Operative Clause.

a. "Right of the People." The first salient feature of the operative clause is that it codifies a "right of the people." . . .

> " '[T]he people' seems to have been a term of art employed in select parts of the Constitution. . . . [Its uses] sugges[t] that 'the people' protected by the Fourth Amendment, and by the First and Second Amendments, and to whom rights and powers are reserved in the Ninth and Tenth Amendments, refers to a class of persons who are part of a national community or who have otherwise developed sufficient connection with this country to be considered part of that community."

This contrasts markedly with the phrase "the militia" in the prefatory clause. As we will describe below, the "militia" in colonial America consisted of a subset of "the people"—those who were male, able bodied, and within a certain age range. Reading the Second Amendment as protecting only the right to "keep and bear Arms" in an organized militia therefore fits poorly with the operative clause's description of the holder of that right as "the people."

We start therefore with a strong presumption that the Second Amendment right is exercised individually and belongs to all Americans.

b. "Keep and bear Arms." We move now from the holder of the right—"the people"—to the substance of the right: "to keep and bear Arms."

Before addressing the verbs "keep" and "bear," we interpret their object: "Arms." The 18th-century meaning is no different from the meaning today. The 1773 edition of Samuel Johnson's dictionary defined "arms" as "weapons of offence, or armour of defence." 1 Dictionary of the English Language 107 (4th ed.) (hereinafter Johnson). Timothy Cunningham's important 1771 legal dictionary defined "arms" as "any thing that a man wears for his defence, or takes into his hands, or useth in wrath to cast at or strike another." 1 A New and Complete Law Dictionary (1771); see also N. Webster, American Dictionary of the English Language (1828) (reprinted 1989) (hereinafter Webster) (similar). . . .

Some have made the argument, bordering on the frivolous, that only those arms in existence in the 18th century are protected by the Second Amendment. We do not interpret constitutional rights that way. Just as the First Amendment protects modern forms of communications, *e.g., Reno v. American Civil Liberties Union*, 521 U.S. 844, 849, 117 S. Ct. 2329, 138 L. Ed. 2d 874 (1997), and the Fourth Amendment applies to modern forms of search, *e.g., Kyllo v. United States*, 533 U.S. 27, 35-36, 121 S. Ct. 2038, 150 L. Ed. 2d 94 (2001), the Second Amendment extends, prima facie, to all instruments that constitute bearable arms, even those that were not in existence at the time of the founding. . . .

From our review of founding-era sources, we conclude that this natural meaning was also the meaning that "bear arms" had in the 18th century. In numerous instances, "bear arms" was unambiguously used to refer to the carrying of weapons outside of an organized militia. The most prominent examples are those most relevant to the Second Amendment: Nine state constitutional provisions written in the 18th century or the first two decades of the 19th, which enshrined a right of citizens to "bear arms in defense of themselves and the state" or "bear arms in defense of himself and the state." It is clear from those formulations that "bear arms" did not refer only to carrying a weapon in an organized military unit. . . .

c. Meaning of the Operative Clause. Putting all of these textual elements together, we find that they guarantee the individual right to possess and carry weapons in case of confrontation. This meaning is strongly confirmed by the historical background of the Second Amendment. We look to this because it has always been widely understood that the Second Amendment, like the First and Fourth Amendments, codified a *pre-existing* right. The very text of the Second Amendment implicitly recognizes the pre-existence of the right and declares only that it "shall not be infringed." As we said in *United States v. Cruikshank*, 92 U.S. 542, 553, 23 L. Ed. 588 (1876), "[t]his is not a right granted by the Constitution. Neither is it in any manner dependent upon that instrument for its existence. The Second amendment declares that it shall not be infringed. . . ."

There seems to us no doubt, on the basis of both text and history, that the Second Amendment conferred an individual right to keep and bear arms. Of course the right was not unlimited, just as the First Amendment's right of free speech was not, *see, e.g., United States v. Williams*, 553 U.S. _____ , 128 S. Ct. 1830, _____ L. Ed. 2d _____ (2008). Thus, we do not read the Second Amendment to protect the right of citizens to carry arms for *any sort* of confrontation, just as we do not read the First Amendment to protect the right of citizens to speak for *any purpose*. Before turning to limitations upon the individual right, however, we must determine whether the prefatory clause of the Second Amendment comports with our interpretation of the operative clause.

2. Prefatory Clause.

The prefatory clause reads: "A well regulated Militia, being necessary to the security of a free State. . . ."

a. "Well-Regulated Militia." In *United States v. Miller*, 307 U.S. 174, 179, 59 S. Ct. 816, 83 L. Ed. 1206 (1939), we explained that "the Militia comprised all males physically capable of acting in concert for the common defense." That definition comports with founding-era sources. . . .

Petitioners take a seemingly narrower view of the militia, stating that "[m]ilitias are the state- and congressionally-regulated military forces described in the Militia Clauses (art. I, §8, cls. 15-16)." Brief for Petitioners 12. Although we agree with petitioners' interpretive assumption that "militia" means the same thing in Article I and the Second Amendment, we believe that petitioners identify the wrong thing, namely, the organized militia. Unlike armies and navies, which Congress is given the power to create ("to raise . . . Armies"; "to provide . . . a Navy," Art. I, §8, cls. 12-13), the militia is assumed by Article I already to be *in existence*. Congress is given the power to "provide for calling forth the militia," §8, cl. 15; and the power not to create, but to "organiz[e]" it— and not to organize "a" militia, which is what one would expect if the militia were to be a federal creation, but to organize "the" militia, connoting a body already in existence, *ibid.*, cl. 16. This is fully consistent with the ordinary definition of the militia as all able-bodied men. From that pool, Congress has plenary power to organize the units that will make up an effective fighting force. That is what Congress did in the first militia Act, which specified that "each and every free able-bodied white male citizen of the respective states, resident therein, who is or shall be of the age of eighteen years, and under the age of forty-five years (except as is herein after excepted) shall severally and respectively be enrolled in the militia." Act of May 8, 1792, 1 Stat. 271. To be sure, Congress need not conscript every able-bodied man into the militia, because nothing in Article I suggests that in exercising its power to organize, discipline, and arm the militia, Congress must focus upon the entire body. Although the militia consists of all able-bodied men, the federally organized militia may consist of a subset of them.

Finally, the adjective "well-regulated" implies nothing more than the imposition of proper discipline and training. . . .

b. "Security of a Free State." The phrase "security of a free state" meant "security of a free polity," not security of each of the several States as the dissent below argued, see 478 F.3d, at 405, and n.10. Joseph Story wrote in his treatise on the Constitution that "the word 'state' is used in various senses [and in] its most enlarged sense, it means the people composing a particular nation or community." 1 Story §208; see also 3 *id.*, §1890 (in reference to the Second Amendment's prefatory clause: "The militia is the natural defence of a free country"). It is true that the term "State" elsewhere in the Constitution refers to individual States, but the phrase "security of a free state" and close variations seem to have been terms of art in 18th-century political discourse, meaning a " 'free country' " or free polity. . . .

There are many reasons why the militia was thought to be "necessary to the security of a free state." See 3 Story §1890. First, of course, it is useful in repelling invasions and suppressing insurrections. Second, it renders large standing armies unnecessary-an argument that Alexander Hamilton made in favor of federal control over the militia. The Federalist No. 29, pp. 226, 227 (B. Wright ed. 1961) (A. Hamilton). Third, when the able-bodied men of a nation are trained in arms and organized, they are better able to resist tyranny.

3. Relationship between Prefatory Clause and Operative Clause

We reach the question, then: Does the preface fit with an operative clause that creates an individual right to keep and bear arms? It fits perfectly, once one knows the history that the founding generation knew and that we have described above. That history showed that the way tyrants had eliminated a militia consisting of all the able-bodied men was not by banning the militia but simply by taking away the people's arms, enabling a select militia or standing army to suppress political opponents. This is what had occurred in England that prompted codification of the right to have arms in the English Bill of Rights. . . .

It is therefore entirely sensible that the Second Amendment's prefatory clause announces the purpose for which the right was codified: to prevent elimination of the militia. The prefatory clause does not suggest that preserving the militia was the only reason Americans valued the ancient right; most undoubtedly thought it even more important for self-defense and hunting. But the threat that the new Federal Government would destroy the citizens' militia by taking away their arms was the reason that right—unlike some other English rights—was codified in a written Constitution. . . .

Like most rights, the right secured by the Second Amendment is not unlimited. From Blackstone through the 19th-century cases, commentators and courts routinely explained that the right was not a right to keep and carry any weapon whatsoever in any manner whatsoever and for whatever purpose. *See, e.g., Sheldon*, in 5 Blume 346; Rawle 123; Pomeroy 152-153; Abbott 333. For example, the majority of the 19th-century courts to consider the question held that prohibitions on carrying concealed weapons were lawful under the Second Amendment or state analogues. *See, e.g., State v. Chandler*, 5 La. Ann., at 489-490; *Nunn v. State*, 1 Ga., at 251; see generally 2 Kent *340, n.2; The American Students' Blackstone 84, n.11 (G. Chase ed. 1884). Although we do not undertake an exhaustive historical analysis today of the full scope of the Second Amendment, nothing in our opinion should be taken to cast doubt on longstanding prohibitions on the possession of firearms by felons and the mentally ill, or laws forbidding the carrying of firearms in sensitive places such as schools and government buildings, or laws imposing conditions and qualifications on the commercial sale of arms.

We also recognize another important limitation on the right to keep and carry arms. *Miller* said, as we have explained, that the sorts of weapons protected were those "in common use at the time." 307 U.S., at 179, 59 S. Ct. 816. We think that limitation is fairly supported by the historical tradition of prohibiting the carrying of "dangerous and unusual weapons." . . .

It may be objected that if weapons that are most useful in military service—M-16 rifles and the like—may be banned, then the Second Amendment right is completely detached from the prefatory clause. But as we have said, the conception of the militia at the time of the Second Amendment's ratification was the body of all citizens capable of military service, who would bring the sorts of lawful weapons that they possessed at home to militia duty. It may well be true today that a militia, to be as effective as militias in the 18th century, would require sophisticated arms that are highly unusual in society at large. Indeed, it may be true that no amount of small arms could be useful against modern-day bombers and tanks. But the fact that modern developments have limited the degree of fit between the prefatory clause and the protected right cannot change our interpretation of the right. . . .

We turn finally to the law at issue here. As we have said, the law totally bans handgun possession in the home. It also requires that any lawful firearm in the home be disassembled or bound by a trigger lock at all times, rendering it inoperable. . . .

In sum, we hold that the District's ban on handgun possession in the home violates the Second Amendment, as does its prohibition against rendering any lawful firearm in the home operable for the purpose of immediate self-defense. Assuming that Heller is not disqualified from the exercise of Second Amendment rights, the District must permit him to register his handgun and must issue him a license to carry it in the home. . . .

It is so ordered. . . .

———————————

CASE QUESTIONS

UNITED STATES v. MILLER

1. How did the Court distinguish a "militia" from a "standing army"? Why did the distinction matter to the Court's holding? Explain.

2. Did the Court appear to interpret the two clauses of the Second Amendment disjunctively or conjunctively? What support can you find for your conclusion?

DISTRICT OF COLUMBIA v. HELLER

1. How did statutory construction play a large part in the Court's holding? Explain.

2. How would the Court respond to an argument that the right to possess machine guns is not protected by the Second Amendment because they did not exist at the time the Amendment was adopted?

3. According to the Court, if the Second Amendment had not been explicitly included in the Bill of Rights would we still have a right to keep and bear arms?

4. Do you think the Court's holding in *Heller* was consistent or inconsistent with its earlier opinion in *Miller*? Explain.

HYPOTHETICAL WITH ACCOMPANYING ANALYSIS

Hypothetical

A recent frenzy has erupted over what the media has dubbed the nation's new "*it*" weapon: the Taser. Originally used by the military and law enforcement as a non-lethal alternative to firearms, the Taser is an electroshock weapon that temporarily incapacitates individuals when used properly. Because state laws regulating Tasers are sparse and individuals can easily acquire them, Tasers have gained unprecedented popularity among private citizens as a means of self-defense. However, several incidents garnered national attention when Tasers were used excessively, resulting in serious injury or death.

Due to the rapidly growing use of Tasers by public and private officials alike as well as the increasing number of deaths associated with them, Congress has enacted the following provision in a legislative package dealing with crime control:

§1219. Tasers. It shall be unlawful for any person to knowingly possess, control, or receive a Taser.

Related sections of the law provide a specific definition of "Tasers," exclude from coverage "peace officers in the performance of their lawful duties," and provide that a violation of §1219 is a felony with a potential punishment of two years' incarceration.

Ben Williams is a husband and father of five children. He lives in a less-than-ideal part of town, so he recently bought a Taser to protect his family because he didn't want to risk having a firearm in his home with so many children. When police were called to his house one evening because his teenage son was playing music too loudly and disturbing the peace, officers came upon Ben's Taser. He was arrested for violating §1219. Ben filed a Motion to Dismiss his indictment, challenging the constitutionality of the statute. Discuss the likelihood that Ben will succeed.

Analysis

The Second Amendment provides that "the right of the people to keep and bear Arms, shall not be infringed." The issue in the instant hypothetical is whether the government has the power under the Second Amendment to ban a citizen from possessing a Taser.

At the outset, it must be determined if the Second Amendment is applicable to the statute. First, the amendment applies only to federal laws because it has not been incorporated against the states. Section 1219 is part of a crime control package enacted by Congress, so it is clearly a federal law. Second, the amendment protects "the *individual* right to possess and carry weapons in case of confrontation." District of Columbia v. Heller, 128 S. Ct. 2783 (2008) (emphasis added). Section 1219 prohibits "any *person*" from knowingly possessing a Taser. Because the federal law restricts an individual's right to bear a weapon, the Second Amendment applies.

Next, it must be determined if §1219 constitutes a permissible regulation on the right to bear arms, because the Court has recognized that "[l]ike most rights, the right secured by the Second Amendment is not unlimited." *Id.* Congress may place certain restrictions on the right to bear arms, including (1) who may possess the weapon; (2) where the weapon may be possessed; (3) what type of weapon may be possessed; and (4) limitations on the commercial sale of arms. Section 1219 implicates only the third category: what type of weapon may be possessed. In United States v. Miller, 307 U.S. 174 (1939), the Court held that the Second Amendment did not protect the possession of short-barreled shotguns. *Heller* later clarified that the Second Amendment does not protect "dangerous and unusual weapons," or "those weapons not typically possessed by law-abiding citizens for lawful purposes." Applying the foregoing law to the instant case, the question that must be answered is whether a Taser constitutes a dangerous and unusual weapon not typically used for self-defense. Evidence exists that citizens *are* using Tasers for self-defense, since they are less volatile than firearms and are not regulated as much. This appears to be the exact reason why Ben Williams acquired his Taser. The counterargument is that since Tasers are relatively new weapons they would be considered "unusual," and, because they have the potential of taking a human life, they are also "dangerous." However, the stronger argument appears to be that a Taser would fall into the first category, because the Supreme Court has given examples of "dangerous and unusual weapons" to include short-barreled shotguns and machineguns. Arguably, Tasers equate to neither in terms of their lethality or dangerousness.

If a court were to hold that Tasers do not qualify as protected weapons under the definition in *Heller*, then §1219 would not violate the Second Amendment. If, on the other hand, a court were to hold that Tasers do qualify as protected weapons, then the statute would be in violation of the Second Amendment.

Regardless of the resolution to this issue, however, §1219 would likely be unconstitutional for another reason. The Tenth Amendment provides that "[t]he powers not delegated to the United States by the Constitution . . . are reserved to the States respectively, or to the people." Included within this concept is the fact that general "police powers" are reserved to the states. As further explained in United States v. Lopez, 514 U.S. 549 (1995), "the States possess primary authority for defining and enforcing the criminal law." In the instant case, §1219 is clearly an attempt by Congress to regulate criminal law, an area left to the states to regulate as they so choose. Because Congress made no attempt to justify the law based on any of its specifically enumerated powers within the Constitution, it exceeded its authority.

In conclusion, Ben will have a very strong case that §1219 is unconstitutional for alternative reasons. First, Ben could succeed in arguing that the statute violates the Second Amendment because it restricts his right to possess a protected weapon. Even if a court were to hold that Tasers are not the types of weapons protected by the Second Amendment, §1219 will likely be struck down as violating the states' police powers to regulate the criminal laws free from interference by the federal government.

For several years the rapidly growing problem of illegal immigrants and smugglers has concerned the citizens living in border states with Mexico. Despite constant promises from the federal government to ensure that more resources and manpower will be devoted to preventing Mexicans from illegally crossing the border, little has been done. So, citizens have decided to take matters into their own hands. Within the last few years, groups of civilian volunteers in Arizona, Texas, New Mexico, and California have begun patrolling the borders in shifts to stop illegal immigration. Some of the groups contain as many as 1,000 volunteers, and some have even coined informal names, such as "The Border Busters," "The Militia Men," and "Smuggler Snuffers." The citizens patrolling the borders are armed with their own weapons, although a large percentage have no military training or real experience with weapons.

Despite the fact that the groups claim they are only peacefully protecting our country from foreign invasion, those opposed to these makeshift border patrols say the groups are nothing more than "vigilante, trigger-happy Mexican-haters" who are looking for an excuse to use violence. They further cite to several recent tragedies to illustrate their point. In Arizona, a late-night border crossing went awry, resulting in the shooting deaths of four Mexicans by Smuggler Snuffers. In Texas, The Militia Men opened fire on several families of illegal immigrants, killing three small children and wounding a dozen others. And in New Mexico, a member of the Border Busters mistook two volunteers for immigrants and shot and killed them both.

The above events have prompted action by the federal government. The proposed law, unofficially titled "The National Border Safety and Security Act," (NBSSA), is designed to allay the increasing violence of these volunteer groups and to ensure that already strained relations with the Mexican government remain civil. The law reads in relevant part:

THE NATIONAL BORDER SAFETY AND SECURITY ACT

§101. Prohibited Persons.

(a) It shall be unlawful for any person or any groups of persons to possess firearms within ten (10) miles of the contiguous border of the United States and another nation. Excluded from this Section are any duly authorized federal or state law enforcement officials. . . .

§501. Enforcement of Provisions.

(a) Local and state law enforcement officials shall conduct periodic unannounced sweeps of the lands within ten (10) miles of the contiguous border of the United States and another nation to ensure the compliance with §101(a) of this Act. . . .

Discuss whether the NBSSA would constitute a permissible regulation of the right to bear arms under the Second Amendment, and whether any other Constitutional provisions would be implicated.

DISCUSSION QUESTIONS

1. Research challenge: Provide a chronology of major gun control laws enacted by Congress since the Second Amendment. For each law, include (A) the title of the law; (B) the year it was enacted; and (C) the major components of the law.

2. Brandon is a senior in a state public high school. One day he is caught with a loaded handgun hidden in his backpack. He is ultimately convicted of violating a federal law that prohibits any individual from "knowingly possessing a firearm in a place known to be a school zone." Do you agree with such a law? Do you think Congress should have the power to criminalize Brandon's conduct in a state public school? Explain. *See* United States v. Lopez, 514 U.S. 549 (1995).

3. Congress, believing that the states aren't doing enough to ensure that guns are being sold to responsible individuals, passes a law requiring state and local law enforcement agencies to run background checks on anyone wishing to purchase a gun. Tom Trotter, the sheriff of a small Midwestern town, challenges the law as unconstitutional. Who wins? *See* Printz v. United States, 521 U.S. 898 (1997).

4. Revisit Questions 2 and 3. What legal authority did the Court rely upon for each decision? What do those cases have in common?

5. Would federal laws restricting the possession of Anthrax violate the Second Amendment? Other biological weapons? Explain.

6. Does the Second Amendment apply *only* to guns? What other weapons, if any, would it apply to? How does the Court's opinion in *Heller* help you answer this question?

7. Research challenge: What is a "Saturday Night Special" and how is it significant to the Second Amendment? What prominent political figure was murdered with this type of weapon?

8. On March 28, 1998, 13-year-old Mitchell Johnson and 11-year-old Andrew Golden opened fire on the playground of their middle school in Jonesboro, Arkansas, killing four students and one teacher. Subsequently, the victims' families filed suit against the manufacturer of a rifle used in the shootings, seeking millions of dollars in damages for failure to install trigger locks on their weapons. On April 20, 1999, teenagers Dylan Klebold and Eric Harris killed 12 students and one teacher during their shooting rampage at Columbine High School in Littleton, Colorado. The parents of Isaiah Shoals, one of the victims, also considered a civil lawsuit against a gun manufacturer for marketing the semi-automatic pistol used in the shootings to make the

weapon attractive to criminals. Do you agree with these lawsuits? Why or why not?

9. Research challenge: Many states have enacted various types of Child Access Prevention (CAP) laws. What, specifically, do these laws regulate? How could such laws have possibly saved the life of six-year-old Kayla Rolland, a first grader at a Michigan elementary school in 2000?

10. Compare and contrast a "militia" during the time period of the Second Amendment with a militia in our society today. In your opinion, should the evolution of the term result in an evolved and perhaps even different interpretation of the Second Amendment than what was originally intended by its drafters? Where else is a "militia" explicitly mentioned in the Constitution?

11. Research challenge: Familiarize yourself with the details of the Virginia Tech campus shooting that occurred on April 16, 2007. How can you reconcile an individual's right to privacy with respect to the disclosure of mental illness versus the public's right to safety? In your opinion, should college students be permitted to carry concealed weapons in order to prevent tragedies like Virginia Tech? Should the faculty be armed? What are the pros and cons?

12. Other than the Second Amendment's right to bear arms, what other portions of the Bill of Rights have not been incorporated against the states via the Fourteenth Amendment? Why do you think these provisions have not yet been incorporated? *See, e.g.,* United States v. Cruikshank, 92 U.S. 542 (1875), and Duncan v. Louisiana, 391 U.S. 145 (1968).

13. What are some categories of individuals who traditionally have been prohibited from purchasing or possessing firearms? Do you agree with these categories? Are there any you would add?

14. What is the "NCIS"? How is it significant to gun control? What are some advantages and disadvantages of it?

15. Research challenge: What laws does your jurisdiction have in place with regard to the right to bear arms? Do you agree with those laws? Explain.

16. Following the September 11, 2001, attacks on the World Trade Center and Pentagon, numerous federal laws were enacted to protect our nation from terrorism. One proposed law, supported by both President Bush and the Justice Department, would give the attorney general discretion to block the sales of a firearm to any suspect on a "terrorist watch list." Would you support such a law? Why or why not?

True/False

1. Although the Second Amendment protects an individual's right to bear arms, it is not an absolute right; the federal government may place restrictions on who may possess a weapon or where it may be possessed.

2. Even if the right to bear arms were not mentioned in the Constitution or Amendments, American citizens would still have the right.

3. The Second Amendment does not protect the right to bear any type of weapon.

4. Although the federal government cannot enact its own laws requiring background checks prior to purchasing weapons, it can enact laws requiring the states to conduct background checks prior to selling firearms to individuals.

5. According to the Court in *Miller*, a militia is the same thing as a standing army.

Multiple Choice

6. Which authority found specifically in the Constitution typically gives the federal government the ability to regulate the right to bear arms?

   A. The Second Amendment.
   B. The Commerce Clause.
   C. Both A and B.
   D. Neither A nor B.

7. According to the Supreme Court's opinion in *United States v. Miller*, which of the following was *not* true about a militia at the time when the Second Amendment was ratified?

   A. The militia was comprised only of men.
   B. An individual had to be within a certain age range to be part of the militia.
   C. An individual had the choice as to whether to join the militia.
   D. Members of the militia used their own weapons.

8. Which of the following factors contributes to making the Second Amendment unique among the protections within the Bill of Rights?

    A. Unlike most protections within the Bill of Rights, it has not been incorporated to apply to the states.

    B. Relatively little Supreme Court case law exists interpreting the amendment.

    C. Both A and B.

    D. Neither A nor B.

9. In *District of Columbia v. Heller*, which of the District of Columbia's provisions did the Supreme Court declare was in violation of the Second Amendment?

    A. The provision that totally banned handgun possession in the home.

    B. The provision that required any lawful firearms in the home to be disassembled or bound by a trigger lock at all times.

    C. Both A and B.

    D. Neither A nor B.

10. Which of the following statements would *best* represent *Heller*'s interpretation of its earlier precedent in *United States v. Miller*?

    A. *Miller* should be overturned because it held that individuals have a right to bear arms only in connection with a militia.

    B. *Miller* was entirely consistent with the Court's determination in *Heller* that the right to bear arms is an individual right, and *Miller* held only that certain types of weapons were not protected by the Second Amendment.

    C. *Miller* is inapplicable to *Heller* because the two cases dealt with different laws.

    D. *Miller* is not worth considering as precedent because it was decided 70 years prior to *Heller*.

Chapter 11

The Constitution and the Criminal Justice System

> "From the very beginning, our . . . constitutions and laws have laid great emphasis on procedural and substantive safeguards designed to assure fair trials before impartial tribunals in which every defendant stands equal before the law."
>
> —**Justice Hugo L. Black, Gideon v. Wainwright, 372 U.S. 335 (1963)**

INTRODUCTION

Imagine this . . . You've been accused of a horrific crime, and your life is literally on the line. An indictment is handed down against you, and that very same day your trial begins. You aren't given an attorney, you aren't allowed to call any witnesses to testify on your behalf, and the evidence admitted against you boils down to nothing short of gossip and rumors. Within a week's time you've been convicted, but you aren't permitted to appeal. Instead, you sit in jail and wait. Yes, you wait, until only a few days later you are hanged. Executed by order of the law for the heinous crimes for which you have been found guilty.

Can you imagine something so unfair, so outrageous actually happening? Well it did. And not in some primitive civilization, but right here in our country. Her name was Bridget Bishop. She was the first of dozens of people accused of witchcraft and supposedly brought to justice during the infamous Salem Witch Trials in the early 1690s. Bridget's story is hardly what we would consider "justice" by today's standards. Sadly, though, she wasn't alone. Many people stood accused of crimes in our nation—some blatantly innocent and others arguably guilty—without any of the basic procedural protections that we now take for granted. The Framers of our founding documents, well aware of cases like Bridget's, decided that "justice" wasn't just a hollow term. Instead, it was a

173

promise to someone accused of a crime that they would be assured fairness and equality in the criminal justice system.

So how did the Framers attempt to prevent atrocities like Bridget's from happening again? The Bill of Rights. Or, more specifically, four constitutional amendments which provided some of the most cherished rights to an individual accused of a crime: the right to an attorney, the right against unreasonable searches and seizures, the right to be free from self-incrimination, the right to due process of law, and the right to confront adverse witnesses, just to name a few. Later, the adoption of the Fourteenth Amendment further enhanced those protections. Collectively, these amendments work to ensure that cases like Bridget's are hopefully a thing of the past. Within this chapter, you'll find a discussion of those protections and what consequences the government will face for violating them.

And by the way, Bridget may have been denied justice in 1692 when she was sent to the gallows, but she did get the proverbial last word on the matter. On Halloween day in 2001, over 300 years after her execution, Bridget was officially exonerated from any wrongdoing. Although late, perhaps Bridget Bishop finally did receive the justice she deserved.

STUDENT *Checklist*

The Constitution & the Criminal Justice System

1. Do the constitutional amendments that offer protection to someone suspected of a crime **apply**?

▪ Was a **government agent** directly involved in the alleged constitutional violation; or

▪ Was an individual involved who was **acting as an instrument or agent** of the government or with the **participation or knowledge** of a government official?

2. Which of the **protections** within the constitutional amendments was/ were **implicated**?

▪ The **Fourth Amendment**
  ▫ The right to be free from **unreasonable searches and seizures**?
  ▫ The **warrant requirement**?

▪ The **Fifth Amendment**
  ▫ The right to be free from **double jeopardy**?
  ▫ The right to be free from **self-incrimination**?
  ▫ The right to **due process of law**?

▪ The **Sixth Amendment**
  ▫ The right to a **speedy** and **public trial**?
  ▫ The right to an **impartial jury**?
  ▫ The right to **confront** witnesses?
  ▫ The right to the **assistance of counsel**?

- The **Eighth Amendment**
  - The right to be free from **excessive bail or fines**?
  - The right to be free from **cruel and unusual punishment**?

- The **Fourteenth Amendment**
  - The right to **due process of law**?
  - The right to **equal protection of the laws**?

3. If a **violation** of an individual's constitutional rights occurred, what is the appropriate **remedy** for that violation?

- The **suppression of evidence** at trial based on the **Exclusionary Rule**?

- The **dismissal of charges** against the accused?

- A **retrial** of the accused?

SUPREME COURT CASES

MAPP v. OHIO, 367 U.S. 643 (1961)

[In *Mapp,* the Supreme Court extended the judicially created exclusionary rule, once applicable only to the federal government, to the states.]

 . . . On May 23, 1957, three Cleveland police officers arrived at appellant's residence in that city pursuant to information that "person (was) hiding out in the home, who was wanted for questioning in connection with a recent bombing, and that there was a large amount of policy paraphernalia being hidden in the home." Miss Mapp and her daughter by a former marriage lived on the top floor of the two-family dwelling. Upon their arrival at that house, the officers knocked on the door and demanded entrance but appellant, after telephoning her attorney, refused to admit them without a search warrant. They advised their headquarters of the situation and undertook a surveillance of the house.

The officers again sought entrance some three hours later when four or more additional officers arrived on the scene. When Miss Mapp did not come to the door immediately, at least one of the several doors to the house was forcibly opened and the policemen gained admittance. Meanwhile Miss Mapp's attorney arrived, but the officers, having secured their own entry, and continuing in their defiance of the law, would permit him neither to see Miss Mapp nor to enter the house. It appears that Miss Mapp was halfway down the stairs from the upper floor to the front door when the officers, in this highhanded manner, broke into the hall. She demanded to see the search warrant. A paper, claimed to be a warrant, was held up by one of the officers. She grabbed the "warrant" and placed it in her bosom. A struggle ensued in which the officers recovered the piece of paper and as a result of which they handcuffed appellant because she had been "belligerent" in resisting their official rescue of the "warrant" from her person. Running roughshod over appellant, a policeman "grabbed" her, "twisted (her) hand," and she "yelled (and) pleaded with him" because "it was hurting." Appellant, in handcuffs, was then forcibly taken upstairs to her bedroom where the officers searched a dresser, a chest of drawers, a closet and some suitcases. They also looked into a photo album and through personal papers belonging to the appellant. The search spread to the rest of the second floor including the child's bedroom, the living room, the kitchen and a dinette.

The basement of the building and a trunk found therein were also searched. The obscene materials for possession of which she was ultimately convicted were discovered in the course of that widespread search.

At the trial no search warrant was produced by the prosecution, nor was the failure to produce one explained or accounted for. At best, "There is, in the record, considerable doubt as to whether there ever was any warrant for the search of defendant's home." 170 Ohio St. at page 430, 166 N.E.2d at page 389. . . .

I

Seventy-five years ago, in Boyd v. United States, 1886, 116 U.S. 616, 630, 6 S. Ct. 524, 532, 29 L. Ed. 746, considering the Fourth and Fifth Amendments as running "almost into each other" on the facts before it, this Court held that the doctrines of those Amendments

> "apply to all invasions on the part of the government and its employees of the sanctity of a man's home and the privacies of life. It is not the breaking of his doors, and the rummaging of his drawers, that constitutes the essence of the offence; but it is the invasion of his indefeasible right of personal security, personal liberty and private property. . . . Breaking into a house and opening boxes and drawers are circumstances of aggravation; but any forcible and compulsory extortion of a man's own testimony or of his private papers to be used as evidence to convict him of crime or to forfeit his goods, is within the condemnation . . . (of those Amendments)."

The Court noted that

> "constitutional provisions for the security of person and property should be liberally construed. . . . It is the duty of courts to be watchful for the constitutional rights of the citizen, and against any stealthy encroachments thereon." At page 635 of 116 U.S., at page 535 of 6 S. Ct.

In this jealous regard for maintaining the integrity of individual rights, the Court gave life to Madison's prediction that "independent tribunals of justice . . . will be naturally led to resist every encroachment upon rights expressly stipulated for in the Constitution by the declaration of rights." I Annals of Cong. 439 (1789). Concluding, the Court specifically referred to the use of the evidence there seized as "unconstitutional." At page 638 of 116 U.S., at page 536 of 6 S. Ct.

Less than 30 years after *Boyd*, this Court, in Weeks v. United States, 1914, 232 U.S. 383, at pages 391-392, 34 S. Ct. 341, at page 344, 58 L. Ed. 652, stated that

> "the 4th Amendment . . . put the courts of the United States and Federal officials, in the exercise of their power and authority, under limitations and restraints (and) . . . forever secure(d) the people, their persons, houses, papers, and effects, against all unreasonable searches and seizures under the guise of law . . . and the duty of giving to it force and effect is obligatory upon all entrusted under our Federal system with the enforcement of the laws."

Specifically dealing with the use of the evidence unconstitutionally seized, the Court concluded:

> "If letters and private documents can thus be seized and held and used in evidence against a citizen accused of an offense, the protection of the Fourth Amendment declaring his right to be secure against such searches and seizures is of no value,

and, so far as those thus placed are concerned, might as well be stricken from the Constitution. The efforts of the courts and their officials to bring the guilty to punishment, praiseworthy as they are, are not to be aided by the sacrifice of those great principles established by years of endeavor and suffering which have resulted in their embodiment in the fundamental law of the land." At page 393 of 232 U.S., at page 344 of 34 S. Ct.

Finally, the Court in that case clearly stated that use of the seized evidence involved "a denial of the constitutional rights of the accused." At page 398 of 232 U.S., at page 346 of 34 S. Ct. Thus, in the year 1914, in the *Weeks* case, this Court "for the first time" held that "in a federal prosecution the Fourth Amendment barred the use of evidence secured through an illegal search and seizure." Wolf v. People of State of Colorado, supra, 338 U.S. at page 28, 69 S. Ct. at page 1361. This Court has ever since required of federal law officers a strict adherence to that command which this Court has held to be a clear, specific, and constitutionally required—even if judicially implied—deterrent safeguard without insistence upon which the Fourth Amendment would have been reduced to "a form of words." Holmes J., Silverthorne Lumber Co. v. United States, 1920, 251 U.S. 385, 392, 40 S. Ct. 182, 183, 64 L. Ed. 319. It meant, quite simply, that "conviction by means of unlawful seizures and enforced confessions . . . should find no sanction in the judgments of the courts . . . ," Weeks v. United States, supra, 232 U.S. at page 392, 34 S. Ct. at page 344, and that such evidence "shall not be used at all." Silverthorne Lumber Co. v. United States, supra, 251 U.S. at page 392, 40 S. Ct. at page 183.

There are in the cases of this Court some passing references to the *Weeks* rule as being one of evidence. But the plain and unequivocal language of *Weeks*—and its later paraphrase in *Wolf*—to the effect that the *Weeks* rule is of constitutional origin, remains entirely undisturbed. In Byars v. United States, 1927, 273 U.S. 28, at pages 29-30, 47 S. Ct. 248, at pages 248-249, 71 L. Ed. 520, a unanimous Court declared that "the doctrine (cannot) . . . be tolerated under our constitutional system, that evidences of crime discovered by a federal officer in making a search without lawful warrant may be used against the victim of the unlawful search where a timely challenge has been interposed." (Emphasis added.) The Court, in Olmstead v. United States, 1928, 277 U.S. 438, at page 462, 48 S. Ct. 564, 567, 72 L. Ed. 944, in unmistakable language restated the *Weeks* rule:

> "The striking outcome of the *Weeks* case and those which followed it was the sweeping declaration that the Fourth Amendment, although not referring to or limiting the use of evidence in court, really forbade its introduction if obtained by government officers through a violation of the amendment." . . .

Since the Fourth Amendment's right of privacy has been declared enforceable against the States through the Due Process Clause of the Fourteenth, it is enforceable against them by the same sanction of exclusion as is used against the Federal Government. Were it otherwise, then just as without the *Weeks* rule the assurance against unreasonable federal searches and seizures would be "a form of words," valueless and undeserving of mention in a perpetual charter of inestimable human liberties, so too, without that rule the freedom from state invasions of privacy would be so ephemeral and so neatly severed from its conceptual nexus with the freedom from all brutish means of coercing evidence as not to merit this Court's high regard as a freedom "implicit in the concept of ordered liberty." At the time that the Court held in *Wolf* that the Amendment was applicable to the States through the Due Process Clause, the cases of this

Court, as we have seen, had steadfastly held that as to federal officers the Fourth Amendment included the exclusion of the evidence seized in violation of its provisions. Even *Wolf* "stoutly adhered" to that proposition. The right to privacy, when conceded operatively enforceable against the States, was not susceptible of destruction by avulsion of the sanction upon which its protection and enjoyment had always been deemed dependent under the *Boyd*, *Weeks* and *Silverthorne* cases. Therefore, in extending the substantive protections of due process to all constitutionally unreasonable searches—state or federal—it was logically and constitutionally necessary that the exclusion doctrine—an essential part of the right to privacy—be also insisted upon as an essential ingredient of the right newly recognized by the *Wolf* case. In short, the admission of the new constitutional right by *Wolf* could not consistently tolerate denial of its most important constitutional privilege, namely, the exclusion of the evidence which an accused had been forced to give by reason of the unlawful seizure. To hold otherwise is to grant the right but in reality to withhold its privilege and enjoyment. Only last year the Court itself recognized that the purpose of the exclusionary rule "is to deter—to compel respect for the constitutional guaranty in the only effectively available way—by removing the incentive to disregard it." Elkins v. United States, supra, 364 U.S. at page 217, 80 S. Ct. at page 1444.

Indeed, we are aware of no restraint, similar to that rejected today, conditioning the enforcement of any other basic constitutional right. The right to privacy, no less important than any other right carefully and particularly reserved to the people, would stand in marked contrast to all other rights declared as "basic to a free society." Wolf v. People of State of Colorado, supra, 338 U.S. at page 27, 69 S. Ct. at page 1361. This Court has not hesitated to enforce as strictly against the States as it does against the Federal Government the rights of free speech and of a free press, the rights to notice and to a fair, public trial, including, as it does, the right not to be convicted by use of a coerced confession, however logically relevant it be, and without regard to its reliability. Rogers v. Richmond, 1961, 365 U.S. 534, 81 S. Ct. 735, 5 L. Ed. 2d 760. And nothing could be more certain that that when a coerced confession is involved, "the relevant rules of evidence" are overridden without regard to "the incidence of such conduct by the police," slight or frequent. Why should not the same rule apply to what is tantamount to coerced testimony by way of unconstitutional seizure of goods, papers, effect, documents, etc.? We find that, as to the Federal Government, the Fourth and Fifth Amendments and, as to the States, the freedom from unconscionable invasions of privacy and the freedom from convictions based upon coerced confessions do enjoy an "intimate relation" in their perpetuation of "principles of humanity and civil liberty (secured) . . . only after years of struggle." . . . The philosophy of each Amendment and of each freedom is complementary to, although not dependent upon, that of the other in its sphere of influence—the very least that together they assure in either sphere is that no man is to be convicted on unconstitutional evidence. Cf. Rochin v. People of State of California, 1952, 342 U.S. 165, 173, 72 S. Ct. 205, 210, 96 L. Ed. 183.

V

Moreover, our holding that the exclusionary rule is an essential part of both the Fourth and Fourteenth Amendments is not only the logical dictate of prior cases, but it also makes very good sense. There is no war between the Constitution and common sense. Presently, a federal prosecutor may make no use of evidence illegally seized, but a State's attorney across the street may, although he supposedly is operating under the enforceable prohibitions of the same Amendment. Thus the State, by admitting evidence unlawfully seized, serves to encourage disobedience to the Federal Constitution which it is bound to uphold. Moreover, as was said in *Elkins*, "(t)he very essence of a healthy federalism depends upon the avoidance of needless conflict between state and federal courts." 364 U.S. at page 221, 80 S. Ct. at page 1446. . . .

Federal-state cooperation in the solution of crime under constitutional standards will be promoted, if only by recognition of their now mutual obligation to respect the same fundamental criteria in their approaches. "However much in a particular case insistence upon such rules may appear as a technicality that inures to the benefit of a guilty person, the history of the criminal law proves that tolerance of shortcut methods in law enforcement impairs its enduring effectiveness." Miller v. United States, 1958, 357 U.S. 301, 313, 78 S. Ct. 1190, 1197, 2 L. Ed. 2d 1332. Denying shortcuts to only one of two cooperating law enforcement agencies tends naturally to breed legitimate suspicion of "working arrangements" whose results are equally tainted. Byars v. United States, 1927, 273 U.S. 28, 47 S. Ct. 248, 71 L. Ed. 520; Lustig v. United States, 1949, 338 U.S. 74, 69 S. Ct. 1372, 93 L. Ed. 1819.

There are those who say, as did Justice (then Judge) Cardozo, that under our constitutional exclusionary doctrine "(t)he criminal is to go free because the constable has blundered." People v. Defore, 242 N.Y. at page 21, 150 N.E. at page 587. In some cases this will undoubtedly be the result. But, as was said in *Elkins*, "there is another consideration—the imperative of judicial integrity." 364 U.S. at page 222, 80 S. Ct. at page 1447. The criminal goes free, if he must, but it is the law that sets him free. Nothing can destroy a government more quickly than its failure to observe its own laws, or worse, its disregard of the charter of its own existence. As Mr. Justice Brandeis, dissenting, said in Olmstead v. United States, 1928, 277 U.S. 438, 485, 48 S. Ct. 564, 575, 72 L. Ed. 944: "Our government is the potent, the omnipresent teacher. For good or for ill, it teaches the whole people by its example. . . . If the government becomes a lawbreaker, it breeds contempt for law; it invites every man to become a law unto himself; it invites anarchy." Nor can it lightly be assumed that, as a practical matter, adoption of the exclusionary rule fetters law enforcement. Only last year this Court expressly considered that contention and found that "pragmatic evidence of a sort" to the contrary was not wanting. Elkins v. United States, supra, 364 U.S. at page 218, 80 S. Ct. at page 1444. The Court noted that

> "The federal courts themselves have operated under the exclusionary rule of *Weeks* for almost half a century; yet it has not been suggested either that the Federal Bureau of Investigation has thereby been rendered ineffective, or that the administration of criminal justice in the federal courts has thereby been disrupted. Moreover, the experience of the states is impressive. . . . The movement towards the rule of exclusion has been halting but seemingly inexorable." Id., 364 U.S. at pages 218-219, 80 S. Ct. at pages 1444-1445.

The ignoble shortcut to conviction left open to the State tends to destroy the entire system of constitutional restraints on which the liberties of the people rest. Having once recognized that the right to privacy embodied in the Fourth Amendment is enforceable against the States, and that the right to be secure against rude invasions of privacy by state officers is, therefore, constitutional in origin, we can no longer permit that right to remain an empty promise. Because it is enforceable in the same manner and to like effect as other basic rights secured by the Due Process Clause, we can no longer permit it to be revocable at the whim of any police officer who, in the name of law enforcement itself, chooses to suspend its enjoyment. Our decision, founded on reason and truth, gives to the individual no more than that which the Constitution guarantees him, to the police officer no less than that to which honest law enforcement is entitled, and, to the courts, that judicial integrity so necessary in the true administration of justice.

The judgment of the Supreme Court of Ohio is reversed and the cause remanded for further proceedings not inconsistent with this opinion. Reversed and remanded.

KENNEDY v. LOUISIANA, 1287 S. CT. 2641 (2008)

[The Petitioner was convicted of the brutal rape of L.H., his stepdaughter. He was convicted of aggravated rape and pursuant to a Louisiana statute was sentenced to death. His conviction and sentence were affirmed by the Supreme Court of Louisiana.]

II

The Eighth Amendment, applicable to the States through the Fourteenth Amendment, provides that "[e]xcessive bail shall not be required, nor excessive fines imposed, nor cruel and unusual punishments inflicted." The Amendment proscribes "all excessive punishments, as well as cruel and unusual punishments that may or may not be excessive." *Atkins,* 536 U.S., at 311, n.7, 122 S. Ct. 2242. The Court explained in *Atkins, id.,* at 311, 122 S. Ct. 2242, and *Roper, supra,* at 560, 125 S. Ct. 1183, that the Eighth Amendment's protection against excessive or cruel and unusual punishments flows from the basic "precept of justice that punishment for [a] crime should be graduated and proportioned to [the] offense." *Weems v. United States,* 217 U.S. 349, 367, 30 S. Ct. 544, 54 L. Ed. 793 (1910). Whether this requirement has been fulfilled is determined not by the standards that prevailed when the Eighth Amendment was adopted in 1791 but by the norms that "currently prevail." *Atkins, supra,* at 311, 122 S. Ct. 2242. The Amendment "draw[s] its meaning from the evolving standards of decency that mark the progress of a maturing society." *Trop v. Dulles,* 356 U.S. 86, 101, 78 S. Ct. 590, 2 L. Ed. 2d 630 (1958) (plurality opinion). This is because "[t]he standard of extreme cruelty is not merely descriptive, but necessarily embodies a moral judgment. The standard itself remains the same, but its applicability must change as the basic mores of society change." *Furman v. Georgia,* 408 U.S. 238, 382, 92 S. Ct. 2726, 33 L. Ed. 2d 346 (1972) (Burger, C. J., dissenting). . . .

Applying this principle, we held in *Roper* and *Atkins* that the execution of juveniles and mentally retarded persons are punishments violative of the Eighth Amendment because the offender had a diminished personal responsibility for the crime. See *Roper, supra,* at 571-573, 125 S. Ct. 1183; *Atkins, supra,* at 318, 320, 122 S. Ct. 2242. The Court further has held that the death penalty can be disproportionate to the crime itself where the crime did not result, or was not intended to result, in death of the victim. In *Coker,* 433 U.S. 584, 97 S. Ct. 2861, 53 L. Ed. 2d 982, for instance, the Court held it would be unconstitutional to execute an offender who had raped an adult woman. See also *Eberheart, supra* (holding unconstitutional in light of *Coker* a sentence of death for the kidnaping and rape of an adult woman). And in *Enmund v. Florida,* 458 U.S. 782, 102 S. Ct. 3368, 73 L. Ed. 2d 1140 (1982), the Court overturned the capital sentence of a defendant who aided and abetted a robbery during which a murder was committed but did not himself kill, attempt to kill, or intend that a killing would take place. On the other hand, in *Tison v. Arizona,* 481 U.S. 137, 107 S. Ct. 1676, 95 L. Ed. 2d 127 (1987), the Court allowed the defendants' death sentences to stand where they did not themselves kill the victims but their involvement in the events leading up to the murders was active, recklessly indifferent, and substantial. . . .

Based both on consensus and our own independent judgment, our holding is that a death sentence for one who raped but did not kill a child, and who did not intend to assist another in killing the child, is unconstitutional under the Eighth and Fourteenth Amendments. . . .

Our decision is consistent with the justifications offered for the death penalty. *Gregg* instructs that capital punishment is excessive when it is grossly out of proportion to the crime or it does not fulfill the two distinct social purposes served by the death penalty: retribution and deterrence of capital crimes. . . .

As in *Coker,* here it cannot be said with any certainty that the death penalty for child rape serves no deterrent or retributive function. . . . This argument does not overcome other objections, however. The incongruity between the crime of child rape and the harshness of the death penalty poses risks of over-punishment and counsels against a constitutional ruling that the death penalty can be expanded to include this offense.

The goal of retribution, which reflects society's and the victim's interests in seeing that the offender is repaid for the hurt he caused, see *Atkins,* 536 U.S., at 319, 122 S. Ct. 2242; *Furman, supra,* at 308, 92 S. Ct. 2726 (Stewart, J., concurring), does not justify the harshness of the death penalty here. In measuring retribution, as well as other objectives of criminal law, it is appropriate to distinguish between a particularly depraved murder that merits death as a form of retribution and the crime of child rape. See Part IV-A, *supra*; *Coker, supra,* at 597-598, 97 S. Ct. 2861 (plurality opinion).

There is an additional reason for our conclusion that imposing the death penalty for child rape would not further retributive purposes. In considering whether retribution is served, among other factors we have looked to whether capital punishment "has the potential . . . to allow the community as a whole, including the surviving family and friends of the victim, to affirm its own judgment that the culpability of the prisoner is so serious that the ultimate penalty must be sought and imposed." *Panetti v. Quarterman,* 551 U.S. ___, ___, 127 S. Ct. 2842, 2847, 168 L. Ed. 2d 662 (2007). In considering the death penalty for nonhomicide offenses this inquiry necessarily also must include the question whether the death penalty balances the wrong to the victim. Cf. *Roper,* 543 U.S., at 571, 125 S. Ct. 1183.

It is not at all evident that the child rape victim's hurt is lessened when the law permits the death of the perpetrator. Capital cases require a long-term commitment by those who testify for the prosecution, especially when guilt and sentencing determinations are in multiple proceedings. In cases like this the key testimony is not just from the family but from the victim herself. During formative years of her adolescence, made all the more daunting for having to come to terms with the brutality of her experience, L.H. was required to discuss the case at length with law enforcement personnel. In a public trial she was required to recount once more all the details of the crime to a jury as the State pursued the death of her stepfather. . . . And in the end the State made L.H. a central figure in its decision to seek the death penalty, telling the jury in closing statements: "[L.H.] is asking you, asking you to set up a time and place when he dies." Tr. 121 (Aug. 26, 2003).

Society's desire to inflict the death penalty for child rape by enlisting the child victim to assist it over the course of years in asking for capital punishment forces a moral choice on the child, who is not of mature age to make that choice. The way the death penalty here involves the child victim in its enforcement can compromise a decent legal system; and this is but a subset of fundamental difficulties capital punishment can cause in the administration and enforcement of laws proscribing child rape.

There are, moreover, serious systemic concerns in prosecuting the crime of child rape that are relevant to the constitutionality of making it a capital offense. The problem of unreliable, induced, and even imagined child testimony means there is a "special risk of wrongful execution" in some child rape cases. *Atkins, supra,* at 321, 122 S. Ct. 2242. See also Brief for National Association of Criminal Defense Lawyers et al. as *Amici Curiae* 5-17. This undermines, at least to some degree, the meaningful contribution of the death penalty to legitimate goals of punishment. Studies conclude that children are highly susceptible to suggestive questioning techniques like repetition, guided imagery, and selective reinforcement. . . .

Similar criticisms pertain to other cases involving child witnesses; but child rape cases present heightened concerns because the central narrative and account of the crime often comes from the child herself. She and the accused are, in most instances, the only ones present when the crime was committed. See *Pennsylvania v. Ritchie,* 480 U.S. 39, 60, 107 S. Ct. 989, 94 L. Ed. 2d 40 (1987). Cf. Goodman, Testifying in Criminal Court, at 118. And the question in a capital case is not just the fact of the crime, including, say, proof of rape as distinct from abuse short of rape, but details bearing upon brutality in its commission. These matters are subject to fabrication or exaggeration, or both. See Ceci and Friedman, *supra;* Quas, *supra.* Although capital punishment does bring retribution, and the legislature here has chosen to use it for this end, its judgment must be weighed, in deciding the constitutional question, against the special risks of unreliable testimony with respect to this crime.

With respect to deterrence, if the death penalty adds to the risk of non-reporting, that, too, diminishes the penalty's objectives. Underreporting is a common problem with respect to child sexual abuse. . . . The experience of the *amici* who work with child victims indicates that, when the punishment is death, both the victim and the victim's family members may be more likely to shield the perpetrator from discovery, thus increasing underreporting. See Brief for National Association of Social Workers et al. as *Amici Curiae* 11-13. As a result, punishment by death may not result in more deterrence or more effective enforcement.

In addition, by in effect making the punishment for child rape and murder equivalent, a State that punishes child rape by death may remove a strong incentive for the rapist not to kill the victim. Assuming the offender behaves in a rational way, as one must to justify the penalty on grounds of deterrence, the penalty in some respects gives less protection, not more, to the victim, who is often the sole witness to the crime. . . . It might be argued that, even if the death penalty results in a marginal increase in the incentive to kill, this is counterbalanced by a marginally increased deterrent to commit the crime at all. Whatever balance the legislature strikes, however, uncertainty on the point makes the argument for the penalty less compelling than for homicide crimes.

Each of these propositions, standing alone, might not establish the unconstitutionality of the death penalty for the crime of child rape. Taken in sum, however, they demonstrate the serious negative consequences of making child rape a capital offense. These considerations lead us to conclude, in our independent judgment, that the death penalty is not a proportional punishment for the rape of a child. . . . *It is so ordered.*

CASE QUESTIONS

MAPP v. OHIO

1. Does the Court conclude that the Exclusionary Rule is a constitutional rule or a rule of evidence? Why would it matter one way or the other?

2. What are some ways in which illegal police conduct might be deterred other than the exclusion of illegally obtained evidence from trial? What potential problems can you foresee with these alternative methods of deterrence and why?

3. Research challenge: *Mapp v. Ohio* deals specifically with the Exclusionary Rule as it applies to the Fourth Amendment. How has the Exclusionary Rule been extended to other constitutional protections in a criminal case, and what case law supports your answers?

KENNEDY v. LOUISIANA

1. What other cases were explicitly discussed by the Court in which the imposition of the death penalty violated the Eighth Amendment? Do you agree with the holdings in those cases? Why or why not?

2. Given the Court's holding, how would you predict the Court might rule if presented with the issue of whether the death penalty constitutes cruel and unusual punishment for "offenses against the State" such as treason, espionage, terrorism, or drug kingpin activity? What led you to your prediction?

3. What justifications does the Court give for its decision in Part IV of the opinion? What arguments can you make that the points raised by the Court perhaps aren't relevant to the issue before it? Explain.

4. Do you agree with the Court's holding? Explain. If it were your job to draft death penalty legislation for your jurisdiction, who would you make eligible for the death penalty and why?

HYPOTHETICAL WITH ACCOMPANYING ANALSYSIS

Hypothetical

Mary was home one evening watching her favorite reruns when there was a knock at her door. As she looked through the peep hole, Mary noticed two uniformed police officers standing on the other side. Mary, somewhat alarmed, cracked the door slightly. "Good evening ma'am," Officer Baker said to her. "We're with the Bayside Police Department. Our agency is collecting clothing for the local homeless shelter, and we were wondering if you had any contributions." "Oh, sure," Mary replied, "I have some old coats and sweaters in my bedroom closet. I live here alone and I don't have much space, so I'd be happy to get rid of some stuff. Come in and have a seat while I get them." Mary invited the officers to make themselves comfortable on her living room couch. "I'll only be a few minutes," she said, and then she disappeared into a back room. Both officers sat patiently and waited, but as the minutes ticked by and Mary never reappeared, they began to wonder. At first they were slightly annoyed, but soon they began to worry. "Ma'am?" Officer Hatfield called. "Ma'am, is everything okay?" No reply. "Maybe something happened to her," Officer Baker said to Officer Hatfield. "Maybe she's hurt or something." After calling for Mary a few more times, the officers decided to investigate. They headed in the direction Mary had disappeared and they came to three doors, one of which was opened and the other two were closed. Officer Baker poked his head through the opened door into what appeared to be an office. "Hello? You in here ma'am?" As he quickly glanced around the room he spotted several plastic baggies of a green leafy substance sitting on a desk along with matches and rolling papers. Baker, who had been on the force almost 20 years and at one point was the commander of the Narcotics Division, immediately recognized the "substance" as marijuana. He seized all of the items on the desk. Hatfield, meanwhile, had pushed opened one of the closed doors to find a small room with numerous sealed boxes labeled "magazines" stacked on top of one another. Hatfield opened one of the boxes and found it full of magazines containing child pornography. Hatfield seized a box.

Finally, Mary reappeared from behind the third door with a shopping bag full of clothes. "I'm so sorry I took so long," Mary said. "Uh, ma'am," Officer Baker said, "you're gonna have to come with me now, you're under arrest." Baker handcuffed Mary while Hatfield searched her pockets, finding a single joint of marijuana. As soon as she was handcuffed she blurted out, "I had to do it! I just lost my job and selling the drugs and porn was the only way I could make ends meet!" "How long have you been selling?" Hatfield asked her. "About six months," Mary sobbed. Officer Baker then informed Mary of her *Miranda* rights and placed her in the back of the squad car. Mary was officially on her way to charges of possession of marijuana and possession of child pornography.

To Be Continued . . .

Analysis

The constitutional amendments offer a variety of protections to ensure that the rights of someone accused of a crime are respected. When analyzing the scenario, three issues must be addressed: First, whether those protections are triggered, thus making the amendments applicable; second, which specific protections are implicated; and third, whether any of the protections were violated, and, if so, what remedy Mary will be entitled to.

The amendments are only triggered if the government was either directly involved in the alleged violation or if an individual was acting as an instrument or agent of the government. *See* Coolidge v. New Hampshire, 403 U.S. 443 (1971). In the instant case, Officers Baker and Hatfield were clearly government officials—they were in uniform and they identified themselves as police officers. The fact that they were at Mary's residence collecting for a charity and not because she was suspected of a crime is immaterial. At all times they were acting on behalf of the government. The various protections within the amendments are, therefore, applicable.

Next, it must be determined which constitutional amendments are implicated. The scenario deals with the Fourth Amendment right against unreasonable searches and seizures, as well as the Fifth Amendment's right against compelled self-incrimination. Each will be discussed separately.

The Fourth Amendment explicitly provides that "the right of the people to be secure in their persons, houses, papers, and effects, against unreasonable searches and seizures, shall not be violated[.]" In the instant case, the officers conducted a search when they looked for Mary. That search occurred in Mary's apartment, where she possessed a reasonable expectation of privacy. *See* Katz v. United States, 389 U.S. 347 (1967). The officers did not have a warrant at any time during their search. The Supreme Court has acknowledged that, while it is preferable for government officials to obtain a warrant *prior* to conducting a search and/or seizure, in limited circumstances officials may search without first obtaining a warrant. The officers initially gained entry to Mary's apartment by her lawful consent. Subsequently, Officers Baker and Hatfield became concerned that Mary had perhaps become hurt. Thus, their search was pursuant to their obligations of ensuring public safety and could lawfully be conducted without a warrant. Brigham City v. Stuart, 547 U.S. 398 (2006). In order to comply with the Fourth Amendment, the scope of a search must be reasonable in light of what is being searched for. Harris v. United States, 331 U.S. 145 (1947). In this case, the officers were searching for Mary. It would thus be reasonable for them to open doors and conduct a room-to-room search. Therefore, Officer Baker was justified in "quickly glancing" around the office while calling for Mary. As he did so, he noticed the marijuana and paraphernalia sitting on the desk. The Supreme Court has also held that if, during the course of a prior valid intrusion, items are discovered that are "immediately apparent" to be evidence of a crime, officers are not expected to ignore such illegality even though inadvertently discovered. *Coolidge v. New Hampshire, supra.* The plain view doctrine described above applies here. Officer Baker was lawfully searching for Mary, and he came upon the marijuana and paraphernalia sitting in open view on a desk. Given Baker's prior training and experience, he immediately recognized the substance as marijuana. Baker was thus entitled to seize the items. Officer Hatfield was also legally permitted to push open the door in order to search for Mary. The child pornography, however, was not in plain view because it was not until Hatfield manipulated the sealed box by opening the lid that he discovered the illicit nature of its contents. The seizure of the magazines, therefore, was unconstitutional. Once Mary was arrested, the officers were permitted to conduct a warrantless search incident to arrest. Chimel v. California, 395 U.S. 752 (1969). The search incident to arrest exception to the warrant requirement permits a search of an arrestee's person, so the joint of marijuana recovered from Mary's pocket was properly seized. In sum, the Exclusionary Rule will require that the child pornography be suppressed as evidence because it was unlawfully seized, Mapp v. Ohio, 367 U.S. 643 (1961), but all other evidence will be admitted at Mary's trial.

In addition to the Fourth Amendment, the right against compelled self-incrimination is also implicated in this scenario. The Fifth Amendment provides that "[n]o person . . . shall be compelled in any criminal case to be a witness against himself." The Supreme Court has held that an individual is entitled to this protection when in custody and prior to interrogation. Miranda v. Arizona, 384 U.S. 436 (1966). With regard to the first component, "custody" occurs when an individual has been "deprived of his freedom of action in any significant way." *Id.* Mary was clearly in police custody when she made both statements because she had just been formally placed under arrest and handcuffed by Officer Baker. It next becomes important to examine Mary's statements separately. Her first statement, "I had to do it! I just lost my job and selling the drugs and porn was the only way I could make ends meet," was not in response to any questioning by either officer but was instead "blurted" out. Because she was not being interrogated when she made the first statement, Mary's Fifth Amendment rights were not violated. Mary's second statement, "About six months," however, was made in direct response to Officer Hatfield's question as to how long she had been selling the illegal items. Mary, therefore, was in custody and was being interrogated when she gave the information. Because she had not been informed of her basic constitutional rights prior to making that statement, it was unconstitutionally obtained. The Exclusionary Rule will prohibit the second statement from being admissible in the prosecution's case against her.

In conclusion, limited violations of both the Fourth and Fifth Amendments will result in the suppression of some evidence against Mary. The majority of evidence, however, will be admissible against her.

. . . As Mary's trial date quickly approached, Prosecutor Gavin Gallow became concerned he might not get a conviction. So, while Mary sat in her tiny cell awaiting trial (she was unable to post bond), Gallow dragged his feet as long as possible. Even though Mary's defense attorney complained on more than one occasion about the delay, her trial didn't begin until three years after she had been arrested. During the jury selection process, Mary noticed that Gallow appeared to be excluding all African Americans from her jury. Mary, who was Caucasian, complained about the alleged exclusions on account of race. The trial judge ruled against her, explaining, "Since you are not a member of the class allegedly being excluded, you have no constitutional right to challenge the exclusion of the jurors." Soon afterward, a jury of all Caucasians was seated. The trial itself lasted a little over two days, and after less than an hour of deliberation, the jury found Mary guilty on all counts. Mary appealed her conviction, but because she had spent all of her money on attorney's fees for the trial, Mary was flat broke. She requested that an attorney be appointed to represent her on appeal, but the judge denied her request, explaining to Mary that the Sixth Amendment right to counsel did not apply to appeals. Mary had no choice but to act *pro se* on appeal. By some miracle Mary was able to win a reversal due to various evidentiary errors at the trial. Mary was ecstatic, but her elation didn't last long because Gallow announced that he planned on retrying Mary for all crimes. Mary objected, arguing that a retrial would violate her right against double jeopardy.

Analyze the relevant constitutional provisions that are implicated in this scenario, and discuss in detail whether any violations of Mary's rights occurred.

DISCUSSION QUESTIONS

1. What are the factors that must be considered when determining whether the accused's Sixth Amendment right to a speedy trial has been violated? What is the remedy for such a violation? Who is Alex Kelly, and did he successfully argue that his 1997 Connecticut trial for alleged rapes committed in 1986 violated his right to a speedy trial? Why or why not?

2. When does the Sixth Amendment right to counsel apply? Is an individual constitutionally entitled to an attorney during the appellate process? Explain.

3. Tiffany is a very jealous person. When her boyfriend broke up with her and began dating Courtney, she couldn't handle it. One night she attacked Courtney with a baseball bat. Courtney was gravely injured and hospitalized in a coma. Nine months after the attack, Tiffany was convicted by a jury of attempted first-degree murder. Exactly one week after the conviction, Courtney died from her injuries. Can Tiffany now be prosecuted for murder?

What if Tiffany had been acquitted of the attempted first-degree murder charge, would your answer change? Explain. *See* Diaz v. United States, 223 U.S. 442 (1912).

4. Are juveniles afforded the same constitutional protections within the criminal justice system as adults? In your opinion, *should* they be afforded the same protections? Explain.

5. A city bank has just been robbed. A call is broadcast over the police radio that the perpetrator was a Caucasian male, over 6 feet in height, wearing a dark sweatshirt. Officer Carr, who is on foot patrol only three blocks from the bank, sees a man fitting the description walking casually along the other side of the street. Can Officer Carr arrest the man? Can he stop the man? Can he search the man? Would your answer to the last question change depending upon whether the man had been lawfully arrested? Explain. *Compare* Chimel v. California, 395 U.S. 752 (1960), *with* Terry v. Ohio, 392 U.S. 1 (1968).

6. How does the Equal Protection Clause of the Fourteenth Amendment (see Chapter 7, *supra*) interact with the other constitutional amendments discussed within this chapter to ensure basic fairness and equality in the criminal justice process? What categories of defendants does the Clause usually offer protection to that might not have traditionally received such protection?

7. Jonathan and Christopher are suspected of having burglarized several homes in an upscale neighborhood. Office Zeigler arrives at Jonathan's house one night, tells him that he is under arrest for the crimes, and while standing in Jonathan's living room, he proceeds to question Jonathan extensively about the burglaries. Jonathan provides Officer Zeigler with a full confession. Meanwhile, Christopher drives himself to the police station. As soon as he enters the front door he comes across Officer Adams, who is completely uninvolved in the burglary investigation and has no idea who Christopher is. Christopher says to Adams, "I have something I need to get off my chest," and he provides Adams with a full confession to the burglaries. Neither suspect was Mirandized prior to their respective confessions. In which case, if either, did the officers violate the Fifth Amendment right against compelled self-incrimination? Explain. *See* Miranda v. Arizona, 384 U.S. 436 (1966).

8. What are the underlying purposes of the Sixth Amendment's Confrontation Clause? Who is Julie Jensen, and why did her "testimony" in a 2008 Wisconsin murder trial present a unique issue regarding the defendant's right to confrontation? What was the ultimate outcome in the case?

9. The police have just arrested Anne for murdering her husband. The officers Mirandize Anne and take her to the police station, where she demands an attorney. The police refuse, and after 72 hours of continual questioning and without the benefit of a lawyer, Anne confesses to the murder. She also informs police that she dumped the gun used in the shooting in a shallow lake. Police dredge the lake and recover the gun. At her murder trial, will Anne's confession be admissible against her? Will the gun be admissible against her? Explain. What if right as Anne was giving officers the location of the murder weapon, teenagers who were swimming in the lake

inadvertently came across the weapon and turned it in to the police. Would the gun be admissible against her then? Why or why not? *See* Nix v. Williams, 467 U.S. 431 (1984).

10. The Jacksons live on a 100-acre farm. They are suspected of drug dealing. In which of the following places would government officials likely need a warrant prior to searching for evidence and why? (A) A detached garage with a guest room overtop and ten yards from the Jackson's main residence; (B) Plastic garbage bags placed on the street curb by the Jacksons for collection early the next morning; (C) A locked tool shed 50 yards from the main residence with a six-foot tall fence around it and a "No Trespassing" sign affixed to its door; or (D) A barn located over 100 yards from the main residence with no doors and no signs. What additional facts might you want to know when answering these questions? *See* Katz v. United States, 389 U.S. 347 (1967).

11. Research challenge: Who is James Graves, and why was he charged with four counts of manslaughter in Florida in 2002? Given what you learned in *Kennedy v. Louisiana*, do you think the Supreme Court would sanction a death sentence against him for the crimes he committed? Explain.

True/False

Read the below hypothetical and answer the questions that follow.

Brady was on trial for raping his 12-year-old niece. Brady's attorney was convinced of his guilt, despite Brady's continual protestations of innocence. After the prosecution rested its case, Brady's attorney declined to offer any evidence and refused to put Brady on the stand despite his wishes to testify. A jury of 12 women found Brady guilty, and he was later sentenced to death for the crime.

1. According to *Kennedy v. Louisiana*, Brady can be sentenced to death for the crime *only* if an aggravating circumstance was present during the rape.

2. Brady's niece may be permitted to testify in a manner other than a direct face-to-face confrontation in the courtroom if it can first be shown that the alternative means of testifying are necessary to protect the welfare of his niece and that she would be traumatized from having to testify in Brady's presence at trial.

3. In order for Brady to succeed in claiming ineffective assistance of trial counsel, Brady will only need to show that his counsel's performance was objectively incompetent regardless of whether Brady was prejudiced by counsel's performance.

4. The fact that Brady's jury consisted only of women will automatically serve as a violation of his Sixth Amendment right to a jury representative of the community.

5. Brady's attorney violated his Fifth Amendment rights by not permitting Brady to testify at trial despite his wishes to do so.

Multiple Choice

6. James is arrested for terrorism, a federal crime. He is read his *Miranda* rights and taken to the police station. He demands an attorney, but the agents fail to provide him with one. James is beaten continually until he confesses to the crime. Which of James's constitutional rights was *not* violated?

   A. His Fifth Amendment right against compelled self-incrimination.
   B. His Fifth Amendment right to due process of law.
   C. His Sixth Amendment right to counsel.
   D. All of the above rights were violated.

7. Revisit the above question. Assuming James is brought to trial on terrorism charges, what will most likely happen to his confession?

   A. It will be kept out at trial based on the Exclusionary Rule.
   B. It will be kept out at trial because it was obtained in violation of *Miranda*.
   C. It will be admitted at trial because the evidence was not obtained in violation of the Fourth Amendment's right to be free from unreasonable searches and seizures.
   D. It will be admitted as evidence at trial with an explanation to the jury regarding the circumstances under which the confession was given.

8. Assume that James is found guilty of his crimes and sentenced to life imprisonment. The sentencing judge then ordered that James's entire sentence be served in solitary confinement. If James wanted to challenge the judge's sentence on constitutional grounds, which amendment(s) would provide him with the best chance of succeeding in his challenge?

   A. The Eighth Amendment prohibition of cruel and unusual punishment.
   B. The Fifth Amendment right to due process of law.
   C. Both A and B.
   D. Neither A nor B.

9. Tracey has been indicted on charges of burglary. She is ordered to appear in a line-up along with five other women before the homeowner/victim in the case. Each woman is required to say, "If you call the cops, I'll kill you," which was allegedly what the burglar said prior to fleeing the crime scene. Tracey requests counsel at the line-up, but her request is denied. Which of Tracey's constitutional rights was most likely violated?

   A. Her Fourth Amendment right to be free from unreasonable searches and seizures, because making her appear in the line-up amounted to a seizure of her person.
   B. Her Fifth Amendment right against compelled self-incrimination, because she was required to utter the words said by the perpetrator of the crime.
   C. Her Sixth Amendment right to counsel, because she had been formally accused of a crime, and a line-up is a critical stage of the criminal justice process.
   D. All of the above were violations of her constitutional rights.

10. Which of the following constitutional provisions, if violated, will result in an outright dismissal of all charges without the ability to reinitiate those charges?

   A. The Fourth Amendment right against unreasonable searches and seizures.
   B. The Sixth Amendment right to a speedy trial.
   C. The Sixth Amendment right to confrontation.
   D. The Fifth or Fourteenth Amendment right to due process of law.

12

Voting Rights

"The vote is the most powerful instrument ever
devised by man for breaking down injustice
and destroying the terrible walls which imprison
men because they are different from other men."

—Lyndon B. Johnson

INTRODUCTION

The right to vote in free and fair elections is the foundation of democracy. That voting rights are core to our system of government and that our democracy has changed over time is evidenced by how rules and regulations regarding voting are interspersed throughout the Constitution and Amendments. Article I established the process of electing Senators. However, that process was changed by the Seventeenth Amendment, which mandated that Senators be elected directly by the people. Article I also established the process of electing the President and Vice President. However, that process was also changed by the Twelfth Amendment.

The Constitution vests the power to establish local electoral processes and voting qualifications to the states. From the infancy of our democracy through the 1960s, some states, especially in the South, undertook practices which limited suffrage of minorities and women. As even the Supreme Court interpreted the body of the Constitution to mean that women and African Americans could not vote, passage of the Fifteenth and Nineteenth Amendments were required to prevent states from denying suffrage on the basis of race or sex, respectively. Although these non-discrimination amendments were passed, the states still undertook practices, such as poll taxes, literacy tests, grandfather clauses, and racial gerrymandering, that indirectly resulted in limitations on suffrage by minorities. The Twenty-fourth Amendment was then passed to eliminate the poll tax, and the Supreme Court invalidated these practices that had a discriminatory impact. *See* Lane v. Wilson, 307 U.S. 268 (1939) (banning grandfather clauses); Smith v. Allwright, 321 U.S. 649 (1944) (preventing whites-only primaries); Harper v. Virginia Board of Elections, 383 U.S. 663 (1966)

193

(eliminating state poll taxes). Ultimately, Congress became involved in ensuring voting rights with the passage of the Voting Rights Act of 1965 (VRA). Although the VRA challengers argued that the Act exceeded Congress's power, the Supreme Court concluded that Congress did have the power to enforce the Fifteenth Amendment (preventing states from denying suffrage on the basis of sex or race), and the VRA finally allowed non-white citizens equal voting rights. South Carolina v. Katzenbach, 383 U.S. 301 (1966).

The political process and democracy itself can be quite messy and lead to raging disputes, which are often partisan in nature. Parties in power pass voting laws and undertake congressional and local districting in manners which will help ensure that the party in power remains in power. Courts are particularly loathe to engage in purely political disputes. As such, historically, they only become involved when it is essential to ensure universal suffrage, that each person's vote is equally counted, and that elections are fair in that there is a real choice in parties or candidates. Otherwise, the courts will refrain from entering partisan disputes.

The Rehnquist Court was criticized for having violated this long-standing practice of staying outside of the political fray in ruling in the case of Bush v. Gore, 531 U.S. 98 (2000). In this case, the 2000 presidential election was hotly contested, and the electoral votes cast by the State of Florida would decide the election. The popular vote was so close in the state that Gore demanded a manual recount. The procedures and timeline for the recount were challenged and litigation ensued. Eventually, the state supreme court extended the time for the recount and held that only certain counties with divergent recount procedures would participate in the recount. The U.S. Supreme Court ruled that the Florida recount process was so arbitrary that voters within the state were treated differently. As such, the recount process violated equal protection and was unconstitutional. However, critics of the Supreme Court's decision do not so much focus on the ruling that the process was arbitrary and unconstitutional as the remedy imposed by the Supreme Court. Many critics consider that the appropriate remedy should have been that all of the votes in the entire state be recounted under the same procedures so that each vote was treated equally. Instead, by a 5-4 vote the Court ruled to stop the recount completely. This effectively declared Bush the winner. Because the only justices who ruled to stop the recount were Republican appointees, critics see this decision as being political in nature and contrary to the principle that courts should be above the political fray in ruling on voting rights cases.

STUDENT *Checklist*

Voting Rights

1. Is there universal suffrage?

2. Does each person's vote count equally? (Is there one person one vote?)

3. Is there a choice of parties or candidates?

SUPREME COURT CASES

HARPER v. VIRGINIA BOARD OF ELECTIONS,
383 U.S. 663 (1966)

[Virginia residents filed suit to have Virginia's poll tax declared unconstitutional. The citizens argued that it violated the First and Fourteenth Amendments of the U.S. Constitution. Although the U.S. Constitution does not explicitly mention the right to vote in state elections, it determined that because Virginia held state elections that the Equal Protection Clause of the Fourteenth Amendment applied. The Court did not review the case on First Amendment issues.]

Mr. Justice DOUGLAS delivered the opinion of the Court. . . .

While the right to vote in federal elections is conferred by Art. I, §2, of the Constitution, the right to vote in state elections is nowhere expressly mentioned. . . . [O]nce the franchise is granted to the electorate, lines may not be drawn which are inconsistent with the Equal Protection Clause of the Fourteenth Amendment. That is to say, the right of suffrage "is subject to the imposition of state standards which are not discriminatory and which do not contravene any restriction that Congress, acting pursuant to its constitutional powers, has imposed." . . .

We conclude that a State violates the Equal Protection Clause of the Fourteenth Amendment whenever it makes the affluence of the voter or payment of any fee an electoral standard. Voter qualifications have no relation to wealth nor to paying or not paying this or any other tax. Our cases demonstrate that the Equal Protection Clause of the Fourteenth Amendment restrains the States from fixing voter qualifications which invidiously discriminate. Thus without questioning the power of a State to impose reasonable residence restrictions on the availability of the ballot, that a State may not deny the opportunity to vote to a bona fide resident merely because he is a member of the armed services. "By forbidding a soldier ever to controvert the presumption of non-residence, the Texas Constitution imposes an invidious discrimination in violation of the Fourteenth Amendment." Previously we had said that neither homesite nor occupation "affords a permissible basis for distinguishing between qualified voters within the State." We think the same must be true of requirements of wealth or affluence or payment of a fee.

Long ago in *Yick Wo v. Hopkins* . . . , the Court referred to "the political franchise of voting" as a "fundamental political right, because preservative of all rights." Recently in *Reynolds v. Sims* . . . we said, "Undoubtedly, the right of suffrage is a fundamental matter in a free and democratic society. Especially since the right to exercise the franchise in a free and unimpaired manner is preservative of other basic civil and political rights, any alleged infringement of the right of citizens to vote must be carefully and meticulously scrutinized." There we were considering charges that voters in one part of the State had greater representation per person in the State Legislature than voters in another part of the State. We concluded:

"A citizen, a qualified voter, is no more nor no less so because he lives in the city or on the farm. This is the clear and strong command of our Constitution's Equal Protection Clause. This is an essential part of the concept of a government of laws and not men. This is at the heart of Lincoln's vision of 'government of the people, by the people, [and] for the people.' The Equal Protection Clause demands no less than substantially equal state legislative representation for all citizens, of all places as well as of all races."

We say the same whether the citizen, otherwise qualified to vote, has $1.50 in his pocket or nothing at all, pays the fee or fails to pay it. The principle that denies the State the right to dilute a citizen's vote on account of his economic status or other such factors by analogy bars a system which excludes those unable to pay a fee to vote or who fail to pay.

It is argued that a State may exact fees from citizens for many different kinds of licenses; that if it can demand from all an equal fee for a driver's license, it can demand from all an equal poll tax for voting. But we must remember that the interest of the State, when it comes to voting, is limited to the power to fix qualifications. Wealth, like race, creed, or color, is not germane to one's ability to participate intelligently in the electoral process. Lines drawn on the basis of wealth or property, like those of race are traditionally disfavored. To introduce wealth or payment of a fee as a measure of a voter's qualifications is to introduce a capricious or irrelevant factor. The degree of the discrimination is irrelevant. In this context—that is, as a condition of obtaining a ballot—the requirement of fee paying causes an "invidious" discrimination that runs afoul of the Equal Protection Clause. Levy "by the poll," as stated in *Breedlove v. Suttles*, is an old familiar form of taxation; and we say nothing to impair its validity so long as it is not made a condition to the exercise of the franchise. *Breedlove v. Suttles* sanctioned its use as "a prerequisite of voting." To that extent the Breedlove case is overruled. . . .

We have long been mindful that where fundamental rights and liberties are asserted under the Equal Protection Clause, classifications which might invade or restrain them must be closely scrutinized and carefully confined.

Those principles apply here. For to repeat, wealth or fee paying has, in our view, no relation to voting qualifications; the right to vote is too precious, too fundamental to be so burdened or conditioned.

Reversed.

CRAWFORD v. MARION COUNTY ELECTION BOARD, 128 S. CT. 1610 (2008)

[The State of Indiana passed a law requiring citizens to present a valid photo identification issued by the government in order to cast a vote. The law provided that if someone was indigent or could not be photographed because of religious reasons they could only cast a provisional ballot, and their votes would not be counted unless they completed an affidavit at the clerk's office within ten days of the election. The State of Indiana would provide free photo identification to qualified voters who could establish their identity and residency.

Two lawsuits were filed challenging this law. The suits were consolidated. The plaintiffs included the state Democratic Party, elected officials and organizations representing the poor, elderly, minority and disabled voters. The plaintiffs asserted that the voter photo identification law violated the Fourteenth Amendment's Equal Protection Clause because it would "arbitrarily disfranchise qualified voters who do not possess the required identification and will place an unjustified burden on those who cannot readily obtain such identification." The plaintiffs also asserted that photo identification was not a necessary and proper way to avoid fraud.

The State of Indiana argued that it passed the law to try to modernize an antiquated election system and to prevent voter fraud.

The trial court, issued summary judgment in favor of the defendants, holding that the plaintiffs had not introduced evidence of any Indiana resident who would actually be unable to vote because of the photo identification requirement, estimating that 99% of eligible voters already possessed a government issued photo identification. The Court of Appeals affirmed the trial court's decision.

The U.S. Supreme Court considered the case and applied the Harper decision discussed above and specifically recognized that "even rational restrictions on the right to vote are invidious if they are unrelated to voter qualifications." It also considered the cases of Norman v. Reed, 502 U.S. 279, 288-289 (1992) (holding that "severe restriction" was not justified by a narrowly drawn state interest of compelling importance" and that even what appears to be a slight burden requires the state to demonstrate legitimate interests "sufficiently weighty to justify the limitation."), and Burdick v. Takushi, 504 U.S. 428, 434 (1992) (holding that in dealing with "reasonable, nondiscriminatory restrictions" that a court must balance the asserted injury to the voting rights against the "'precise interests put forward by the State as justifications for the burden imposed by its rule.'" (quoting Anderson v. Calabrezze, 460 U.S. 780, 789 (1983)).]

Justice STEVENS announced the judgment of the Court and delivered an opinion in which THE CHIEF JUSTICE and Justice KENNEDY join.

* * *

ELECTION MODERNIZATION

Two recently enacted federal statutes have made it necessary for States to reexamine their election procedures. Both contain provisions consistent with a State's choice to use government-issued photo identification as a relevant source of information concerning a citizen's eligibility to vote.

In the National Voter Registration Act of 1993 (NVRA), Congress established procedures that would both increase the number of registered voters and protect the integrity of the electoral process. The statute requires state motor vehicle driver's license applications to serve as voter registration applications. While that requirement has increased the number of registered voters, the statute also contains a provision restricting States' ability to remove names from the lists of registered voters. These protections have been partly responsible for inflated lists of registered voters. For example, evidence credited by Judge Barker estimated that as of 2004 Indiana's voter rolls were inflated by as much as 41.4%, and data collected by the Election Assistance Committee in 2004 indicated that 19 of 92 Indiana counties had registration totals exceeding 100% of the 2004 voting-age population.

In HAVA, Congress required every State to create and maintain a computerized statewide list of all registered voters. HAVA also requires the States to verify voter information contained in a voter registration application and specifies either an "applicant's driver's license number" or "the last 4 digits of the applicant's social security number" as acceptable verifications. If an individual has neither number, the State is required to assign the applicant a voter identification number.

HAVA also imposes new identification requirements for individuals registering to vote for the first time who submit their applications by mail. If the voter is casting his ballot in person, he must present local election officials with written identification, which may be either "a current and valid photo identification" or another form of documentation such as a bank statement or paycheck. If the voter is voting by mail, he must include a copy of the identification with his ballot. A voter may also include a copy of the documentation with his application or provide his driver's license number or Social Security number for verification. Finally, in a provision entitled "Fail-safe voting," HAVA authorizes the casting of provisional ballots by challenged voters.

Of course, neither HAVA nor NVRA required Indiana to enact [the voter photo identification statute] but they do indicate that Congress believes that photo identification is one effective method of establishing a voter's qualification to vote and that the integrity of elections is enhanced through improved technology. That conclusion is also supported by a report issued shortly after the enactment of [the statute] by the Commission on Federal Election Reform chaired by former President Jimmy Carter and former Secretary of State James A. Baker III. . . .

> "A good registration list will ensure that citizens are only registered in one place, but election officials still need to make sure that the person arriving at a polling site is the same one that is named on the registration list. In the old days and in small towns where everyone knows each other, voters did not need to identify themselves. But in the United States, where 40 million people move each year, and in urban areas where some people do not even know the people living in their own apartment building let alone their precinct, some form of identification is needed.
>
> "There is no evidence of extensive fraud in U.S. elections or of multiple voting, but both occur, and it could affect the outcome of a close election. The electoral system cannot inspire public confidence if no safeguards exist to deter or detect fraud or to confirm the identity of voters. Photo identification cards currently are needed to board a plane, enter federal buildings, and cash a check. Voting is equally important. . . ."

VOTER FRAUD

The only kind of voter fraud that [the statute at issue] addresses is in-person voter impersonation at polling places. The record contains no evidence of any such fraud actually occurring in Indiana at any time in its history. Moreover, petitioners argue that provisions of the Indiana Criminal Code punishing such conduct as a felony provide adequate protection against the risk that such conduct will occur in the future. It remains true, however, that flagrant examples of such fraud in other parts of the country have been documented throughout this Nation's history by respected historians and journalists, that occasional examples have surfaced in recent years, and that Indiana's own experience with fraudulent voting in the 2003 Democratic primary for East Chicago Mayor—though perpetrated using absentee ballots and not in-person fraud—demonstrate that not only is the risk of voter fraud real but that it could affect the outcome of a close election.

There is no question about the legitimacy or importance of the State's interest in counting only the votes of eligible voters. Moreover, the interest in orderly administration and accurate recordkeeping provides a sufficient justification for carefully identifying all voters participating in the election process. While the most effective method of preventing election fraud may well be debatable, the propriety of doing so is perfectly clear.

. . . Even though Indiana's own negligence may have contributed to the serious inflation of its registration lists when [the statute] was enacted, the fact of inflated voter rolls does provide a neutral and nondiscriminatory reason supporting the State's decision to require photo identification.

SAFEGUARDING VOTER CONFIDENCE

Finally, the State contends that it has an interest in protecting public confidence "in the integrity and legitimacy of representative government." While that interest is closely related to the State's interest in preventing voter fraud, public confidence in the integrity of the electoral process has independent significance, because it encourages citizen participation in the democratic process. As the Carter-Baker Report observed, the "electoral system cannot inspire public confidence if no safeguards exist to deter or detect fraud or to confirm the identity of voters."

III

States employ different methods of identifying eligible voters at the polls. Some merely check off the names of registered voters who identify themselves; others require voters to present registration cards or other documentation before they can vote; some require voters to sign their names so their signatures can be compared with those on file; and in recent years an increasing number of States have relied primarily on photo identification. A photo identification requirement imposes some burdens on voters that other methods of identification do not share. For example, a voter may lose his photo identification, may have his wallet stolen on the way to the polls, or may not resemble the photo in the identification because he recently grew a beard. Burdens of that sort arising from life's vagaries, however, are neither so serious nor so frequent as to raise any question about the constitutionality of [the statute], the availability of the right to cast a provisional ballot provides an adequate remedy for problems of that character.

The burdens that are relevant to the issue before us are those imposed on persons who are eligible to vote but do not possess a current photo identification that complies with the requirements of [the statute]. The fact that most voters already possess a valid driver's license, or some other form of acceptable identification, would not save the statute under our reasoning in *Harper*, if the State required voters to pay a tax or a fee to obtain a new photo identification. But just as other States provide free voter registration cards, the photo identification cards issued by Indiana's BMV are also free. For most voters who need them, the inconvenience of making a trip to the BMV, gathering the required documents, and posing for a photograph surely does not qualify as a substantial burden on the right to vote, or even represent a significant increase over the usual burdens of voting.

Both evidence in the record and facts of which we may take judicial notice, however, indicate that a somewhat heavier burden may be placed on a limited number of persons. They include elderly persons born out-of-state, who may have difficulty obtaining a birth certificate; persons who because of economic or other personal limitations may find it difficult either to secure a copy of their birth certificate or to assemble the other required documentation to obtain a state-issued identification; homeless persons; and persons with a religious objection to being photographed. If we assume, as the evidence suggests, that some members of these classes were registered voters when [the statute] was enacted, the new identification requirement may have imposed a special burden on their right to vote.

The severity of that burden is, of course, mitigated by the fact that, if eligible, voters without photo identification may cast provisional ballots that will ultimately be counted. To do so, however, they must travel to the circuit court clerk's office within 10 days to execute the required affidavit. It is unlikely that such a requirement would pose a constitutional problem unless it is wholly unjustified. And even assuming that the burden may not be justified as to a few voters, that conclusion is by no means sufficient to establish petitioners' right to the relief they seek in this litigation.

IV

Given the fact that petitioners have advanced a broad attack on the constitutionality of [the statute], seeking relief that would invalidate the statute in all its applications, they bear a heavy burden of persuasion. . . .

Petitioners ask this Court, in effect, to perform a unique balancing analysis that looks specifically at a small number of voters who may experience a special burden under the statute and weighs their burdens against the State's broad interests in protecting election integrity. Petitioners urge us to ask whether the State's interests justify the burden imposed on voters who cannot afford or obtain a birth certificate and who must make a second trip to the circuit court clerk's office after voting. But on the basis of the evidence in the record it is not possible to quantify either the magnitude of the burden on this narrow class of voters or the portion of the burden imposed on them that is fully justified.

First, the evidence in the record does not provide us with the number of registered voters without photo identification. . . . Much of the argument about the numbers of such voters comes from extrarecord, postjudgment studies, the accuracy of which has not been tested in the trial court.

Further, the deposition evidence presented in the District Court does not provide any concrete evidence of the burden imposed on voters who currently lack photo identification. . . .

The record says virtually nothing about the difficulties faced by either indigent voters or voters with religious objections to being photographed. . . .

In sum, on the basis of the record that has been made in this litigation, we cannot conclude that the statute imposes "excessively burdensome requirements" on any class of voters. . . . The " 'precise interests' " advanced by the State are therefore sufficient to defeat petitioners' facial challenge to [the statute]. . . .

In their briefs, petitioners stress the fact that all of the Republicans in the General Assembly voted in favor of [the statute] and the Democrats were unanimous in opposing it. In her opinion rejecting petitioners' facial challenge, Judge Barker noted that the litigation was the result of a partisan dispute that had "spilled out of the state house into the courts." It is fair to infer that partisan considerations may have played a significant role in the decision to enact [the statute]. If such considerations had provided the only justification for a photo identification requirement, we may also assume that [the statute] would suffer the same fate as the poll tax at issue in Harper.

But if a nondiscriminatory law is supported by valid neutral justifications, those justifications should not be disregarded simply because partisan interests may have provided one motivation for the votes of individual legislators. The state interests identified as justifications for [the statute] are both neutral and sufficiently strong to require us to reject petitioners' facial attack on the statute. The application of the statute to the vast majority of Indiana voters is amply justified by the valid interest in protecting "the integrity and reliability of the electoral process."

The judgment of the Court of Appeals is affirmed.

CASE QUESTIONS

HARPER v. VIRGINIA BOARD OF ELECTIONS

1. What is a poll tax?

2. Why do you think the U.S. Constitution does not explicitly mention the right to vote in state elections?

3. Explain why the *Harper* Court considered the poll tax unconstitutional?

4. What level of constitutional scrutiny did the Court apply in this case? Why did it apply this level of scrutiny?

5. Assume that your state government did away with voting machines and public sites where citizens cast ballots. Instead, to cast his/her vote, a citizen can only do so online, using a computer connected to the Internet. Applying the principles in *Harper*, do you believe that this practice is constitutional?

CRAWFORD v. MARION COUNTY ELECTION BOARD

1. Describe the two federal laws that evidence why election modernization is a legitimate governmental interest.

2. Why did the Court say that it is important to carefully identify all voters?

3. If the plaintiffs had provided evidence that a substantial number of Indiana voters would not be able to vote because of the law, do you think that the *Crawford* decision would have been different? Explain why or why not.

4. In your opinion, how many burdened voters would there need to have been to change the outcome of the case? Explain how you reached this number.

5. Why did the outcome of the case not change when the Court recognized that the voter photo identification statute was highly politicized and was passed by a unanimous vote of Republicans in the General Assembly for the statute and a unanimous vote of Democrats against the statute?

HYPOTHETICAL WITH ACCOMPANYING ANALYSIS

Hypothetical

The State of Utropia holds primary elections for the U.S. President in which the legislature only allows a citizen to vote for a candidate within their party, and the primary election is closed to anyone who is a not a party member. The Republicrat Party has three candidates running in the primary. The Republicrat Party has a rule that no women may be a member of the Republicrat Party.

Women residents of Utropia sued, asserting that this was an unconstitutional limitation on their voting rights.

Analysis

The Supreme Court has consistently ruled that states have the power to establish voting procedures and voter qualifications. However, when there are challenges to such rules by those groups who have been historically disenfranchised and lacked political clout, the courts have agreed to conduct a "more searching judicial inquiry." United States v. Carolene Products, 304 U.S. 144 (1938). At first glance this appears to not be a state action, as the Republicrat Party is a private organization. This, too, has been the conclusion of the Supreme Court in several cases, including Newberry v. United States, 256 U.S. 232 (1921), and Grovey v. Townsend, 295 U.S. 45 (1935). In *Grovey*, the Court ruled that a whites-only Democratic primary was permissible, because the Texas State Democratic Party was a private party that could exclude non-white members with no constitutional implications. However, in 1944, the Supreme Court overturned the *Grovey* decision, determining that a state-established electoral process that resulted in a whites-only primary because of discriminatory private political party membership practices indirectly denied non-whites the right to vote. Smith v. Allwright, 321 U.S. 649 (1944). Therefore, the Court concluded that a whites-only primary violated the Fifteenth Amendment.

The case at issue is very similar to the *Smith* case, in that the State of Utropia's electoral process indirectly denies women the right to vote. Such indirect discrimination does not violate the Fifteenth Amendment, but it does violate the Nineteenth Amendment, which provides that the "right of citizens . . . to vote shall not be denied or abridged by . . . any state on account of sex." As such, the State of Utropia's primary does not provide for universal suffrage and is unconstitutional.

In the State of Xenophobia, there has been a large influx of legal immigrants from other countries over the past two generations. These immigrants and their progeny are proud of their heritages and have kept using their native languages to the exclusion of English. In the State of Xenophobia, the ballot and ballot instructions are provided only in English. The non-English speaking residents have sued the State of Xenophobia arguing that English-only ballots and instructions unconstitutionally prevent non-English speaking citizens who are otherwise eligible to vote from exercising that right. Which party will prevail in this lawsuit and why?

DISCUSSION QUESTIONS

1. Define "legislative malapportionment."

2. Research challenge: Which Framer of the U.S. Constitution considered democracy a form of mob rule and a threat to liberty and property? Why did he believe this?

3. Under the U.S. Constitution and its Amendments, how are Senators elected?

4. Under the U.S. Constitution and its Amendments, how are Representatives elected?

5. Read Bush v. Gore, 531 U.S. 98 (2000). Do you believe that the 2000 Presidential election was decided by the Supreme Court? Do you believe that the decision was correct or incorrect? Explain why or why not.

6. Do you think that the electoral college method of presidential elections is a good method? Explain why or why not. If not, explain what method you would rather see used.

7. List the pros and cons of casting votes over the Internet. Do you think that Internet voting should be implemented?

8. Assume that a court has declared congressional districts to have been racially drawn, what is the remedy? Does the court have the power to redraw the lines?

9. The United States has two strong political parties: the Republican Party and the Democratic Party. Explain how these parties have collaborated to prevent competition by rival third parties in elections.

10. What is partisan gerrymandering? Is it constitutional? Does the Supreme Court believe that it should involve itself in cases of partisan gerrymandering? Why or why not? *See* Davis v. Bandemer, 478 U.S. 109 (1986).

11. Explain the role of the states in establishing processes for elections for federal officials. *See* Lassiter v. Northhampton County Board of Education, 360 U.S. 45 (1959).

12. Research Challenge: Eavesdropping is a felony in Illinois. Jack was convicted of eavesdropping. Can Jack constitutionally be denied the right to vote? Explain why or why not. Do you think that Jack should be denied his right to vote for having committed eavesdropping?

13. Can a state design districts to help increase the number of minorities voting in that district so as to help increase the number of minority elected officials? Why or why not? *See* Hunt v. Cromartie, 526 U.S. 541 (1999).

True/False

1. The U.S. Supreme Court has, over the course of history, generally been adverse to entering into the politics of an election.

2. Political gerrymandering is unconstitutional.

3. Women had the right to vote before African Americans in the United States.

4. The Supreme Court determined that Congress has the power to enforce the Fifteenth Amendment.

5. Congress, and not the Supreme Court, eliminated the use of literacy tests as a means of racial discrimination in elections.

Multiple Choice

6. The _____ Amendment establishes a voting age of 18.

   A. Fourteenth
   B. Fifteenth
   C. Twenty-fourth
   D. Twenty-sixth

7. The President of the United States is elected by:

   A. The vote of the popular majority.
   B. An Electoral College.
   C. The vote of majority of Senators and Representatives.
   D. The vote of the majority of the Supreme Court.

8. The _____ Amendment essentially gave women the right to vote.

   A. First
   B. Fifteenth
   C. Nineteenth
   D. Twenty-sixth

9. Which of the following was not an attempt to prevent African Americans from voting after the passage of the Fifteenth Amendment?

   A. Poll Taxes
   B. Racial Gerrymandering
   C. Political Gerrymandering
   D. Grandfather Clauses

10. Every ten years, Congress determines the number of representatives to Congress each state has based upon

   A. A plan generated by the incumbent President.
   B. A ruling of the Supreme Court.
   C. The U.S. Census.
   D. Individual state censuses.

TABLE OF CASES

Principal cases indicated by italics.

Aetna Life Ins. Co. v. Haworth, 26
Agins v. City of Tiburon, 79
Ashcroft v. Free Speech Coalition, 126, 131

Babbit v. United Farm Workers National Union, 22
Bailey v. Drexel Furniture, 30
Baker v. Carr, 23
Barenblatt v. United States, 40
Bell v. Burson, 80
Bolling v. Sharpe, 104
Bowers v. Hardwick, 95
Boy Scouts of America v. Dale, 135
Brigham v. Stuart, 185
Brown v. Board of Education of Topeka Kansas, 105, 112, 115
Buck v. Bell, 98
Bush v. Gore, 59, 116, 194, 203

Chimel v. California, 185, 188
Church of the Lukumi Babalu Aye, Inc. v. Hialeah, 150
Clinton v. City of New York, 60
Clinton v. Federal Election Commission, 135
Coolidge v. New Hampshire, 184, 185
Craig v. Boren, 114
Crawford v. Marion County Election Board, 196, 201

Dames & Moore v. Regan, 60
Davis v. Bandemer, 204
Davis v. Beason, 149
DeFunis v. Odegaard, 23
Diaz v. United States, 188
District of Columbia v. Heller, 156, *159*, 164, 165, 168, 171
Division v. Smith, 150
Duncan v. Louisiana, 169

Eisenstadt v. Baird, 95
Elk Grove Unified School District v. Newdow, 18, 21

Employment Division, Department of Human Resources of Oregon v. Smith, 148
Everson v. Board of Education, 149

Federal Communications Commission v. Fox Television Stations, Inc., 134
Flast v. Cohen, 25
Frazee v. Illinois Dep't of Soc. Sec., 149
Frothingham v. Mellon, 25

Gideon v. Wainright, 173
Gillette v. United States, 152
Goldberg v. Kelly, 79
Golder v. Zwickler, 23
Goldman v. Weinberger, 152
Gomez v. United States, 25
Gonzales v. O Centro Espirita Beneficente Uniao do Vegetal, 143, 148, 152
Gonzales v. Raich, 34, 38
Goss v. Lopez, 77
Griswold v. Connecticut, 95, 96
Grovey v. Townsend, 202
Grutter v. Bollinger, 107, 113

Hamdi v. Rumsfeld, 79
Hammer v. Dagenhart, 30
Harper v. Virginia Board of Elections, 193, *195*, 201
Harris v. United States, 185
Heart of Atlanta and Katzenbach v. McClung, 30
Heart of Atlanta Motel v. United States, 31
Hodel v. Virginia Surface Mining and Reclamation Association, Inc., 30
Holtzman v. Schlesinger, 41
Hunt v. Cromartie, 204
Hurley v. Irish-American Gay Group of Boston, 131

Jacobsen v. Massachusetts, 152
Jones v. Clinton, 58

Katz v. United States, 185, 189
Katzenbach v. Morgan, 41
Kelo v. City of New London, Connecticut, 72, 76
Kennedy v. Louisiana, 180, 183, 189, 190

Lane v. Wilson, 193
Lassiter v. Northhampton County Board of
    Education, 204
Lawrence v. Texas, 90, 95, 97
Lemon v. Kurtzman, 140, 148, 154
Lujan v. Defenders of Wildlife, 23

M'Culloch v. Maryland, 30, 40
Mapp v. Ohio, 175, 183, 185
Marbury v. Madison, 13, 21
Marshall v. Marshall, 26
Massachusetts v. Oakes, 23
Matthews v. Eldridge, 77
McConnell v. Federal Elections Commission, 135
McCreary County v. ACLU of Kentucky, 139,
    148, 153
Medellín v. Texas, 51, 57, 62
Miller v. California, 30, 131, 134
Miranda v. Arizona, 185, 188, 190, 191
Morey v. Doud, 79

Near v. Minnesota, 133
New York Times v. United States, 123, 130
New York v. Ferber, 131
Newberry v. United States, 202
Nix v. Williams, 189
Nixon v. Fitzgerald. 58

Okanogan Indians v. United States, 60

Palazzolo v. Rhode Island, 79
Paul v. Davis, 77
Peretz v. United States, 25
Planned Parenthood of Southeastern Pa. v.
    Casey, 83, 95
Plessy v. Ferguson, 103, 113
Poe v. Ullman, 23
Printz v. United States, 168

Ravin v. State, 98
Regents of the University of California v.
    Bakke, 113
Roe v. Wade, 84, 94, 97, 99, 101
Romer v. Evans, 95
Rostker v. Goldberg, 113, 114
Rumsfeld v. Forum for Academic and Institutional
    Rights, Inc., 134

Santa Clara County v. Southern Pacific R.R. Co., 78
Scott v. Sandford, 79, 80
Sell v. United States, 99
Sherbert v. Verner, 148, 150
Skinner v. Oklahoma, 96
Smith v. Allwright, 193, 202
South Carolina v. Katzenbach, 194
Spencer v. Kemna, 26

Terry v. Ohio, 188
Torasco v. Watkins, 149
Truax v. Raich, 79

United States v. Ballard, 149
United States v. Carolene Products, 202
United States v. Cruikshank, 169
United States v. Curtiss-Wright Export Corp., 60
United States v. Lopez, 31, 38, 166, 168
United States v. Miller, 156, 164, 165, 170, 171
United States v. Morrison, 31, 38
United States v. Nixon, 40
United States v. Seeger, 149, 152
United States v. Virginia, 115

Van Orden v. Perry, 139, *141*, 148

Warth v. Seldin, 22
West Coast Hotel Co. v. Parrish, 67, 75
West Coast Hotel v. Parrish, 80, 81
Wickard v. Filburn, 38

Yick Wo v. Hopkins, 79
Younger v. Harris, 23
Youngstown Sheet & Tube Co. v. Sawyer, 47, 56, 61